THE EN

Published t

Compiled I

C000256127

A LEXIC

8000 caref

will enrich everyday language

USEFUL AND INTERESTING

Aegis protection, support; **axiomatic** self-evident;
caveat a warning; **embrangle** to confuse;
epeolatry the worship of words; **gricer** railway enthusiast;
kylie a boomerang; **miff** a small quarrel; **nadir** lowest point;
ochlocracy mob rule; **prolix** long-winded;
vitilitigation vexatious litigation.

MISUNDERSTOOD

Childish or childlike? Masterful or masterly?
Suppositious or supposititious?
Transcendent or transcendental?

CORRECT USAGE

Between you and I or between you and me?
Compare to or compare with?
Less or fewer? Who or whom?

FOREIGN IMPORTS WITH USEFUL MEANINGS

Comme il faut as it should be
de mal en pis from bad to worse
samizdat clandestine publishing
schadenfreude enjoyment of another's misfortune
verligte liberal
zweite gesellschaft second-rate people

A REFERENCE SOURCE OF OBSCURE FACTS
(A QUIZ CRIB)

Greek myths, philosophers, artists, food, drink, places,
animals, plants, religions etc.

*Let the English Wordsmith help you and every Scrabbler, quiz
aficionado, student, crossword enthusiast, journalist, lawyer or
academic who has ever been lost for a word or in need of a phrase.*

First published in 2011 by

THE GREAT WORDSMITH LLP

Text and cover design: Temple Design

Illustrations: Matthew 'Moz' English
www.mozthecartoonist.com

ISBN: 978-0-9567364-0-6

The English Wordsmith
was dedicated by David
to his daughter Laura.

INTRODUCTION

Old English as spoken by the Anglo-Saxons was later influenced by various languages – in particular Latin and French. Today, English is a constantly changing language, taking in new words on an almost daily basis. The result is a world language with a vast vocabulary.

David Andrews' collection of 8,000 words and phrases shows the diverse nature of that language. The words he collected together include the common and the not-so-common. Portmanteau is a case with two compartments: French *porter* to carry and *manteau* a cloak. Common enough. However, a portmanteau word meaning one word that is a blend of two other words – brunch (breakfast and lunch) is not quite so common.

Latin has its place in *The English Wordsmith*. "*Reductio ad absurdum*: proving the falsity of a proposition by showing its logical consequence is absurd or contradictory."

Usage also has its place: Who or whom? Is none used with a singular or plural verb? "None of the partners is in the office today... None of the delegates in the hall were listening to the speech."

Following his retirement from the partnership of a major London law firm, David Andrews devoted many years of his life to writing – not only law books – but this collection of words. He completed his book shortly before his death in 2010.

It is appropriate perhaps that, in the year that he finished writing *The Wordsmith*, the supremacy of the English language was finally acknowledged, even in France. The fact that English is now the language of business and commerce, of the internet and of everyday life, seems to have been accepted in Paris. Frederic Martel, author of *Mainstream*, in which he attacked French-only orthodoxy, was reported as saying: "If the French want to exist in the world today they have to speak English" (*The Times*, October 8, 2010: "Paris elite say writing on the wall is in English").

Another illustration of the emergence of English as the world language is the situation in India. With the exception of Hindi, more Indians speak English than any other language: it is estimated that over 125 million Indians speak English as their second language (*The Times of India*, March 14, 2010).

In *The English Wordsmith*, David Andrews illustrates the richness and diversity of the English language. It is a book for your bookshelf, a book to dip into, a gift for a friend, a companion.

Anthony Connerty
Temple, London EC4

A

aa *Hawaiian* lava

Aachen city and spa in western Germany near Dutch and Belgian borders, part of France 1801-15, French name Aix-la-Chapelle; principal court of Charlemagne who died there in 814

aardvark *'earth-pig'*, a large burrowing nocturnal mammal of southern Africa, with a long tubular snout, a long sticky extensile tongue and large ears; it feeds on ants and termites

abactinal away from or opposite the mouth (of an animal); **aboral**

abacus 1) a counting-board, counting-frame 2) *archit.* the flat slab on the top of a column supporting the architrave of the entablature

abaft in or towards the back of a ship; aft, astern, behind

abalone an edible, rock-clinging shellfish of warm seas; related to snails and limpets, its shallow ear-shaped shell is lined with a type of mother-of-pearl used in jewellery

abase to humiliate, belittle or degrade (somebody) esp. **abase oneself**

abashed ashamed and embarrassed; disconcerted

abate 1) to make or become less strong; (to cause) to die down 2) to bring to an end

abatis, abattis a defence made of felled trees placed together with the boughs pointing outwards

abattoir a slaughterhouse

abdabs, habdabs usu. in pl. **the screaming abdabs** nervous anxiety or irritation

abdicate 1) to renounce, to give up the throne 2) to give up one's responsibilities

aberrant abnormal

aberration departure from the norm; a deviation from the expected course

ab extra Lat. from without

abeyance suspension

abhor to detest

abhorrent loathsome, disgusting

abide 1) to tolerate 2) to last for a long time, to endure

abide by (to) to accept or act in accordance with

abiding lasting for ever

abigail a lady's maid

ab imo pectore *Lat.* from the bottom of the heart

ab incunabulis *Lat.* from the cradle

ab initio *Lat.* from the beginning

ab intra *Lat.* from within

abiogenesis the supposed first spontaneous generation of living organisms on earth from non-living matter

abiosis absence of life

abiotic not involving or derived from living organisms

abject experienced to the maximum degree: 1) hopeless, miserable, wretched *(poverty)* 2) without pride or dignity, humble, respectful, submissive *(apology)* 3) despicable, shameless, contemptible *(liar, coward)*

abjure to renounce, to give up, to abstain from

ablation 1) surgical removal of part of the body 2) the wearing away of something; melting, evaporation, erosion

abligurition extravagance with regard to food

ablutions the act of washing

abnegate to give up, to deny to oneself a right or pleasure; to renounce

abominate to abhor, detest, loathe

abomination 1) an object of disgust or hatred 2) a feeling of hatred

aboral away from or opposite the mouth; **abactinal**

abortive unsuccessful

abrade to scrape or wear away

abrasive harsh, curt, insensitive in speech or manner

abreaction the release of pent-up emotions; catharsis

abrogate to cancel, to repeal

abscissa *maths* the distance to a point along the horizontal x-axis of a graph

abscond to steal away, to leave secretly and hurriedly

abseil to descend, as from a cliff top or helicopter by a supporting rope around one's body

absinthe a potent green liqueur; aniseed-flavoured, it turns milky when water is added; it is technically a gin

absolutism 1) unlimited power 2) the belief that principles cannot be diluted or be made relative; authoritarian form of government – dictatorship, absolute monarchy

absolve 1) to clear of guilt, to free from blame 2) to pardon (a sin)

absquatulate to leave abruptly

abstemious moderate, not self-indulgent, in eating and/or drinking

abstergent cleansing or scouring

abstinence abstaining totally in certain activities esp. drinking alcohol i.e. a teetotaller

Acadia
*the Atlantic provinces of Canada: New Brunswick,
Prince Edward Island, Nova Scotia, Newfoundland and
Labrador esp. their French-speaking areas*

abstract *adj.* having no physical existence; theoretical; (of art) not representing things pictorially *n.* a summary *v.* to extract, take out, remove

abstruse hard to understand, esoteric, recondite

abundant present in large quantities; plentiful

abut to touch, join, be adjacent to

Abyssinia the former name of Ethiopia

Acadia the Atlantic provinces of Canada: New Brunswick, Prince Edward Island, Nova Scotia, Newfoundland and Labrador esp. their French-speaking areas

a cappella *mus.* sung without instrumental accompaniment

acarid a tick or mite

acaroid like a tick or mite

accablant Fr. overwhelming

accablé Fr. overwhelmed

accede usu. **accede to** 1) to assent, to agree to 2) to assume, to take up, a position or office

acceptation the conventional or accepted meaning of a word or phrase

accidence inflectional morphology – the part of grammar concerned with the inflections of words

accidie, acedia spiritual or mental sloth, apathy

acclivity a slope upwards

accolade 1) an honour, award, praise 2) a touch on the shoulder with a sword conferring knighthood

accord *n.* 1) an agreement or treaty 2) agreement or harmony

accord *v.* to grant

accord with *v.* to fit in with; to be consistent with

accoudoir *Fr.* elbowrest, armrest *fig.* something to lean on for support

accoutred attired, equipped

accoutrement clothing or equipment for a particular activity

accrue to accumulate, to add or increase

acephalous without a head; descriptive of a society without central political organization or a recognized head

acerbic sour, bitter, harsh

acervate *adj.* growing in heaps or clusters

acescent turning sour

acetic to do with vinegar

acharnement *Fr.* 1) bloodthirsty ferocity 2) relentless determination

Achates 1) the faithful companion of Aeneas in Virgil's Aeneid 2) a loyal friend

Achilles' heel weakness or flaw, small and apparently unimportant but fatally vulnerable

achromatic without colour or of neutral colour – black, white, grey

achromic, achromous colourless

acidic 1) having a high chemical acid content 2) *fig.* sour, sharp (of a personality or humour)

acme the highest point

acmeism (in Russian poetry) a movement, begun in 1910, against symbolism and in favour of simple everyday language

acolyte an assistant, a follower; an assistant to a priest at the altar

acoustic 1) relating to sound or hearing 2) referring to a musical instrument that does not use electric amplification

acoustics 1) the scientific study of sound 2) the overall effect of sound in an enclosed space

acrid bitter, unpleasantly pungent

acrimonious bitter in language or tone

acrimony bitterness

acronym a word formed from the initial letters of other words – scuba = *self-contained underwater breathing apparatus*

acrophobia fear of heights

acropolis a citadel in ancient Greece

acrostic
writing, esp. a poem, in which the first letters of each
line, read down the page, spell out a word or words –
double acrostic uses first and last letters – triple acrostic
uses middle letters to form a third word or words

acrostic writing, esp. a poem, in which the first letters of each line, read down the page, spell out a word or words – double acrostic uses first and last letters – triple acrostic uses middle letters to form a third word or words

acuity acuteness, keenness, sharpness of the senses or the mind – thought, vision, or hearing

aculeate 1) having a sting e.g. of bees and wasps 2) pointed, prickly

acumen the ability to make good judgments; keen discernment; insight

acuminate tapering to a sharp point

adage a maxim, proverb or saying

adagio *mus.* in slow time

adamant 1) unshakable in determination or purpose 2) refusing to be persuaded or to change one's mind

adamantine 1) unbreakable, very hard, unyielding 2) having the lustre of a diamond 3) *n.* a legendary rock or mineral associated at times with both diamond and lodestones

addled 1) muddled, confused 2) (of an egg) rotten

adept (a person who is) very skilled or proficient at something

adherent a supporter; sticking to something

adhibit to apply or affix to something else

ad hoc for a particular purpose

adhocracy an organisation in which teams work on individual projects on an ad hoc basis; the teams are flexible and informal, often changing their personnel, their shape and relationship to one another.

ad hominem *'to the man'*, personal; *(of an argument)* based on personal, rather than objective, considerations

ad infinitum endlessly; forever

adipescent becoming fat

adipose fat

adjacent next to, adjoining

adjure to solemnly appeal to or urge (someone to do something)

ad-lib to improvise (usually something spoken)

admixture a mixture with something else

admonish to warn, to reprimand

ad nauseam tiresomely, sickeningly and tediously to an extreme degree

adobe 1) sun-dried brick 2) the clay from which such bricks are made 3) a building made of the bricks

Adonis a beautiful, young man

adrenalin a hormone secreted by the adrenal glands in response to stress; it increases heart rate, pulse rate, and blood pressure

adroit skilful

adscititious additional, added, supplementary

adsorb to hold (molecules) as a thin film on a surface

adulation excessive admiration; adoration

adumbrate to foreshadow, to outline

aduncous hooked, curved inward

adventitious 1) accidental, by chance, unexpected 2) coming from outside; not native

adversary an opponent

adverse turned against, opposed; unfavourable cf. **averse**

adversity difficulty or misfortune

advert to refer to

advertence, **advertency** heedfulness, attentiveness *adj.* **advertent**

advoutry adultery

advowson the right to nominate a priest to a vacant benefice or living in the Church of England

adze, **adz** a tool with a cutting blade at right angles to the handle

aegis protection, backing, support

aegrotat 1) a sick note 2) an examination pass awarded to a student too ill to take the exam

aeolian, **eolian** related to, carried, deposited, or produced by the wind

aeon, eon 1) an infinitely long time 2) a thousand million years in astronomy and geology

aerobe a micro-organism that cannot live without oxygen

Aesculapian medical, relating to healing, to doctors

aesthete one who claims to appreciate art and beauty

aesthetic concerned with (the appreciation of) beauty; in good taste, tasteful; pertaining to **aesthetics, aestheticism**

aesthetics the study of the nature of beauty; the theory of taste

Aestheticism late 19th- century European arts movement based on 'art for art's sake'

aestival, estival to do with the summer

aestivate to spend the summer in a dormant state

aestivation spending the summer in a dormant state

aetiology = etiology

affable good-natured and sociable

affect to pretend to have or feel or be; use for show; have an effect on

affectation an artificial way of speaking, dressing, or behaving

affecting touching the feelings of; moving; evoking feelings of pity, sympathy, or pathos

affective emotional

afferent conducting, bringing inwards or towards

affidavit a written, sworn statement for use in court

affinity close connection or resemblance; strong liking, attraction; tendency to combine

afflatus poetic inspiration or other creative impulse, thought to be of divine origin

affluence wealth

affluent wealthy

affront an insult; to insult

aficionado an enthusiast, a devotee

a fortiori all the more so, for an even stronger reason

aga an Ottoman commander, leader

agamic involving asexual reproduction

agamogenesis reproduction without sex – as in some lower animals and plants

agape 1) Christian love 2) open-mouthed

agaric a mushroom or other fungus with gills on the underside of its cap

agastric having no stomach

agate a hard semi-precious stone, usu. banded chalcedony, of varying colour and transparency

agave fine, architectural, succulent plant with strongly-toothed, sharply-pointed leaves

agent provocateur one who incites suspects to break the law so that they can be convicted

ageusia lack of the sense of taste

ageustia the loss of the sense of taste

aggiornamento (R.C. Church) the process of bringing in up-to-date methods, ideas etc.

agglomerate to collect or form into a mass

agglomeration a mass of things

agglutinate to stick things together

aggrandize 1) to make greater in size, power, or rank 2) to cause to appear greater than is the case; to exaggerate

aghast astounded

agile quick, nimble, lively

agio the mark-up or percentage charged on the exchange of one currency into another that is more valuable

agist to take in and feed (livestock) for payment

agitprop political, esp. Communist or left-wing propoganda

aglossia congenital absence of the tongue

agminate gathered or clustered together

agnate (one who is) descended esp. by the male line from the same male ancestor

agnostic one who holds that it is impossible to know if there is a God because there is no evidence one way or the other

agog amazed, eager, expectant

à gogo in abundance, galore

agonistic argumentative; aggressive; polemical; combative

agoraphobia fear of large open spaces

agraphia loss of the power to express ideas in writing

agrarian relating to land, farming, or the country

agrestic 1) to do with the country; rural; rustic 2) unpolished; uncouth

ague 1) malaria 2) a shivering fit

ahistorical lacking a sense of the past

aigrette a long plume of egret (white) feathers worn as a headdress

aiguillettes tagged points of braid hanging from the shoulder on some military and naval uniforms

aileron a hinged flap on the trailing edge of an aircraft wing to provide lateral control

ailurophile one who likes cats

ailurophobe one who dislikes, is afraid of cats

aitch-bone the rump bone

ait, eyot a small island in a river

akimbo with hands on hips and elbows outwards

akin 1) related by blood 2) of similar character

alabaster a white, marble-like stone mainly from Italy. It is a kind of opaque or translucent gypsum

alacrity speedy and cheerful eagerness, readiness

alalia loss of speech, inability to speak

à la mode 1) fashionable, trendy 2) (of beef) braised in wine 3) *N.Amer.* served with ice cream

alb long white vestment worn by some Christian priests and servers

albatross 1) very large seabird of the southern oceans; it has long narrow wings. It was traditionally feared by mariners as an ill omen 2) a burden or encumbrance

albedo the amount of light reflected back by the earth, a planet, or the moon

albeit although

albescent turning white

albino a person or animal with a congenital lack of pigment in the skin and hair (which are white) and the eyes (which are usually pink)

Albion ancient and literary name for Britain or England, probably from the white (*albus*) cliffs of Dover

albumen white of an egg

alcalde a mayor or magistrate in Spain, Portugal or Latin America

alcatraz a pelican

alchemy the quasi-scientific forerunner of chemistry concerned with turning base metals into gold, finding an elixir to prolong life, and a panacea or universal remedy to cure all diseases

al dente (of food) firm, after being lightly cooked

aldrin a highly poisonous chlorinated insecticide

aleatoric, aleatory 1) depending on chance or the throw of dice 2) (of a musical performance) improvisatory, random

alembic 1) an obsolete type of distilling apparatus 2) anything that distills or purifies

alembicated refined, precious, esp. of a literary style

aleph *(ox)* the first letter of the Hebrew (Jewish) alphabet

alfalfa a pea-like leguminous plant grown for fodder, aka **lucerne**

alfresco outside, in the fresh air

algolagnia sadomasochism

algorithm a step-by-step procedure for solving a mathematical problem using a computer

alguacil, alguazil a mounted official at a bull fight

Alhambra ornate palace of the Moorish kings of Granada in Spain built in the 13th and 14th centuries

alias a false name

alibi evidence that an accused was elsewhere when a crime took place

alidade 1) a surveying instrument which measures vertical angles 2) the upper rotatable part of a theodolite

alienate 1) to transfer property to another 2) to cause to become unfriendly

alienation a sociological term used variously to describe: a sense of estrangement from society; a feeling of powerlessness to affect social change; a depersonalisation of the individual in a large and bureaucratic society

alimentary pertaining to food, nutrition, or digestion

alkahest the hypothetical universal solvent sought by alchemists

allegory a story, poem, or picture which has a deeper, hidden meaning

allegro *mus.* in a brisk, lively manner; at a rapid tempo

alleviate to lighten, to make less severe, to ease symptoms without providing a cure

alliaceous to do with garlic or onion

alliaphage a garlic-eater

alliteration the repetition of initial consonant sounds in adjacent or neighbouring words – *Love's Labour's Lost*

allochthonous originating elsewhere

allocution a formal speech

allopathy the treatment of disease by conventional methods

allopatric occurring in separate, non-overlapping areas

allotrope, allotropic each different physical form in which an element can exist e.g. carbon as graphite, as charcoal, and as diamond

alloy 1) a mixture of metals 2) to mix (metals) to form an alloy

allspice the spice from a Caribbean tree of the same name

allure appeal, attraction, or fascination

allusion an indirect reference

allusively referentially

alluvium fertile soil consisting of clay, mud, silt, gravel, and sand, as well as organic matter, deposited by flowing water during a flood

alma, almah an Egyptian dancing-girl

alma mater one's old university, college or school

almoner one who distributes alms

aloe a plant with fleshy, lightly-toothed, pointed leaves whose bitter resin is used as a laxative, less architectural than agave

alopecia baldness

alphameric made up of letters and numbers

altercation a heated and noisy argument

alter ego another side to oneself; a second self; an intimate friend or confidant

alterity the state of being other or different; otherness

alternate *adj.* every other; (of two) each following and succeeding the other in turn repeatedly *n.* a deputy or substitute

alternative available as a different option

altiloquent speaking in high-flown, pompous, inflated language

altisonant high-sounding, noisy, loud

altricial (esp. of a bird) hatched in an immature and helpless condition and needing care for some time after birth

altruism self-denying, unselfish concern for the welfare of others

alumnus, alumna; alumni a former student; former students

alvine to do with the belly

amah a maid or nursemaid in the Far East

amalgamate to combine or unite into one organization or structure

amanuensis a person who takes dictation or copies manuscripts

amaranthine 1) unfading 2) purplish 3) pertaining to the amaranth plant whose purple, slow-fading flowers were regarded as an emblem of immortality

amaurosis blindness without obvious damage to the eye

amazon a tall, strong, well-built woman

ambagious 1) roundabout, vague 2) indefinite

ambiance, ambience atmosphere

ambidextrous able to use both hands equally well

ambient 1) surrounding, in the immediate environment 2) relaxing, creating a pleasant atmosphere

ambit boundary or circuit; scope, bounds, or range of something

ambivalent in two minds, undecided

ambivert a person who fluctuates between being an introvert and an extrovert

ambrosia the food of the gods; something delicious

ambulatory 1) pertaining to walking 2) (of a will) able to be changed or revoked

ambuscade 1) an ambush 2) to ambush

âme damnée Fr. a mere tool of someone

ameliorate to improve *n.* **amelioration**

amenable responsive

amend to correct and improve

amercement a fine

American lion the cougar, the puma

amethyst a purple/violet type of quartz from which drinking cups used to be made; regarded as a gemstone it was once thought to ward off drunkenness

Amharic the language of Ethiopia

amicus curiae 'a friend of the court' a person not involved in a case who advises the court

amity friendship

ammonite the flat spirally-coiled fossil shell of an extinct marine mollusc

ammophilous sand-loving

amnesty 1) a pardon 2) an agreement to take no action in relation to specified offences for a fixed period

amok, amuck wildly in an uncontrollable frenzy

amoral 1) concerning places or situations where moral considerations do not arise 2) concerning people who reject or have no concept of the difference between right and wrong 3) lacking a sense of ethics

amoretto a representation of Cupid in artwork

amorous to do with (sexual) love or desire

amorphous having no definite shape, or form, or organization

amortize 1) to pay off a debt by instalments or by payments into a sinking fund 2) to write off gradually the initial cost of an asset

amour-propre self-respect, self-esteem; vanity

ampersand the sign '&' for and

amphibian a frog, toad, newt, etc. that lives on land but breeds in water

amphibious 1) living on or in or suited for both land and water 2) (of a military operation) involving forces landed from the sea

amphibology ambiguity of expression – 'You'll be lucky to get Smith to work for you' in reply to a request for a reference

amphigory, **amphigouri** nonsense writing usu. in verse

amphora (in Ancient Greece and Rome) a jar with a narrow neck and two handles

amphoric like the sound of blowing into a bottle

amplify to expand and clarify by adding details; to make louder

amulet a trinket or piece of jewellery worn as a protection against harm or misfortune

amphibology
*ambiguity of expression – 'You'll be lucky to get Smith
to work for you' in reply to a request for a reference*

amuse-bouche Fr. an appetizer before a meal – the term used in restaurants

amuse-gueule Fr. an appetizer

amygdaloid almond-shaped

amylaceous of or resembling starch

Anabaptists 1520s/1530s onwards, radical Protestant reformers who insisted on baptism for adult believers only; they rejected infant baptism and held that those baptized in infancy should be baptized again

anabiosis revival after apparent death; suspended animation

anachronism something which does not belong to, or is out of keeping with the time in which it is placed

anachronous belonging to a different time

anacoluthon a construction in which there is no logical or grammatical sequence; a *non sequitur*; 'If you don't come – how is your father?'

anaconda a very large snake of tropical South America

Anacreontic in the manner of Anacreon, 6th- century b.c. Greek poet who celebrated love, wine, song and revelry

anadromous (of a fish) swimming upriver from the sea to spawn as salmon do

anaemia, anemia a deficiency in red blood cells, in haemoglobin, causing pallor, tiredness, and lack of energy *adj.* **anaemic, anemic** listless and weak; pallid; lacking in vigour

anaglyph 1) an ornament e.g. a cameo carved in low relief 2) a picture with a three- dimensional effect when viewed through special glasses

anagnorisis *Gk.* 'discovery', 'recognition'; the turning point in a drama when the characters realise the true state of affairs; dénouement

anagoge, anagogy an allegorical or mystical version of certain texts such as the Bible stories

analects, analecta extracts from various literary or philosophical passages

analepsis a 'flashback' in storytelling

analeptic restorative

analgesic relieving pain

analogue 1) something that is similar or comparable to something else 2) displaying information by means of a dial

anal retentive *n.* a meticulous, fussy, finicky person

anamorphosis a distorted image which appears normal from a particular angle or with a suitable mirror or lens

ananas a pineapple

anaphora 1) the repetition, for rhetorical effect, of a word or phrase at the beginning of successive clauses 2) (to avoid repetition) the use of a substitute word esp. a pronoun, to refer to a preceding word or phrase

anaphylaxis, anaphylactic a severe, potentially fatal, allergic reaction to an antigen e.g. to a bee sting, to an injection

anarchism the abolition of all forms of government and the organisation of society on a voluntary, cooperative basis

anarchist one who believes in anarchism

anathema 1) a detested thing or person 2) a solemn ecclesiastical curse involving denunciation of a doctrine or excommunication of a person

anatomize 1) to dissect 2) to examine

anchorite *fem.* **anchoress** a religious recluse; a hermit

ancillary 1) extra; additional; providing support 2) of secondary importance; subsidiary

ancipital, ancipitous flattened and having two edges

andante *mus.* in a moderately slow tempo

androcentric considering men or males to be central, primary

androgynous partly male and partly female; hermaphrodite

android a robot that looks like a human being

andrology the branch of medicine dealing with diseases in men, esp. of the reproductive organs

anele to anoint esp. to administer extreme unction

aneroid 1) not containing a liquid 2) a type of barometer

aneurysm an abnormal localized swelling of the wall of an artery

anfractuous winding, twisting and turning, bending; sinuous, circuitous

angary the right of a country at war to requisition the property of neutrals (e.g. vehicles on its territory and ships in its ports) provided it pays full compensation

anglophone one who speaks English

angora mohair

angst anxiety

anguine pertaining to a snake

anhydrous containing no water

anile feeble and frail like an old woman

anima 1) the part of the psyche directed inwards to the subconscious 2) (in Jung) the feminine part of a man's personality

animadversion criticism

animatronics making and operating lifelike robots for use in films

animism 1) the belief that inanimate objects, plants, etc. have souls 2) the belief that there is an unseen force that animates the universe

animosity hostility, hatred

animus 1) animosity, hostility 2) (in Jung) the male personality in a woman's unconscious

anneal to strengthen (metal or glass) by heating followed by cooling

annelids a phylum of worms including leeches

annihilate to destroy, to reduce to nothing *Lat.* nihil, nothing

annular ring-shaped

Annunciation 1) the announcement to the Virgin Mary by angel Gabriel that she was to be the mother of Christ; feast-day is Lady Day 25th March 2) an announcement

anodyne 1) something that relieves pain or distress 2) neutral; inoffensive; bland; uncontroversial

anoestrus, **anestrus** a period of sexual inactivity when a female mammal is not on heat

anoint to smear with oil e.g. at baptism, consecration

anomaly, **anomalous** something deviating from the standard, the normal, the expected or the usual

anomie, **anomy** lack of the customary social, moral or ethical standards; more loosely used to describe a condition akin to rootlessness, alienation, instability, purposelessness etc.

anonymous of unknown identity; not identified by name

anorak 1) a waterproof jacket with a hood 2) a social misfit with boring hobbies

anorexia nervosa an obsessive desire to lose weight by refusing to eat

anorexic, anorectic suffering from anorexia; very thin; marked by loss of appetite

anosmia loss of the sense of smell

Anschluss the annexation of Austria by Germany in 1938

anserine to do with a goose or geese; goose-like

antagonism active hostility or opposition

antecedents a person's ancestors and background esp. the previous convictions of someone found guilty of a criminal offence

antediluvian before the biblical flood

antelucan before dawn or daylight

antenna one of a pair of mobile sense organs on the heads of insects, crustaceans, etc.; (pl.) an aerial

anthropic to do with human beings

anthropic principle the fact that human beings exist and that there is life in the universe must place limits on the ways in which the very early universe could have evolved

anthropocentric considering humankind as the centre of existence

anthropoid 1) manlike 2) apelike

anthropology the study of all facets of humankind –
society, culture, evolution, human zoology, and the
distribution of races

anthropomorphism the attribution of human
characteristics to a deity, animal or any non-human
thing; an associated architectural movement of the
1980s resulting in certain buildings being designed
on the basis that windows, doors and porches etc.
could be seen as faces or parts of the human body.

anthropophagi cannibals

anthropophagy the eating of human flesh by other
human beings; cannibalism

antibody a protein produced in the blood which
destroys bacteria

anticoagulant (agent) that prevents clotting of the
blood

antigen a substance, usually a toxin, that causes the
body to produce antibodies

antilogy a contradiction in terms

antimacassar a cover over upholstery esp. the back
of a chair or sofa to protect from grease in the hair,
or as a decoration

antimony a brittle, silvery-white, semi-metal

antinomy a contradiction between two assertions
that are in themselves apparently valid; often loosely
termed a paradox

antipathy an aversion; repugnance; a feeling of strong dislike or hostility

antiperiodic effective against recurrent attacks of a disease

antiphrasis the shortest form of irony – using a single word to mean its exact opposite, such as calling a short man 'Lofty'

antipyretic (a drug) preventing or reducing fever

antiquated outdated, old-fashioned

antithesis a direct opposite

antithetical directly opposed or contrary

antonomasia 1) the use of an epithet or title instead of a proper name e.g. *the father of history* for Herodotus 2) the use of a proper name to express a general idea e.g. *a Lothario* for a womaniser

antonym a word of opposite meaning e.g. the antonym of young is old

antrorse directed or pointing upwards or forwards

anuran a frog or toad

anxiety of influence the feelings of inadequacy experienced by writers, esp. poets trying to compete with the wealth of the literary tradition that precedes them (Harold Bloom)

aorta the main artery taking oxygen-rich blood from the heart to the circulatory system

à outrance Fr. to the utmost; to excess; to the death; to the bitter end

apatetic concerning colouration that disguises and protects an animal

apathetic having no interest or enthusiasm; indifferent

apathy indifference, lack of interest or feeling

ape to imitate

aperçu Fr. 1) an insight; a glimpse, a moment of suddenly understanding, appreciating something 2) an outline, a summary

aperient (a drug) that relieves constipation

apex the top or highest point of something

aphasia total or partial loss of the ability to understand or produce speech or writing following brain damage

aphelion the point in its orbit at which a body is furthest from the sun

aphemia loss of the power of speech due to disease in the brain

aphesis the loss or gradual disappearance of a letter at the beginning of a word e.g. *squire* from *esquire*

aphid an insect which feeds off plants by sucking sap from them e.g. greenfly, blackfly

aphonia, aphony loss of voice

aphorism a concise, pithy saying; an apothegm

aphotic without light, having no light

aphrodisiac (a food, drink or drug) that arouses sexual desire

Aphrodite the Greek goddess of erotic love

aphtha 1) a small ulcer in the mouth or on the tongue 2) foot and mouth disease

apiarist a bee-keeper

apiculture bee-keeping

aplomb self-confidence; self-assurance; poise

apnoea, apnea temporary cessation of breathing

apocalypse the end of the world

apocope *n.* cutting off the end of a word e.g *photo* for *photograph*

apocryphal of doubtful authenticity, unlikely to be true

apodal without feet

apodictic, apodeictic absolutely certain, demonstrably true, proven beyond dispute

apodosis the main clause of a conditional sentence

apogamy, apogamic asexual reproduction without fertilisation

apogee 1) the point in the moon's or a satellite's orbit farthest from the earth 2) the highest point, the climax

apograph an exact copy

apolaustic dedicated to enjoyment; pleasure-seeking; hedonistic

Apollo Belvedere an ancient statue of Apollo in the Belvedere Gallery in the Vatican

Apollonian characteristic of or embodying the rational, orderly and sober as one side of human nature is (Nietzsche)

apologia a formal defence of a cause or of one's conduct, beliefs, or opinions

apologist somebody who makes an apologia or defence of some other person or cause esp. one that is controversial or unworthy

apology for a poor example or specimen of, a poor substitute

apolune the point at which a spacecraft in lunar orbit is furthest from the moon

apophthegm a pithy, witty, instructive saying, a maxim

apoplectic relating to apoplexy; furious, in a rage

apoplexy extreme anger or fury, a rage; a fit or a stroke

apoptosis the death of cells occurring as a normal part of the development of an organism

aporia, aporetic 1) an impasse in the deconstructive criticism of Jacques Derrida 2) *in rhetoric* dithering, indecision when faced with a difficult question 'To be or not to be...'

aposematic descriptive of the usual bright colouration of an animal that warns off predators that it is poisonous or foul-tasting; warning

aposiopesis a sudden breaking off in speech or in writing in mid-sentence for dramatic effect – a rhetorical device

apostate one who abandons his party, principles, a cause, or religion; a defector, deserter, turncoat

a posteriori proceeding from effect to cause, involving inductive reasoning from the particular to the general, from observed facts or effects to a general principle; empirical, based on experience

apostil a marginal note

apostrophe *'a turning away'* a rhetorical device whereby the text digresses from the subject in hand to address some person, idea or thing present or absent

apostrophize *rhetorical* to address someone or something absent or imaginary

apothecary a chemist, pharmacist

apothegm a variant spelling of **apophthegm**

apotheosis 1) the highest point in the development of something; apogee 2) making a god of, deification, idealization, giving God-like stature to

apotropaic purportedly able to ward off evil or bad luck

appanage, apanage 1) provision for the younger children of a royal family 2) a natural or customary accompaniment or perk with a job or position

apparatchik a (communist) party activist

apparel clothing

apparition a ghost; a sudden or unusual sight

appease to pacify

appellation a name or title

apperception assimilation of a new concept into the mind

appetence, appetency a craving or desire

apposite appropriate; apt

appraise to evaluate

appreciable significant; perceptible; considerable

appreciate 1) to recognize the value or significance of; to be grateful for 2) to rise in value or price

appreciative grateful

apprise to inform

appurtenance an accessory; an adjunct; an appendage

a priori based on theoretical, deductive reasoning, not actual observation or experience

apropos 1) with reference to 2) appropriate(ly) 3) by the way; incidentally

apse an arched or domed recess, semicircular or polygonal, usu. at the east end of a church

apteral, apterous without wings

apteryx a kiwi

aquamarine light, bluish-green; a gemstone of that colour

aqua vitae *(water of life)* brandy

aqueous to do with water, watery

aquifer a body of rock that holds water

aquiline 1) like an eagle 2) *(of a nose)* curved like an eagle's beak

arabesque 1) a ballet posture 2) an ornamental design of intertwined flowing lines 3) music with a highly ornamental melody

arable (of land) suitable for growing crops

arachnid *zool. term* for a scorpion, spider etc.

Aramaic an ancient language of the Middle East, still spoken in parts of Syria and Lebanon

arbalest a large medieval crossbow designed to fire arrows, stones, and other missiles

arbiter a judge; a person who settles disputes, an arbitrator; one who sets standards for others: *an arbiter of taste*

arbitrage the speculative buying and selling of currencies, securities, commodities or the like, in different markets to take advantage of the differences in price

arbitrary 1) based on personal whim; subjective; capricious; discretionary 2) not subject to control, constraint, review or appeal

arbitration the determination of a dispute by an impartial third party

arboreal 1) relating to trees 2) living in trees

arboretum a place where trees and shrubs are cultivated for exhibition or study

arbour a shady garden retreat enclosed by trees, climbing plants etc.; a bower

Arcadia a mountain retreat in the Peloponnese in southern Greece; an idealized rural setting, a pastoral paradise

arcana secrets; matters known to only a few

arcane mysterious; obscure; technical; esoteric; understood by only the few who have secret knowledge

arch 1) playfully teasing, roguish or mischievous 2) leading, principal, chief 3) expert, very experienced 4) superior or knowing

arch – chief, principal; pre-eminent

archaic out of date; no longer in everyday use

archetype a very typical example

archipelago a group of islands

architrave 1) *archit.* a main beam that rests across the tops of columns 2) the frame round a doorway or window 3) the exterior moulding round an arch

archives historical records; place where they are kept

arcology an ideal city fully integrated with and allowing maximum conservation of its natural environment: the vision in 1969 of U.S. architect Paolo Soleri

arcuate curved

ardency ardour, fervour

ardour great enthusiasm, burning passion or fiery devotion for a person or activity

arduous requiring great effort or endurance

arenaceous sandy

argent silver

argil clay *adj.* **argillaceous, argilliferous**

Argive 1) to do with Argos (ancient Greek city) 2) *literary* for Greek

argon the most common of the noble gases; colourless, odourless and tasteless, it makes up about 1% of the earth's atmosphere; *fig./colloq.* artificial light, from its association with electric light bulbs in which it is used to prolong the life of the filament

argosy a large merchant ship

argot the slang or jargon of a particular group

argufy to argue about something trivial

Argus *Gk. myth* a giant guardian with 100 eyes; a watchful, vigilant person

aria song for a solo voice

Arianism the doctrine named after the Greek theologian Arius (c.250 – c.336) that the divinity of Christ is inferior to the divinity of God

arid dry and consequently infertile

ark a chest

armadillo a burrowing, edentate mammal of Central and South America, covered in a flexible armour of strong bony plates; feeds chiefly on insects

Armageddon the final battle at the end of the world between the forces of good and evil

armature 1) (in sculpture) a framework to support the clay or other material used in the moulding 2) the protective covering of an animal or plant 3) a revolving structure in an electric motor or generator, wound with the coils that carry the current

armiger a person entitled to a coat-of-arms *adj.* **armigerous**

armoire a cupboard or wardrobe

armorial relating to heraldry, heraldic arms

Armorica ancient name for Brittany

aroma a pleasant and distinctive smell

arpeggio notes of a chord played in rapid succession

arquebus = harquebus

arrack, arak a coarse alcoholic spirit distilled in Eastern countries from grain, rice, coco sap, sugar cane etc.

arraign to accuse or charge esp. before a court of law

arrant downright, complete, utter, out-and-out

arras a tapestry

arrhythmia irregularity in the heartbeat

arride to please, to gratify

arrière-pensée a concealed thought or intention

arriviste one who has recently 'arrived', and who is determined to succeed at any price; a person who has ambition but no scruples; a newcomer or upstart

arrogate (to oneself) to claim or appropriate as one's own without justification

Arromanches one of the D-day *(6th June'44)* beaches on which the Allies landed in Normandy before driving the Germans out of France; also the site of a Mulberry Harbour

arsenal a weapons store, armoury

arsis a stressed syllable in verse

art deco 1920s and 1930s bold, decorative, style with symmetrical designs, stylised natural forms, geometric shapes, bright, contrasting colours and sharp edges esp. in houses and household objects

artefact , **artifact** a man-made object

articulate 1) to express clearly and distinctly 2) able to express oneself coherently and fluently; clear, distinct

articulated connected by joints

artifice the use of cunning tricks or deceptions

artificer a skilled mechanic in the armed forces esp. the Navy

artiodactyla ungulates with an even number of toes on each foot – pigs, hippos, camels, and ruminants

artisan a skilled manual worker, craftsman, mechanic

artiste a professional singer or dancer

art nouveau 1890s to early 1900s, was characterized by long, sinuous, undulating lines, based on natural, asymmetrical forms such as flowers, plants and leaves etc.

Aryan 1) a person supposedly descended from the Indo-Europeans 2) (for the Nazis) a non-Jewish Caucasian of the Nordic type

ascetic one who practises self-denial and leads an austere life *adj.* austere in appearance, manner, or attitude

asceticism strict abstinence and self-denial – no pleasure; denying oneself physical comforts and necessities enables one to move beyond material needs and desires and to focus on loftier things

ascribe to assign or attribute, to impute

asexual 1) having no apparent sex or sex organs 2) (of reproduction) not involving sexual activity

ashram a religious retreat for a Hindu holy man

asinine stupid like an ass or donkey

askance with a look of suspicion or disapproval; sideways

askew not in a straight or level position; twisted to one side

Asperger's syndrome a mild autistic disorder involving awkwardness in social relationships, pedantic speech, and preoccupation with very narrow interests

asperity harshness of tone or manner; roughness

asperse to attack the reputation of; to defame

aspersion a slur; a disparaging or malicious remark esp. on a person's character or reputation

asphyxiate to suffocate; to smother

aspic savoury jelly

aspiration 1) ambition 2) breathing

assail to attack

assay 1) the testing of a metal or ore to find out its ingredients and quality 2) to carry out such a test 3) to attempt

assegai, assagai a slender, hardwood spear with an iron tip, used mainly by tribesmen in southern Africa

asseverate to assert, to affirm solemnly, emphatically

assiduous hard working, persevering and taking great care; sedulous; diligent and persistent

assignation a meeting of lovers, a tryst

assimilate 1) to take in and understand (information, ideas) 2) to absorb and digest (food) 3) to absorb and integrate (people, ideas, culture)

assonance the vowel equivalent of alliteration or consonance – the repetition, matching or correspondence of the vowel sounds of nearby words

assuage 1) to soothe, relieve 2) to satisfy, quench *adj.* **assuasive**

astatic not standing still, not static; unstable, unsteady

asteism genteel irony; a polite and ingenious way of deriding somebody

aster a daisy-like garden plant

astigmatism an optical defect of a lens or of the eye causing it not to focus properly and resulting in distorted images

Astraea Roman goddess of justice

astringent 1) severe or harsh (manner or style) 2) sharp or bitter (taste or smell)

asunder apart, into separate pieces

asymmetry having parts which do not match, i.e. do not correspond in size, shape, proportion, arrangement, or relative position

asyndeton the absence or omission of words usu. conjunctions

asyntactic ungrammatical

ataraxia, ataraxy mental tranquillity, serene calmness, peace of mind; stoical indifference

atavism 1) ancestral, not parental, features in organisms, animals or plants 2) reversion to a former type 3) a throwback

ataxy, ataxia loss of control of bodily movements, of muscular coordination

at bay trapped or cornered

atheist one who denies the existence of God

Athena Greek goddess of wisdom

atheology opposition to theology, religion and the study of God

athwart 1) across from side to side 2) across the path or line of

atimy public disgrace

atlantes *archit.* figures of men used as pillars to support the entablature of a Greek building aka **telamones** cf. **caryatides**

Atlantis fabled island in the ocean west of Gibraltar, said by Plato to have sunk beneath the sea

atoll a coral reef surrounding a lagoon

atom the smallest particle of an element that can exist and still retain the chemical properties of that element. It comprises a positively charged nucleus surrounded by orbiting negatively charged electrons. The nucleus consists of neutrons which have no charge and positively charged protons which, in neutral atoms, are equal in number to the orbiting electrons.

atonal (of music) not written in any key

atrabilious, atrabiliar 'black bile'; melancholic, bad-tempered, irritable

atrophy wasting away through undernourishment or lack of use

attar perfume or fragrant oil made from rose petals

attenuate to make thin or thinner; to reduce in strength, force, value, size or degree

attest to confirm as existent, true, correct, or genuine

attic classically elegant, simple, or pure

attributive (of an adjective, adjectival phrase, or modifying noun) preceding the word it modifies and expressing an attribute – an up-to-date report but not the report is up to date which is predicative

attrition wearing down

atypical not typical

aubade music or a poem about the dawn

au courant Fr. fully informed, up to date, 'up to speed'

audacious bold

audacity fearless, reckless, daring boldness

audible able to be heard, hearable

audile relating to the sense of hearing

audiophile a lover of music in high-fidelity sound

augean filthy, dirty

Augeas a king in Gk. myth whose stables had never been cleaned. Hercules cleaned them in a day by diverting the River Alpheus through them

auger a drilling tool

augment to increase, enlarge

augur *v.* to bode, to predict, to presage; to serve as an omen or indication

augury an omen

august grand, imposing and dignified; majestic

Augustan refined, and classically elegant

Augustan age the golden age in a nation's literature *Latin*, the reign of the Emperor Augustus (27 b.c. to a.d.14) includes Horace, Ovid, Virgil and Livy *England*, the reigns of Queen Anne (1702 -14) and George 1 (1714 – 27) extended to the deaths of Pope and Swift (1744-5) *France*, the 17th century to include Corneille, Molière and Racine.

auk a diving seabird – guillemot, puffin, razorbill

aura atmosphere surrounding a person or thing

aural to do with the ear or hearing

aureole a halo

auricle the external ear, the pinna

aurora the dawn – **Aurora**, Roman goddess of the dawn

auscultation listening to the heart, lungs, usu. through a stethoscope

Ausonia *Latin* Italy

auspice an omen – **under the auspices of** with the support or protection of

auspicious showing signs of future success; propitious

aussitôt dit, aussitôt fait Fr. no sooner said than done

austere 1) severe or strict in appearance or manner 2) lacking comforts, luxuries, or adornment

austral southern

autarchy absolute power

autarky economic self-sufficiency – no need for imports!

authoritarian dictatorial, domineering

authoritative 1) reliable because true or accurate 2) commanding and self-confident

autism abnormal self-absorption usu. present from childhood, characterized by difficulty responding to or communicating with the outside world

autochthon an aborigine, a native; the first or an indigenous inhabitant of a place

autochthonous indigenous; native; originating where found

autocrat 1) a ruler who has absolute power 2) a domineering person

auto-da-fé 1) the sentence on heretics by the Spanish Inquisition 2) the execution of the sentence – burning to death

autodidact a self-taught person

autogenous self-produced; self-generated

autogeny 1) a mode of spontaneous generation 2) abiogenesis

autological (of an adjective) having the property it describes e.g. polysyllabic

Autolycus 1) *Gk. myth* a thief 2) 'a snapper-up of unconsidered trifles' (The Winter's Tale)

automaton a robot; a person who responds in a mechanical way

autonomous independent; self-governing; self-sufficient

autopsy a post-mortem examination

autotelic having or being an end or purpose in itself

autotomy casting off a body part by an animal under threat in order to escape capture e.g. a lizard's tail

auxesis growth

auxiliary helping, supporting

avail to be of help, value, or advantage to

avant-garde Fr. new and experimental

avant la lettre Fr. before the term existed (Hercules was an industrial cleaner *avant la lettre*) see **Augeas**

avarice extreme greed for wealth; cupidity

avaricious greedy

avast a nautical command to stop

avatar 1) an incarnation 2) a movable image that represents a person in a virtual reality environment or in cyberspace

avaunt begone!

Ave, Avete Hail!

avenge to get back at

aver to state or assert as a fact

averruncate to avert, ward off; to extirpate

averse (to) opposed; disinclined, loath

avert 1) to prevent or ward off (danger, disaster) 2) to turn away (one's eyes, gaze, etc.)

avian bird-like, to do with birds

aviary a place for keeping birds

avid eager in a greedy way; enthusiastic, keen

avocation a matter one devotes time to, a subsidiary occupation; a hobby

avoirdupois the system of weights based on a pound of 16 ounces – sometimes used humorously to mean excess weight

avow to admit, to confess, to affirm openly

avulsion forcible separation; a forcible tearing away

avuncular like an uncle; kindly, helpful, genial and friendly

awash washed over by water, the sea, waves; flooded

aweigh (of an anchor) raised clear of the sea bed: hanging by its **rode**

awn a bristle growing from the grain-sheath of grasses and cereals e.g. barley, rye

awning a canvas stretched on a frame to protect a shop window, doorway etc. against the sun or rain

awry away from the correct course, with a twist to one side, askew; amiss or faulty

axial to do with an axis

axilla the armpit

axillary to do with the armpit

axiom a rule or principle that is widely accepted or seems self-evident

axiomatic self-evident

axis the axle or line about which a body rotates

ayurveda traditional Hindu system of medicine based mainly on herbal remedies, diet, homeopathy, naturopathy, yogic breathing, etc.

azimuth a horizontal angle which, taken together with an accompanying vertical angle, enables the position of an object in the sky to be pinpointed

azoic without life; before the existence of life

azonic not limited to a zone, not local

azure sky-blue

azygous single; not yoked or joined with another

B

Baal 1) an ancient semitic fertility god 2) the Phoenician sun god and supreme national deity

baas *S.Afr.* boss

baasskap *S.Afr.* white supremacy

Babbitt *esp. in N. America* a bourgeois, materialistic businessman

babel a din, a hubbub; a noise and confusion of many voices

Babel, Tower of biblical tower where the confusion of many languages took place; a hubbub

bacchanal a wild, drunken party; an occasion of wild and drunken revelry

bacchanalian involving drunken revelry; orgiastic

bacchant, bacchante 1) a drunken reveller 2) a priest, priestess, follower or votary of Bacchus

Bacchus *Gk. myth* god of wine (aka Dionysus), hence Bacchanalian tendencies

bacciform berry-shaped

back formation making a new word, esp. a verb, from an existing noun or adjective that might itself have been supposed to derive from the verb – to edit comes from editor and not vice versa

bacteriophage a virus that destroys a bacterium, aka **phage**

Bactrian camel camel with two humps

badinage banter

bagatelle 1) a game in which small balls are struck into holes on a board with pins as obstacles 2) something of no consequence 3) a short, light piece of music, esp. for piano

bagnio a brothel

bailiwick 1) the district or jurisdiction of a bailiff 2) one's area of expertise

baize woollen, usu. green, felt-like fabric used for covering snooker and card-tables

bakelite an early brittle form of plastic

baksheesh a gift of a small sum of money as a gratuity, a tip, alms or a bribe

baleful 1) (*often of facial expression*) menacing, threatening 2) sinister, harmful, evil

ballast heavy material placed in the hold of a ship to steady it

balletomane one who has a passion for ballet

ballistic *(to do with projectiles)* moving under the force of gravity only

ballistic missile initially propelled and guided but in descent it hits its target under gravity

go ballistic to fly into a rage

ballon d'essai Fr. something put forward tentatively or experimentally to gauge reactions to it; a feeler

balneology the science of the therapeutic effects of baths and mineral springs

bamboozle 1) to cheat, trick or deceive 2) to mystify or confuse

banal trite, unoriginal, commonplace

banausic for artisans, materialistic, utilitarian

bandanna a type of handkerchief or neckerchief

bandicoot a ratlike Australasian marsupial

bane 1) the cause of ruin, great harm, or serious trouble; a major annoyance; the curse (menstruation) 2) poison

baneful harmful, destructive

banns official proclamation of a forthcoming marriage

banter good-humoured, playful, friendly exchange of teasing remarks in conversation

Bantustan *S.Afr.* homeland

baraguin unintelligible language; gibberish

barb a biting, intentionally hurtful remark

Barbary ape a tailless macaque monkey of North Africa and Gibraltar

Barbary Coast the former name for the Mediterranean coast of North Africa from Morocco to Egypt

barbican the outer defence of a fortified city or castle esp. a tower above a gate or drawbridge

barcarole song of a Venetian gondolier

bardolatry excessive reverence for Shakespeare, 'the bard'

Barmecide, Barmecidal illusory, imaginary and consequently disappointing – from the name of the wealthy Persian in the Arabian Nights who gave a beggar a feast of ornate but empty dishes

barmkin the rampart of a castle

baroque *(of a style)* ornate and extravagant, bold, elaborate, flamboyant

barouche a four-wheeled, horse-drawn carriage, popular in the 19th century

barque a sailing-ship, a boat

barracuda a large voracious and predatory fish of warm seas

barrage a continuous bombardment or firing of artillery over a wide area

barrage balloon a balloon anchored singly or as one of a series, supporting cables or nets in order to hinder the passage of low-flying enemy aircraft

barratry loss or damage caused to the owners/charterers of a ship by its master or crew

barrow a mound of earth over an ancient burial place; a tumulus

bar sinister = bend sinister

barter to exchange goods or services for other goods or services without the exchange of money

barton a farmyard

basalt dark volcanic rock; it is sometimes found in columns as in the Giant's Causeway, Northern Ireland and the cliffs of Fingal's Cave at Staffa, an island of the Inner Hebrides, Scotland

bascule a type of drawbridge

bashaw 1) a pasha; an important man 2) a haughty or pompous person

basilica a large, oblong, public building in ancient Rome; many were subsequently converted into Christian churches

basilisk a mythical reptile with lethal breath which was also able to 'look anyone dead on whom it fixed its eyes'

basinet a light, close-fitting steel helmet used in medieval times

bas-relief sculpture in low relief in which the forms project only slightly from the background

bassinet a baby's basket-like wicker cradle with a hood

bastinado a beating on the soles of the feet; stick used for such beating

bastion 1) a projecting part of a fortification allowing an increased angle of fire 2) a strongly defended position 3) any person or thing considered a defender or a stronghold

bated, with bated breath in anxious suspense

Batesian mimicry imitation whereby a harmless species is protected against predators by its resemblance to a harmful or inedible species

batiste *Fr.* cambric

bathos a sudden, unintended lapse from the exalted to the trivial – a ludicrous descent from the sublime to the ridiculous *adj.* **bathetic**

batman officer's personal servant

batrachian *n. & adj.* (pertaining to) toads and frogs; anuran; salientian

baulk, balk to stop short, to hold back from, to refuse; (*tr.*) to thwart, to foil

bavardage chit-chat, idle gossip

bawdy humorous but indecent

baying barking, howling (of pursuing hounds)

Bayreuth town in Bavaria, holds festivals of Wagner's music; he lived and is buried there

beadsman one employed to pray for others

beastings the first milk from a cow after calving

beatific 1) feeling and displaying blissful happiness in a serene or saintly way 2) having a divine aura; imparting holy bliss

beatification declaring a dead person 'blessed', often the first step towards canonization

beau monde the world of fashionable society

beaux-arts fine arts, poetry, music but esp. painting, sculpture and architecture

becalmed (of a sailing ship) motionless through lack of wind

béchamel Fr. white cream sauce

bedizened dressed gaudily

bedlam 1) a disorderly scene of uproar and confusion 2) a madhouse, an asylum

bedlamite a lunatic

bedraggled wet and dirty as if having been dragged through mud

bee *N. Amer.* a gathering for a specified purpose or amusement

beggar *v.tr.* to be so extraordinary or unusual as to make something difficult or impossible; to defy – (belief, description)

beguile 1) to charm, to fascinate, to enchant; to trick into doing something 2) to help (time) pass pleasantly

behemoth *in scripture*, Job XL: 15 an enormous creature; a hippopotamus or possibly a rhinoceros

behest order, request, command, bidding

behove to be necessary or fitting for, **it behoves someone to do something** it is a duty, responsibility, or appropriate response for someone to do something

belabour to attack physically or verbally

belamy a good friend

beldam an old woman, an old bag, a hag

beleaguered 1) besieged by an enemy 2) struggling against difficulties or criticism

belie 1) to give a false impression of (something); to disguise, conceal 2) to show (something) to be false; to falsify

bell, book and candle a colloquial term for ceremonial excommunication from the R. C. Church

belle laide = jolie laide Fr. an intriguingly plain or ugly woman, whose manner and charm make her attractive

bellicose warlike

belligerent aggressive; engaged in warfare

Bellona the Roman goddess of war; a woman of great spirit and vigour

Bells and smells the Anglo-Catholic or High Church wing of the Church of England, i.e. the altar bells and the incense as used in the Eucharist in the R. C. Church

Bell's palsy paralysis of the muscles on one side of the face

bellwether 1) the leading sheep of a flock often with a bell fastened to its neck 2) a leader or trendsetter

below the salt common, lowly

beluga 1) a large white sturgeon of the Caspian and Black Seas from which caviar is obtained 2) a small white whale

belvedere a summer-house or open-sided gallery at rooftop level

Belvedere Apollo the perfection of youthful manhood – the epitome of a handsome man from the statue of Apollo in the Belvedere Gallery in the Vatican

bemused puzzled, bewildered or confused

benchmark a standard or point of reference against which things may be measured, compared, or assessed

bend sinister a broad diagonal stripe from top right to bottom left of a shield – a supposed sign of bastardy aka **bar sinister**

Benedick, Benedict a newly married man esp. a former confirmed bachelor, from Shakespeare's *Much Ado About Nothing*

benediction blessing

beneficent doing good; charitable; generous

beneficial having a helpful or useful effect

benevolent kindly and helpful

benighted 1) overtaken by the night, in the dark *(lit. and esp. met.)* 2) ignorant, unenlightened

benign kind, friendly; not dangerous to health

béni-oui-oui Fr. somebody who systematically and automatically approves the words and acts of those in authority; a 'yes' man

benison a blessing

benjamin the youngest and favourite son; used loosely esp. by the French to mean one of the stars of the next generation

benthos the flora and fauna on the bottom of a sea or lake *adj.* **benthic**

Beowulf hero of the Old English epic poem of the same name, set in Scandinavia in the early sixth century

berate to criticize angrily

berceuse a lullaby

bereaved having recently lost a close relative or friend through death

bereft deprived, desolate

bergamask a kind of rustic dance originally from Bergamo in Italy

bergamot 1) a type of pear or orange 2) a type of herbaceous plant grown for its scarlet red flowers

berserk out of control; wild or frenzied

beryl a transparent, hard mineral used as a gemstone

beseech to ask earnestly; to beg

beset to surround

besiege to surround with armed forces with a view to capturing or obtaining a surrender

besmirch to tarnish or sully; to make dirty; to stain

besom a broom made of a bundle of twigs tied round a stick

besotted infatuated

bespeak to order in advance **bespoke** made-to-order

bestride 1) to ride, sit, or stand astride (something); to straddle 2) to tower over (something); to dominate

bête noire Fr. someone, something detested

bethel a chapel, a place of worship for nonconformists

bêtise Fr. a stupid remark or action; a blunder

betoken to be a warning or sign of

between each, between every one often reads this type of instruction: 'Sow the seeds in rows, with at least two feet between each row.' It should be clear to anyone that between cannot exist with one singular word, so that between each or between every is nonsense. Correct versions would be: 'Sow the seeds in rows, with at leat two feet between adjacent rows' or ' … with at least two feet between each pair of rows' or 'sow the seeds in rows, the rows being at least two feet apart'.

between you and I may have a vaguely superior air (hence its soubriquet – 'the toff's error') but it is bad grammar and should be **between you and me**; between, as a preposition, takes the accusative or object case

bevel a slope, a slant

bevy a group or gathering

bey (in the Ottoman Empire) a provincial governor

bezant a gold coin

bibacious given to drinking (alcohol)

bibelot a small ornament or trinket

bibliophile a lover of books

bibulous excessively fond of or addicted to alcoholic stimulation

bicker to argue about petty matters

bicuspid having two points, horns, or cusps

biddable obedient, docile

bifurcation a division into two forks or branches

biggin a child's cap or hood

bight 1) a bay 2) a loop in a rope

between you and I
may have a vaguely superior air
(hence its soubriquet – 'the toff's error')
but it is bad grammar and should be
between you and me; between, as a preposition,
takes the accusative or object case

bigot a dogmatist, a person who is obstinately or intolerantly unreceptive to views other than his own

Bildeberg Group a powerful secret gathering of international political and business leaders

bildungsroman Ger. a novel dealing with a person's early life and development into adulthood

bilious 1) to do with (a disorder of) the bile 2) bad-tempered, irritable

bilk to cheat, to swindle (out of money)

billet-doux a love letter

binary opposition(s) form the basis of digital systems of communication and involve the reduction of continuous variations to separate either/or distinctions. Western metaphysics is structured in terms of binary oppositions or dichotomies, e.g. man/woman, presence/absence, mind/matter, culture/nature, speech/writing, etc, the first term is privileged over the other which is relegated to being all that the first term is not.

bind *inf.* an annoyance; a problematical situation

binomial nomenclature, binomial system for naming plants and animals by means of two latin names; the first indicating the genus and the second the species to which the organism belongs

biodegradable capable of decomposing, decaying, rotting

biomorphic a term used in abstract art and surrealism to describe non-geometrical forms based on living organisms and natural shapes, found, for example, in the works of Hans Arp, Yves Tanguy and Joan Miró.

bionic having electromechanical body parts instead of or as well as living ones

biopsy the taking of living tissue from a body to test for disease

biorhythm a cyclically recurring pattern of physiological states in an organism or organ believed by some to affect physical and mental states and behaviour

bipolar disorder the modern name for manic depression

biretta a square cap worn by R.C. clergy – by priests, black; bishops, purple; cardinals, red

Bismarck, Prince von *(1815-1898)* autocratic, authoritarian Prussian statesman; after driving through the unification of Germany *(1871)*, he became the Chancellor of the new German Empire and continued in office until forced out in 1890.

bittern a type of heron

bitumen tar

bivouac an overnight encampment with little or no cover

blackguard a scoundrel

black hole (in astronomy) a region of space having a gravitational field so intense that no matter or radiation can escape

bladderwrack seaweed

blanch 1) to whiten 2) to go white or pale from sickness, shock, fear etc. 3) to prepare (vegetables) by immersing them briefly in boiling water 4) to peel (almonds) by scalding them

blandishment(s) flattery

blasé not interested, unimpressed, indifferent

blather, blether 1) nonsense 2) to talk nonsense

blazon 1) to proclaim (b. abroad) 2) to describe (heraldic arms) in correct, technical terms; to depict them 3) a correct description or depiction of heraldic arms

blight a disease in plants esp. one caused by fungi

bling-bling, bling *adj. & n.* flashy, glitzy (jewellery)

Blücher commander of the Prussian army at the time of Waterloo; the arrival of his troops early evening 18th June 1815 contributed to Napoleon's defeat

Bluebeard a wife killer

bluestocking a scholarly, intellectual or literary woman

blue whale the largest of all the animals

bluff a high steep bank, cliff or headland

blurb a promotional description

blush, at first blush on first impression

Boanerges a speaker or preacher with a loud voice and impassioned delivery

bob a dangling weight on a plumb-line, pendulum or kite tail

bodacious outstanding, impressive, remarkable, excellent

bode to be a portent of (a good or bad outcome)

bodkin a blunt, thick, large-eyed needle

bohemian an artist or writer living an unconventional, gypsy-type existence

bolas *S. Amer.* a number of balls on a cord for throwing at and entangling the legs of a running quarry

bole a tree-trunk

boll the rounded pod containing the seeds of cotton, flax, poppy and similar plants

boll weevil small N. Amer. beetle whose larvae feed on and destroy cotton bolls

bologna a large, smoked sausage

bolus 1) a soft ball of chewed food 2) a large pill

bombardon a bass tuba

bombast high-sounding, pompous, padded, pretentious language with little content

bombilating, bombinating buzzing, humming

bon mot a short, witty saying; a clever remark

booby a foolish or ignorant person

boon something helpful, useful, or beneficial; a timely benefit; a stroke of good luck

boondocks rough, wild, desolate country; the backwoods; the sticks

boondoggle *n.* an activity which is a complete waste of time or money or dishonest *v.* to engage in such activity

boongarry the tree-kangaroo of North Queensland

boor a rude, uncouth, loutish type without manners and social graces

boorish ill-mannered, insensitive, without charm or refinement

booty valuable, stolen goods; loot

borborygmus flatulence in the bowels, tummy rumbling

bordello a brothel

bore a tidal wave

boreal relating to the north or the north wind

Borglum, Gutzon *(1867-1941)* American sculptor who carved the faces of four U.S. presidents (Washington, Jefferson, Lincoln and Theodore Roosevelt) on Mt. Rushmore, S. Dakota

bort inferior diamonds used in cutting tools or, in powdered form, as an abrasive

bosky covered by bushes, trees; wooded

boss a knob, a stud, a round ornamental bump

bothy *Sc.* a humble cottage or hut esp. for housing farm workers or as a mountain shelter

botryoidal shaped like a bunch of grapes

bottomry a contract by which a ship is pledged as security for a loan to finance a voyage

botulism a dangerous form of food poisoning

boudin, boudin noir a French black pudding

boudoir a woman's bedroom or small private room

bouffant puffed out, full

bounder a dishonourable man

bountiful 1) abundant 2) giving generously

Bourbon European royal dynasty, kings of: **France** *(1589-1793)* and *(1815-1848)*: **Spain** *(1700-1931)* (with minor interruptions) and since *1975* (Juan Carlos)

bourbon 1) a chocolate biscuit 2) an American whisky 3) a reactionary *(U.S.)*

bourgeois a typically, middle class, urban type with materialistic values and conventional attitudes

boustrophedon written ploughwise, alternately from right to left and from left to right

bovarysme living in a fantasy world far removed from the realities of everyday life; apart from Madame Bovary in Flaubert's novel (1857) of the same name, other well-known characters in fiction, Don Quixote and Walter Mitty were afflicted in this way.

bovine cattle-like; dull, sluggish, phlegmatic; hebetudinous

bowdlerize to expurgate, to 'clean up' a text

bowyer a maker/seller of archery bows

Box and Cox *n.* the using of the same facilities by different people at different times *v.* to act in this way

boycott to refuse to buy from or deal with

boysenberry 1) a bramble hybrid 2) its large red edible fruit

brachial to do with the arm; arm-like

brachycephalic having a broad, short skull

brachylogy 1) conciseness or over-conciseness of expression 2) a colloquial shortened form of expression e.g. *Thanks!* or *Evening!* in every day speech

brackish slightly salty (of water)

bract a type of leaf

bradycardia abnormally slow heartbeat

braggadocio boasting

Brahman, Brahmin 1) (in the Hindu caste system) a member of the priesthood, the highest caste 2) a superior person

braid 1) plaited threads for edging/trimming 2) to plait

brainstorm 1) a moment in which one is suddenly unable to think clearly 2) *N.Amer.* a brainwave

brainstorming a group discussion to produce ideas and solutions to problems

brainwave a sudden clever idea

branks *(pl.)* an iron bridle for a scold with a bit to compress the tongue

brassica the cabbage genus of plant, a type that includes swede, rape, and mustard

bratwurst a German pork sausage

bravado a swaggering show of boldness to impress; bogus bravery, counterfeit courage

bravo a hired assassin

bravura a brilliant, showy, stylish performance

bray the hee-haw of a donkey

brazen 1) bold, impudent, shameless 2) to do with brass

breastsummer a summer or beam across a broad opening in a building, holding up the wall or structure above it in the same way as a lintel supports the structure above a door or window

breloque a charm, a trinket attached to a watch-chain

breviary a book containing the service for each day in the R.C. Church

brickbat a highly critical remark

bridewell a prison

bridgehead a military position or foothold established in enemy territory by advance troops

brigand a member of a band of robbers

brigantine a two-masted sailing ship favoured by brigands or pirates

brimstone sulphur

brio vigour, liveliness, gusto, vivacity, spirit

broach 1) to raise a subject for discussion 2) to pierce a cask to draw liquor

broadside guns along one side of a warship, or their combined firing simultaneously; scathing criticism or verbal attack *adv.* sideways on

Brobdingnagian a giant; gigantic – from Swift's *Gulliver's Travels* (1726)

brocade a rich fabric woven with a raised design

brocante Fr. second-hand trade; a second-hand shop

brocard an elementary law or principle; a canon

brock a badger

bromide 1) a sedative 2) a platitude 3) a dull or boring person

bromidrosis the giving off or discharge of foul-smelling perspiration

brook to put up with, to bear, to tolerate – usually used in the negative; 'I can't brook bad manners'

brouhaha hubbub; commotion

brown-nose a person who acts obsequiously

brown study, in a in a reverie; absorbed in one's thoughts

Bruegel, Pieter (c. 1525-1569) Flemish artist – painter of landscapes, peasant life, legless beggars and every variety of cripple

bruit to spread widely (a report or rumour)

Brumaire the month of mist; the second month of the French revolutionary calendar from October 23 to Nov. 21

Brummagem 1) relating to Birmingham 2) *dated* cheap and flashy, worthless, counterfeit (in relation to goods esp. imitation jewellery formerly made there)

brumous misty

brusque abrupt, offhand, blunt

brut (of a wine) very dry esp. champagne

bruxism the grinding of the teeth unconsciously

bryony a wild climbing plant with red berries, common in hedgerows

Brythonic the southern group of Celtic languages, Cornish, Welsh, and Breton

bubo *pl.* buboes inflammation and swelling of a lymph node esp. in the armpit or groin

bubonic plague an acute infectious disease characterized by the formation of buboes

buccal pertaining to the cheek

buccaneer a pirate

buccinatory pertaining to a trumpet, a trumpeter or trumpeting

buckshee free of charge

buckram material used for lining and bookbinding

bucolic pastoral, rural, rustic, typical of the countryside

buffo a comic actor in Italian opera

buffoon a clown; one whose ridiculous behaviour means he is perceived as such

bulimia, bulimia nervosa an emotional eating disorder, mostly in females, resulting from compulsive overeating, periods of fasting or self-induced vomiting, associated with depression, anxiety, and low self-esteem

bullace a wild plum tree; a wild plum

bully beef canned corned beef

bulwark 1) a defensive wall; a rampart 2) a mole or breakwater 3) an extension of a ship's sides above upper deck level

bum-bailiff (formerly) an officer empowered to collect debts or arrest debtors

bumptious offensively self-assertive; conceited; overbearing, pushy

bum steer false information or bad advice

bumpkin a yokel, a rustic person

Bundestag the lower house of the German legislature

bunkum, buncombe nonsense

bunting 1) a type of finch 2) flags, pennants, streamers and other decorations

buoyant 1) keeping afloat 2) cheerful and optimistic, light-hearted and uplifted 3) (of an economy or market) engaged in much activity

burgeoning growing rapidly, putting out buds

burgher a citizen

burin a hand-held tool for engraving

Burj Khalifa, Dubai at 2,717 feet is the tallest building in the world; opened in January 2010

burnish to polish to a shiny finish

bushwacked exhausted

buss a kiss; to kiss

bust a sculpture of the upper half of the body

bustier a strapless close-fitting top for women

buttery a room in a university or college from which students can obtain food and wine

buttonhole to detain a person in conversation

buttress a construction or prop against a wall to strengthen it; a reinforcement or support

butyric descriptive of the foul-smelling fatty acid found in rancid butter

buxom (of females) full-bosomed

buzzword a word in fashionable use such as iconic or parameters

bwana (in East Africa) boss, master; sir

byre a cowshed

byword 1) a familiar saying; a proverb 2) somebody or something taken as representing or being a typical example of a specified quality: *a byword for excess*

Byzantine 1) to do with a) Byzantium (Constantinople as it was later called or Istanbul as it is now known) or b) the Eastern Roman Empire or the Eastern Orthodox Church or c) the rich and highly decorated artistic and architectural style which developed in the Byzantine empire and spread elsewhere 2) excessively complicated and detailed 3) underhand, devious

C

cabal a group of plotters

cabala, cabbala, kabala, kabbala ancient Jewish mystical tradition of interpretation of the Old Testament to find its hidden meanings and predictions

cabalistic relating to the cabala, the occult; mysterious, having a secret or apparently magical significance

caboched *(her.)* showing an animal's head full face without any part of the neck

cabochon a precious stone that has been polished but not cut

caboodle a collection or crowd

cabriole 1) a curved furniture leg 2) a leap in the air in ballet

cabriolet 1) a car with a folding or detachable roof; a convertible 2) a two-wheeled carriage with a hood, pulled by a single horse

cacafuego 1) a loud arrogant boaster; one who browbeats, bullies, intimidates, a spitfire *lit*. shit-fire 2) the name of a Spanish galleon taken by Drake in 1577

cache a hoard of weapons, stolen goods, etc.

cachet prestige or distinction; some extra quality

cachinnate to laugh loudly

cack-handed clumsy; inept

cacoethes an urge to do something unwise

cacoethes scribendi an urge to write

cacography 1) bad handwriting 2) bad spelling

cacology bad grammar; bad choice of words; bad pronunciation; faulty speech generally

cacophony harsh, discordant, jarring sound(s)

cadastral showing the ownership, boundaries and value of land for taxation purposes

cadaver a corpse

cadaverous corpse-like, pale, thin, bony, gaunt, haggard

caddy a container for tea

cadenas a medieval locked casket (often in the form of a ship) containing a gentleman's cutlery requirements – knife, fork, spoon etc.

cadence modulation or inflection of the voice

cadenza a complex, solo passage in a concerto near the end

cadi, kadi, qadi a judge in Islamic countries

cadre a small group of people forming the centre of a military unit or political organisation

caducity 1) perishability, transitoriness, frailty 2) the infirmity of old age; senility

caducous easily detached and shed at an early stage during the life of an organism

caesarean section surgical incision into the womb to deliver a baby

Caesar's wife was divorced by her husband on a mere accusation of adultery; the expression is used to describe someone who must be wholly above suspicion

caespitose = cespitose

caesura a pause in a line of verse

cafard severe mental depression; melancholia

cagoule a type of windcheater, anorak

caird an itinerant tinker, a tramp, a gypsy, a vagrant

cairn a mound of stones built as a memorial or landmark

caisson a watertight chamber enabling construction and other work to be carried out under water

caitiff a contemptible person; a coward

cajole to persuade by flattery; to coax

calabash a large, round, woody gourd that grows on a tropical American tree of the same name

calaboose a prison

calamari squid served as food

calamus quill of a feather

calcaneus the heel bone

calcareous chalky

calcariform shaped like a spur

calcine to heat (something) so as to oxidize, reduce or dessicate it

calculus stone-like object (e.g. gallstone or kidney stone) formed in the body from mineral salts

calefacient making warm, warming

calescence *n.* increasing warmth

calibrate to determine the calibre of

calibre 1) the internal diameter of a gun barrel or tube; the diameter of a bullet or shell 2) a person's ability or worth

calico a type of cotton fabric

caliginosity dimness, darkness

caliginous dark, dim, obscure

caliph the chief Muslim ruler in former times, successor of Muhammad

caliphate the office, jurisdiction of a caliph – abolished in 1924

calligraphy elegant handwriting – regarded as an art form

calliope *N. Amer.* a steam organ

Calliope *Gk. myth* the muse of epic poetry

calliper(s) 1) an instrument for measuring thickness, diameter; internal or external dimensions and (small) distances 2) a metal splint supporting a person's leg

callipygian, callipygous having beautiful buttocks

callous 1) unfeeling, insensitive; hard-hearted 2) (of skin) hardened

callow inexperienced, immature

callus a hard, thick patch of skin

caloyer Greek Orthodox Church monk

calque = loan translation

calumny 1) the making of false accusations against someone 2) a false accusation

Calvados French apple brandy

calvities baldness

calyx the outer ring of sepals that protect a flower in bud

camaraderie comradeship; a spirit of good humour and trust among colleagues and friends

camarilla a cabal, a clique of confidential, unofficial, secret, scheming advisers esp. formerly, to the Spanish kings

camber a slight convexity or arched shape of a horizontal surface e.g. a road

cambist 1) a dealer or specialist in foreign currency 2) a manual showing exchange rates and similar equivalents of weights and measures

Cambria *Latin* for Wales

cambrousse, la Fr. the country, 'the sticks'

came thin lead strip securing the panes in a stained-glass or leaded window

camelopard a giraffe

Camelot the site of the mythical Court of King Arthur and his knights of the Round Table

cameo 1) a piece of jewellery with a profile head carved in relief on a different background 2) a short piece of writing neatly encapsulating something 3) a small but distinctive role in a play or film played by a distinguished actor or actress

camera, in camera in private, with the public excluded

camp (of a man) exaggeratedly effeminate and theatrical in style

campanile a free-standing bell tower

campanology bell-ringing

campanula bellflower, usually blue or white

campestral relating to the open country or uncultivated fields

camstairy perverse, unruly

canaille Fr. the common people, the rabble; riff-raff

canapé a small piece of bread or pastry with a savoury topping

canard a false report, an unfounded rumour or story; a hoax

cancroid 1) resembling a crab, crab-like 2) resembling cancer 3) *n.* skin cancer

candide Fr. ingenuous

candour openness, honesty, frankness

Candy, Candia the former English name for Crete

candytuft a plant with clusters of white,red or purple flowers

canephor *archit.* a female figure bearing a basket on her head

canescent turning white

canicular relating to the dog days of considerable heat

canine pertaining to or resembling a dog

canities whiteness of the hair

canker 1) an ulceration or ulcerous disease 2) something evil that spreads and corrupts

cannelure a groove round the cylinder of a bullet

cannibalize 1) to use (a machine) as a source of spare parts for another similar machine 2) (of a company) to reduce (the sales of one of its products) by introducing a similar, competing product

cannonade artillery bombardment

canon (secular and non-musical meanings) 1) a general rule or standard by which something is judged; a yardstick 2) a list which is accepted as representing the authentic works of a particular author or artist 3) the 'great works' of literature in a particular language or a nation's literary tradition 4) (religious meaning) a decree in Church law; a member of a cathedral clergy

canonization making a dead person a saint

canoodle to caress; to kiss and cuddle amorously

canophilist a lover of dogs

canopic designating an ancient Egyptian vase, urn or jar used to hold the remains of the dead

canopy awning-like or roof-like covering

canorous musical, melodious, tuneful

cant insincere, hypocritical language

cantabile *music* in a smooth singing style, flowingly, melodiously

Cantabrigian of or from Cambridge or its university = **Cantab.**

cantankerous bad-tempered, quarrelsome

cantharides = **Spanish Fly**

canthus either corner of the eye, where the upper and lower eyelids meet

cantilever a long, projecting beam or girder, fixed at only one end

cantrip a trick

canvas strong, coarse cloth; a painting on it

canvass to seek votes for; to question in order to ascertain someone's opinion on something

caoutchouc rubber

Capability Brown (Lancelot Brown) *(1715-1783)* English landscape gardener; laid out gardens at Kew, Blenheim and Chatsworth

capacious having considerable space inside; roomy

caparison a decorated covering for a horse's saddle or harness

capillary one of the very fine, hair-like blood vessels *adj.* hair-like, of hair-like thinness

capitulate to surrender, to admit defeat, to give in

capon a castrated male chicken, fattened for eating

capricious unpredictable, whimsical, prone to sudden unexplained changes of mood, behaviour or attitude

caprine to do with a goat or goats; goat-like; hircine

capsicum 1) the pepper plant 2) the pepper fruit of this plant

capstone 1) same as copestone 2) acme, a crowning achievement

captious carping; looking to find fault; quibbling; making trivial criticisms, nitpicking

captivate to fascinate, to charm

carabinieri Italian national police

carapace the shell of a tortoise or a crustacean – crab, lobster, shrimp etc.

carbuncle 1) a bright red gem esp. a garnet 2) an abscess, ulcer or boil

carcinogen a substance that can cause cancer

card an eccentric or amusing person

caribou North American name for a reindeer

caricature 1) a depiction of a person in which distinguishing characteristics are exaggerated for comic or grotesque effect 2) a hopelessly inadequate or inaccurate imitation: *he is a caricature of an actor*

caries decay of teeth or bones

carminative relieving flatulence

carmine crimson

carnage slaughter; the killing of a large number of people

carnal relating to physical esp. sexual matters

carnal knowledge sexual intercourse

carnivorous meat-eating

carob 1) the locust tree 2) the locust bean

carouse (to have) a merry drinking party, to drink freely

carousel a merry-go-round at a fair

carp cavil, complain, find fault, criticize

carpal 1) to do with the carpus or wrist 2) a bone of the wrist

carpe diem Lat. 'seize the day!' make the most of the present opportunity

carpetbagger a politician who seeks election in an area where he has no local connections

carpus the wrist

Carrara marble high-grade, white, Italian marble, prized for sculpture

carrion dead decaying flesh

carte blanche unrestricted power to act, a free hand

cartel an association of businesses to maintain high prices and restrict competition

Cartesian to do with the French philosopher René Descartes (1596-1650)

cartography *n.* making maps

cartomancy divination or fortune telling by the interpretation of playing cards

cartouche an ornament resembling a scroll of paper

cartulary, chartulary the charters or records of a monastery or an estate esp. a register of titles to all its property

carvel-built (of a boat) that has the planks of its hull laid flush

caryatid, caryatids, caryatides a structural column sculpted in the form of a draped female figure used instead of a column to support an entablature

carzey, carsey a lavatory

Casanova 18th-century Italian adventurer, whose name has become a byword for a promiscuous lover

Casaubon the stock character of a dry, out-of-touch scholar or pedant – from the character of that name in George Eliot's *Middlemarch (1871-2)*

casemate chamber or compartment in which guns are mounted

cashier to dismiss from the armed forces with dishonour because of a serious misdemeanour

Cassandra *Gk. myth* had the gift of prophecy but when she refused the advances of Apollo he caused her (true) prophecies to be disbelieved; a prophet of doom

cassiterite raw tin, mostly mined in Malaysia

caste 1) the Hindu class system 2) one of the classes

castellan a governor of a castle

castellated having battlements

castigate to criticize, reprimand severely

castrato a male singer castrated in boyhood to keep his high-pitched voice

casuist one who supposedly resolves cases of conscience and conflicting moral rules with clever but false reasoning; a sophist

casus belli Lat. something that triggers off a war

catachresis the incorrect use of a word, sometimes ineptly e.g. noisome for noisy or in a mixed metaphor

cataclysm 1) a great flood, a deluge 2) a violent upheaval or disastrous change

catacombs underground chambers and tunnels esp. in Rome used for worship and burial by persecuted early Christians

catadromous *(of a fish)* migrating down rivers to the sea to spawn

catafalque a support for a coffin before or during a funeral

catalepsy a state of seizure involving loss of sensation and of consciousness, accompanied by rigidity of the body; occasionally mistaken for death

Catalonia a region of N.E. Spain; cap. Barcelona

catalyst 1) a substance that causes an increase in the rate of a chemical reaction without itself undergoing any permanent chemical change 2) a person or thing that causes something to happen

catamaran 1) a boat with twin hulls side by side 2) a raft of logs or floats tied together

catamite a boy kept for homosexual purposes; a rent boy

cataplexy a medical condition in which strong emotion or laughter brings on a sudden physical collapse that causes the patient to fall to the ground remaining immobile, speechless, but fully conscious

cataract 1) a waterfall 2) a clouding of the lens of the eye resulting in blurred vision

catarrhine denoting primates, including humans, that have a narrow partition between the nostrils

catatonia, catatonic a disturbed mental condition in which the patient is in a state of rigid stupor looking like a statue; catalepsy as a symptom of schizophrenia

catchpole in medieval times, a sheriff's officer who arrested debtors

catechism teaching (Christianity) by question and answer

catechumen a person being taught Christianity prior to baptism or confirmation

categorical absolutely clear and certain; without doubt or reservations

cater-cornered diagonally opposite

caterwauling the howling or wailing of a cat on heat

catgut cord made from the dried intestines of an animal (not a cat) and used for stringed instruments

Cathars heretical Western European Christian sect in the Middle Ages; believed that only the spiritual world was good: the material world was evil

catharsis 1) the release of pent-up emotions through drama e.g. through the evocation of pity and fear, as in tragedy 2) relieving tensions by bringing repressed ideas, experiences, feelings into consciousness and expressing them esp. during psychoanalysis 3) evacuation of the bowels

cathartic to do with catharsis; strongly stimulating the evacuation of the bowels *n.* a strong laxative

Cathay medieval European name for China

cathexis *in psychology* the concentration of mental or emotional energy in one channel on a single goal – a person, object, or idea

catholic comprehensive, of broad scope, covering a wide range

catholicon a cure-all, a panacea

catoptric to do with a mirror and reflections

cat's paw a person used by someone else to do unpleasant things for him or her (referring to the proverbial image of a monkey grasping a cat by the paw to scrape roasting nuts from the fire)

Caucasian, Caucasic, Caucasoid 1) a white European 2) of or relating to the Caucasus mountains between the Caspian Sea and the Black Sea

caucus 1) *N.Amer.* a meeting of the members of a division of a political party to select candidates or agree policy 2) a smaller group or faction within a larger party

caudal of or like a tail, as in the caudal fin of a fish

caudillo a military or political leader in a Spanish-speaking country

cauliflower ear a permanently swollen and distorted ear suffered by boxers and rugby players

caulk 1) a waterproof filler and sealant 2) to seal, to make watertight

cause célèbre a controversial court case or an issue that attracts a great deal of public attention

causerie an informal talk or article

causeway a raised path or road across water or marshland

caustic 1) burning, corrosive 2) sarcastic

cauterize to burn a wound with a hot iron or caustic agent to stop bleeding or prevent infection

cavalier high-handed, off-hand, supercilious, haughty, arrogant

cavatina 1) a short form of aria 2) a lyrical instrumental composition without repeated sections

caveat a warning

caveat emptor a Latin tag from the law of the sale of goods – 'Let the buyer beware'

cavil to carp, complain, make petty objections

cavort to skip about

cayenne pepper a very hot, red pepper

cayman an alligator-like crocodile from tropical America

cecity blindness

celeriac a type of celery

celerity speed, swiftness

celestial relating to the sky or heaven; extremely good, heavenly

celibate 1) unmarried 2) not sexually active

Celtic the Brythonic and Goidelic languages – Irish, Scottish Gaelic, Welsh, Breton, Manx, and Cornish

cembalo a harpsichord

cenade 1) a discussion group or literary clique 2) the room in which the last supper was held

cenobite = **coenobite**

censer a container in which incense is burned esp. one swung at religious ceremonies

censor to impose censorship upon *adj.* **censorial** *n.* **a censor**

censorious harshly critical, judgmental

censor morum Lat. guardian of public morals

censure to criticise strongly *adj.* **censorious** *n.* a **censurer** decides what deserves censure

centaur *Gk. myth* creature with the upper body of a man and the lower body and legs of a horse

centrifugal moving outwards away from a centre; moving away from central authority or unity

centripetal moving towards a centre; directed inwards; favouring centralised authority or unity

cephalic to do with the head

cephalopod a large class of predatory molluscs, well-developed in the head region – octopus, squid, cuttlefish, nautilus, with fork-like tentacles growing around or out of the head

ceraceous waxy, wax-like

ceramics pottery, porcelain

cerate a medicinal preparation for external application; with a basis consisting of wax in whole or in part, it can be spread on the skin without melting

ceratoid horn-like in shape or texture

ceraunic to do with thunder

Cerberus *Gk. myth* three-headed dog guarding the entrance to the underworld

cerebellum the back part of the brain which controls balance and muscular coordination

cerebral palsy impaired muscle coordination and spasticity caused by brain damage before or at birth

cerebrate to think

cerebration the using of the mind; thinking

cerebrotonia the alert, cautious, intellectual personality-type allied to the ectomorph body-type

cerebrum the brain

cerecloth waxed cloth formerly used as a shroud

cerise cherry-pink

cerulean sky-blue; azure

cerumen earwax

cespitose growing in tufts or clumps

cesspool a cistern, pool or sump for sewage

cetacean a whale, dolphin or porpoise

ceteris paribus *Lat.* other things being equal

cetology the study of whales (cetaceans)

ceviche S. American dish of marinaded raw fish or seafood

chacun à son goût Fr. each to his/her own taste

chafe to make worn or sore by rubbing; to rub against

chagrin annoyance or shame at having failed

chalcedony a type of quartz composed of very fine blue or greyish crystals

chamade a signal to an enemy for a parley or surrender

chambré (served) at room temperature

chameleon changeable or fickle person

chamfer 1) a slant or slope made by paring off the edge of anything originally right-angled e.g. an edge or corner 2) to make a bevelled edge or corner

chamois 1) a goat antelope 2) a soft kind of leather originally made from its skin, now obtained from the skin of sheep, goats, or deer

champaign an expanse of level open country; a plain

chandler a dealer in specified items e.g. ship's chandler, corn chandler, a person who makes or sells candles

chanticleer a cock

Chantilly a town north of Paris noted for its 1) whipped cream 2) delicate lace 3) racecourse 4) forest 5) château

chantry 1) a chapel or altar for the singing or 'chanting' of masses for the soul of its founder 2) an endowment for that

chaparral a dense area of tangled shrubs, thorn bushes or dwarf trees esp. evergreen oaks

chaprassi a messenger; an attendant; an orderly

charabia gobbledegook

charade 1) a ludicrous pretence 2) *in pl.* a guessing game

charisma compelling magnetism or personal charm

charivari a noisy mock serenade to a newly-married couple or to an unpopular person

charlatan a fraud

charm collective term for birds, esp. finches

charnel to do with a burial-place; sepulchral, death-like

charnel-house a building or vault housing corpses or bones

Charterhouse 1) a Carthusian monastery 2) an English public school

Chartism *(1837-1848)*, most of its demands for parliamentary and social reform in England became law but not until after the movement had collapsed.

Chartreuse 1) a green or yellow liqueur 2) **chartreuse** a colour varying from a clear yellowish-green to a strong greenish-yellow

chary cautious

Chasid (Hasid) a strictly orthodox Jew in Palestine in the second century b.c. opposed to Hellenising (ancient Greek) influences

Chasidism same as **Hasidism**

chasm a deep gap

chassis a frame

chaste 1) virginal; not sexually active 2) pure, virtuous (in thought and behaviour) 3) simple, unadorned, austere (style)

chasten 1) to have a demoralizing effect on; to subdue 2) to discipline or correct by punishment

chastise to reprimand severely

chatelain a governor of a castle; a castellan

chatelaine the mistress of a large house

chatoyant having a changing lustre like a cat's eye

chattel a possession; a peice of movable, personal property

chauvinism 1) belligerent patriotism, jingoism 2) excessive devotion, loyalty or support for a cause esp. one's own sex or social group

chef d'oeuvre Fr. masterpiece

chef de rang Fr. the waiter in a restaurant who ranks immediately below the head waiter

chela a pincer-like claw of e.g. a lobster, crab, scorpion or similar crustacean

chelate 1) a chemical compound whose atoms include a metal atom e.g. iron chelate used to increase acidity in soil 2) of or having chelae

chenille 1) a thick, soft, tufty cord or yarn 2) a fabric made of this

cheongsam Chinese woman's traditional straight, close-fitting dress with a high neck and a slit skirt

cheroot a cigar with both ends cut off

cherub *pl*. **cherubim** a chubby child – winged, angelic, beautiful, innocent, sweet

chesterfield a padded sofa with arms and back of the same height

chestnut a worn-out, old story or joke

cheval-de-frise a spiked, defensive, military structure of pointed stakes supporting barbed wire used to stop or contain cavalry

cheval glass full-length mirror, hinged so as to swivel in its frame

chevalier d'industrie Fr. a spiv, a swindler

chevron 1) a V-shaped line or stripe 2) in heraldry an inverted V-shape

chiaroscuro the arrangement of light and shade in a picture or drawing; contrast as a literary or artistic technique

chiasmus the inversion in a second phrase or clause of the order of words in the first *adj*. **chiastic**

chicanery trickery

chichi 1) frilly, showy 2) (of a person) fussy, affected

chickpea a kind of bushy plant with edible pealike seeds

chicory 1) a blue-flowered plant with edible leaves used in salads; its carrot-like root roasted and ground to mix with or as a substitute for coffee 2) *N.Amer.* term for endive

chide to scold, rebuke, reprimand

chiffchaff a common warbler with drab plumage and a repetitive call

chiffon a light, diaphanous fabric of silk or nylon

chiffonier ornamental cabinet with a mirror attached

chignon a woman's hair done in a bun at the back of the head

Chihuahua 1) a state of northern Mexico and its capital 2) a breed of very small dog with short, smooth hair and large eyes originally from this part of Mexico

childish silly and immature

childlike simple and innocent

chiliad 1) a thousand 2) a thousand years

chiliasm the belief that Christ will reign bodily on earth for 1000 years – see **millenarianism**

chillum a short, clay pipe used for smoking cannabis; a hookah

chimera 1) *Gk. myth* a fire-breathing female monster with the head of a lion, body of a goat, and tail of a serpent 2) a wild, unrealizable fantasy; an impossible dream

chimerical wildly fanciful or imaginary

Chinook a Northwest coast American Indian originally inhabiting the Columbia river basin in Oregon

chintz printed, patterned, multicoloured cotton fabric with a glazed finish, used for curtains, upholstery, and chair coverings

chintzy cheap, garish, gaudy; fussy, flowery, over-elaborate

chipmunk a type of small squirrel from North America, a burrowing rodent with black striped fur

chipolata a type of small sausage

chirognomy palmistry as a means of judging character

chirography calligraphy, (beautiful) handwriting

chirology sign language used esp. by the deaf

chiromancy palmistry as a means of fortune telling

chironomy the art of gesticulation in oratory

chiropodist one who treats minor foot complaints like corns; a podiatrist

chiropractic manipulative treatment of mis-alignments of the joints esp. of the spine

chit 1) a cheeky young girl or woman 2) a note or voucher

chitin, chitinous the horn-like substance that forms the chief component of the shells of lobsters, crabs or the like

chitterlings the smaller intestines of a pig, prepared as food

chivalrous courteous and gallant

chlamydia a very small parasitic bacterium responsible for such diseases as trachoma, psittacosis and some that are sexually transmitted

choleric bilious, bad-tempered, irascible

cholesterol fatty steroid of animal origin thought to cause hardening of arteries

chordate a creature with a backbone

choreography arranging dance sequences

chough a small black crow

chowder a thick fish soup

chrematistic to do with finance, money-making

chrematistics the science of wealth; money-making

chrestomathy a collection of literary passages used in the study of a foreign language

chrism consecrated oil used for anointing at baptisms, confirmations, ordinations etc.

chrisom a white cloth put on a child at baptism and used as its shroud if it died within the month

chromatic to do with colour

chromosome thread-like structure within plant and animal cells carrying genetic information (genes) that determines and transmits hereditary characteristics

chronic 1) long-lasting, developing slowly, or constantly recurring 2) *Brit. slang* very bad, terrible

chronogram an inscription in which certain letters can be taken as Roman numerals giving a specific date

chrysalis 1) an insect in a cocoon in the stage between larva and adult – the inactive pupa of a butterfly or a moth 2) the hard outer case – the cocoon – enclosing it

chthonic, chthonian to do with or inhabiting the underworld

chukka a period of continuous play in polo lasting 7.5 minutes

chum *n.* chopped fish used as bait v. to fish using chum as bait

churl an impolite, ill-bred person

churlish surly, rude

chutzpah impudence, cheek, shameless audacity

Ciao *Ital.* Hello, Goodbye

cicatrice, cicatrix a scar

cicerone an informative guide for sightseers

cicisbeo (in Italy) a married woman's gigolo

Cid, El 11th-century Spanish soldier and national hero; champion of Christianity against the Moors from whom he captured Valencia in 1094; he ruled there until his death in 1099; immortalised by the French dramatist Corneille

cinnabar a bright red mineral; bright red

cipher, cypher 1) a code 2) the key to this 3) the numeral 0 4) a person or thing of no importance; a nonentity 5) a monogram

cippus 1) the stocks 2) a monumental pillar

circadian recurring regularly at 24-hour intervals

Circassian to do with Circassia, a region of South Russia

Circe *Gk. myth* sorceress who turned Odysseus' (Ulysses') companions into pigs

circuitous roundabout, indirect

circumbendibus a roundabout method, a circumlocution

circumscribe 1) to restrict; to limit 2) to draw

circumspect cautious, prudent, careful not to take risks

circumvent to find a way around (an obstacle or problem), to bypass

ciré *adj. & n.* (having) a glazed, wax-like finish

cirrus thin wispy white cloud at the highest altitudes; often a sign of bad weather to come

citadel a fortress

citrus a fruit or plant of this genus which includes the lemon, the lime, the orange, the citron, and the grapefruit

civet 1) a type of cat native to Africa and Asia 2) the musky secretion of its scent glands used in making perfumes

clade a group of organisms descended from a common ancestor

cladistics the classification of animals and plants by reference to shared characteristics indicating common ancestry; classification strictly according to the order of evolutionary branching cf. **phenetic classification**

clair de lune misty-blue glaze on Chinese porcelain

clairvoyance the supposed facility of perceiving events in the future; seeing or knowing things by supernatural or telepathic means

clam a type of mollusc adhering fast to rocks

clamour shouting, noisy outcry

clandestine secret and hidden, often for an illegal purpose

clangour loud or repeated discordant metallic ringing

claque a group of theatregoers hired to applaud a performance

claret 1) red Bordeaux wine 2) dark, purplish red

claudication limping; lameness

Clausewitz, Karl von *(1780-1831)* Prussian general and military strategist; wrote *On War* advocating total destruction of the enemy

claustrophobia fear of enclosed spaces

clavate, claviform shaped like a club with the thicker end uppermost

clavecin a harpsichord

clavicle collarbone

clavis a key; a key to solving a cipher or code

claymore a two-edged Scottish broadsword

cleat a projection 1) to which a rope is attached 2) to prevent slippage esp. on the sole of a boot or athletic shoe

cleave 1) to split 2) to make one's way through something as if by cleaving

clemency 1) leniency, mercy 2) general pleasantness and mildness of weather

clement 1) (of the weather) pleasantly mild 2) lenient, merciful

clementine a type of tangerine

clepsydra an ancient type of water-clock

clerestory the upper part of the central nave of churches containing a series of windows

clerihew a four-line comic verse about a famous person; it usu. consists of two rhyming couplets with lines of unequal length.

clerisy educated people regarded as a social group

climacteric *n.* 1) a major turning point or critical stage 2) the menopause 3) the male menopause when sexual activity in men is reduced *adj.* 1) critically important 2) to do with a climacteric

climactic *adj.* to do with a climax

climatic regarding the climate, the weather

clinamen an inclination

clinker-built or **clincher-built** (of a boat) having a hull made with overlapping planks

cliometrics the science of quantitative history – the study of economic history using statistics and computer analysis

clove 1) a dried flower-bud used as a pungent aromatic spice 2) any of the small bulbs making up a compound bulb of garlic, shallot, etc.

clove gillyflower or **clove pink** a clove-scented pink, the ancestor of the Carnation and other double pinks

clove hitch a knot by which a rope is secured by passing it twice round a spar or rope that it crosses at right angles

cloven split, partly divided

cloy to overfill with an excess of sweetness, richness, or sentiment

coagulate to clot, curdle, congeal, solidify

coalesce to unite into a whole; to merge

cob 1) a sturdy, thickset, short-legged horse 2) a male swan

cobalt hard silvery-white metallic chemical element used in alloys

cobalt blue deep blue

cochineal a scarlet dye made from the crushed bodies of the Mexican scale insect of the same name

Cockaigne, Cockayne imaginary land of luxury

cockatrice legendary monster, part snake and part cock

cocotte a fashionable prostitute

cod imitation, mock, fake

coda conclusion, the tail-end of something – Latin *cauda*, tail

codex 1) of the same age 2) a contemporary

codger an elderly or eccentric man, an 'old codger'

codicil addition or appendix that revokes a will or part of it

codicology the study of manuscripts

codpiece a pouch at the crotch of breeches worn by men in the 15th and 16th centuries

coeliac to do with the abdomen

coenobite a member of a monastic community; a monk

coerce to force

coetaneous of the same age or period; contemporary; coeval

coeval 1) of the same period of time 2) a contemporary

coffer a chest or strongbox

cogent forceful and convincing

cogitate to meditate, ponder, think deeply

cognate *adj.* 1) (of a word) having the same derivation as another 2) related; connected *n.* 1) a cognate word or language 2) a relative

cognition the mental processes of acquiring knowledge

cognitive dissonance confused, mixed-up thinking from having inconsistent thoughts, attitudes and beliefs that cannot be reconciled

cognizance knowledge; understanding; awareness

cognomen an ancient Roman's third (and usually last) name i.e. his family name and surname; orig. his nickname

cognoscenti people 'in the know'; specialists; connoisseurs

cohere to hold or stick together

coherent 1) logical and consistent 2) able to speak clearly and logically

cohort 1) one of the ten divisions of an ancient Roman legion; it was made up of three hundred to six hundred men 2) a group or band of people with a shared unifying objective 3) a companion or supporter

coign also **quoin** and **coin** position, especially in 'coign of vantage', a favourable viewpoint

coinage the inventing of a new word or phrase

coitus sexual intercourse

col a pass in a mountain range

cold turkey the abrupt and total cessation of taking a drug to which one is addicted; withdrawal symptoms (e.g. sweating and nausea) caused by this

coleslaw salad made of shredded cabbage and other vegetables with mayonnaise

Colette, Sidonie-Gabrielle, *(1873-1954)* French novelist and the foremost French woman author of her day; noted for analytical studies of women

colic abdominal pain

collage a composition, collection or combination of various things arranged and stuck to a backing

collate to bring together

collateral 1) security held by a lender 2) promotional material *(N. Amer.)*

collateral damage inadvertent casualties and destruction in civilian areas caused by military operations esp. civilian casualties of bombing raids

collation a light meal

collect a short prayer for a particular day or season

collimate 1) to adjust the line of sight of (an optical instrument – a telescope, theodolite, etc.) 2) to make parallel (e.g. rays of light)

collocation a combination of two or more words that is well established by usage e.g. a *quick temper* but not a *fast temper*

collocutor one who has conversation with another

colloquial conversational, informal

colloquium an academic conference or seminar

colloquy conversation; dialogue

colluctation strife; opposition

collude conspire

colluvium a mixture of rock fragments from the bases of cliffs

Colonel Blimp caricature of a stuffy, pompous, ultra-conservative, elderly man, often a (former) army officer

colonnade a row of evenly-spaced columns supporting a roof or entablature

coloratura 1) elaborate ornamentation of a basic vocal melody 2) a soprano who specializes in such music

colossus a huge statue

colostomy opening made surgically in the surface of the abdomen, through which the bowel can empty

colourable 1) seemingly valid or genuine; plausible 2) pretended; feigned

colporteur formerly a hawker of cheap, popular, and religious books esp. bibles

colubrine to do with a snake; resembling a snake

comely good-looking, handsome

comestibles eatables, food

comity courtesy and considerate behaviour towards others

comity of nations nations recognizing one another and respecting each other's different laws and customs

comme il faut Fr. 'as it should be', correct, proper

commensal 1) eating at the same table 2) to do with commensalism

commensalism a relationship in which two organisms 'dine at the same table (mensa)' i.e. live in close association; one may derive some benefit but neither harms or is parasitic on the other cf. **symbiosis**

commensurate proportionate

comminate to threaten

commination threat of punishment or revenge

comminute to reduce to minute particles

comminuted fracture the breaking of a bone in several places with much splintering

commis a junior

commiserate to express sympathy (with); to sympathize

commode a chair with a hinged flap concealing a chamber pot

commodious spacious, roomy

compact a contract, a covenant, an agreement

compass to encircle or surround; to comprehend

complacent smug, self-satisfied, feeling that nothing more needs to be done

complaisance a desire to please

complaisant eager to please; calmly accepting mistreatment

complement to complete, to make whole

compliant tending to do what others want; flexible, submissive, cooperative

compliment to praise

comport, comport oneself to behave, to conduct oneself

composite made up of several parts

compos mentis *Lat.* of sound mind, sane

compossible possible in coexistence with something else

compotation the act of tippling, drinking together in company

compound an enclosure

comprise to contain; to be made up of; to consist of; *comprising of, comprised of,* and *comprises of* are solecisms and always incorrect

compromise *n.* settlement reached by making concessions on each side *v.* 1) to make such a settlement 2) to expose to suspicion or commit to a policy etc. unwisely

compte rendu *Fr.* a formal report or review; a statement of account

comptroller a controller: a title for various financial executives

compunction a feeling of guilt or regret; the pricking of conscience; remorse; moral scruple

con a swindle, a confidence trick; to swindle

conation a desire, a striving to do something purposefully *adj.* **conative**

conatus a natural tendency or impulse

con brio *Italian* with vigour and brilliance; in a lively way

concatenate to link together

concatenation a series of linked events

concave curved inwards

concede to admit; to surrender or yield

conceit a far-fetched analogy

concentric sharing the same centre

concetto an ingenious turn of phrase; a conceit

conchology the study or collection of seashells

conciliate to placate, to pacify; to act as a mediator

conciliatory intended to end a disagreement; irenic

concinnity (of literary style) a harmonious, elegant, and neat arrangement

concipient that which conceives

conclave 1) the meeting of the cardinals of the R.C. Church to select a new pope 2) a private meeting

concomitant accompanying; existing or occurring with something else

concord agreement, harmony

concordance 1) agreement or harmony 2) an alphabetical list of words in a work with the context and often the meaning

concrescence the growing together of separate parts

concupiscence sexual desire, lust

condign (usu. of punishment) fitting and deserved

condominium 1) joint control of one state's affairs by other states 2) *N.Amer.* a building of individually-owned flats 3) one of the flats

condone to forgive or overlook

condor a very large, rare, mountain-dwelling vulture of the Andes or California

condottieri Italian mercenaries

condyle the rounded knuckle or knob at the end of some bones

coney, cony a rabbit

confabulate to converse, to chat

confect to make by putting things together

confection 1) any sweet food, such as a cake, pastry or a sweet 2) the act of combining or mixing

configuration an arrangement

conflagration a large, destructive fire

conflate to combine two or more things (esp. two variant texts) into one

confound to confuse

confounded damned (a confounded nuisance!)

confute to prove (a person or thing) to be wrong; to disprove

congé 1) formal permission to leave 2) an abrupt, unceremonious dismissal

congee Chinese broth or porridge

congenial pleasing through having tastes, habits, or temperament similar to one's own

congenital present from birth; occurring at or during birth

congeries a disorderly collection or mass of things heaped together

congruent 1) in agreement, in harmony, congruous 2) geometrically identical

congruous in agreement, in harmony

conjure to call upon, to urge, to implore someone to do something

connictation *n.* winking

conning tower the superstructure of a submarine and its periscope

connive 1) to allow or encourage (something) by ignoring it 2) to conspire

connoisseur a specialist or expert in (one of) the arts or with regard to food, drink, or matters of taste generally

connotation an idea or feeling invoked by a word in addition to its primary meaning; implication

conquistador a conqueror esp. one of the Spanish conquerors of Mexico or Peru in the 16th century

consigliere counsellor, adviser

consommé clear soup of meat or chicken stock

consonance 1) agreement, compatibility, harmony 2) the recurrence of similar-sounding consonants in neighbouring words e.g. *shilly-shally*

conspectus an overview; a summary

conspissate to inspissate; to thicken as by boiling or evaporation; to condense

conspurcation defilement

constituent *n.* 1) a resident of an area represented by an elected official 2) a component part *adj.* 1) being a part of a whole 2) having the power to appoint or elect; able to make or change a political constitution

constrict to make narrow or narrower; to compress

consubstantiation the belief that the body and blood of Christ are actually present with the bread and wine in the Eucharist

consuetude an established custom having the force of law

consummate 1) to complete esp. a marriage or relationship by having sexual intercourse 2) showing great skill and flair; perfect 3) descriptive of the highest, most complete or perfect form of some quality – positive (a consummate politician) or negative (a consummate liar)

consumption 1) the former name for tuberculosis 2) the act of consuming e.g. by eating or burning

contabescent wasting away, atrophied

contagion the transfer of disease from one body to another by touching

contemn to regard or treat with contempt

contemptible despicable, deserving contempt

contemptuous feeling or showing scorn for

contention 1) an argument 2) an assertion

contiguous sharing a common border; touching

continual always happening, frequently recurring

continuous without interruption e.g. a flowing tap

contrarian one who thinks otherwise

contrary *(kon-trare-ree)* perverse, obstinate

contre-jour (taking photographs) into the light i.e. with the light behind the subject

contretemps an unfortunate minor disagreement

contrite full of guilt, regret, or remorse

contumacious contemptuously disobedient to authority; rebellious

contumely abusive or contemptuous language or behaviour

conundrum a puzzle, a riddle

conventicle a clandestine religious meeting of dissenters or nonconformists

convexity a bulge on the outside

convoluted 1) intricately folded, twisted, or coiled in overlapping folds 2) confusing, intricate, extremely complex

convulsion an uncontrollable, violent fit or seizure esp. as occurring in epilepsy

coolie cheaply hired native servant in India

cooper one who makes, repairs, casks, barrels, etc.

cooperage the work, workshop, or products of a cooper

coot a water-bird with dark plumage and a white bill

copacetic, **copasetic**, excellent, in good order, first-rate

cope an ecclesiastical cloak

Copernicus *(1473-1543)* Polish astronomer who demonstrated that, contrary to Ptolemy and the geocentric view of cosmology, the planets (including the earth) orbit the sun

copestone the stone at the top of a building or wall

coprolite fossilized dung

coprology = scatology

coprophilia an abnormal interest in faeces

Coptic a Christian Egyptian

copula a connecting word esp. a form of the verb to be connecting a subject and predicate

cordage the cords or ropes in the rigging of a ship

cordate heart-shaped

cordial warm and friendly

cordillera the system of parallel mountain ranges

cordovan, cordwain a kind of fine leather

cordwainer a shoemaker

coriaceous to do with leather

corkage a charge made by an establishment for serving drink brought in by a customer

corn the chief cereal crop of an area – in England, wheat; in Scotland, oats; in N. Amer. + Austral./N.Z. maize

cornice 1) a projection around or along the top of buildings esp. the top part of an entablature above the frieze 2) an ornamental moulding around the wall of a room just below the ceiling

cornucopia 1) a goat's horn overflowing with flowers, fruit, and corn as a symbol of plenty 2) an abundance

corps a close-knit group

corpulent (of a person) fat

corpus vile someone or something fit only to be the object of an experiment

corral 1) a pen for livestock 2) a defensive enclosure formed by a circle of covered wagons

correlate 1) to have a reciprocal, complementary or mutual relationship 2) to establish such a relationship between things

corroborate to confirm, to support

corrode to wear away, to be worn away by chemical action

cortex an outer layer; bark

corundum a very hard mineral used as a gemstone and an abrasive

coruscate to flash; to sparkle; to glitter

cos lettuce

coscinomancy divination by means of a sieve and a pair of shears

cosi fan tutte It. so do they all: they're all like that (of women)

cosmogony the study of the origin of the universe

cosmology the study of the origin, nature and structure of the universe

cosmopolitan 1) composed of people or elements from many different countries or cultures 2) (a person who has) lived and travelled in many countries

costermonger one who sells fruit from a barrow

costive constipated

coterie a select group of people

Couéism a method of treating one's problems by autosuggestion; it involves repeating 15 to 20 times daily the mantra 'every day and in every way, I am getting better', invented by the French chemist Emile Coué *(1857-1926)*

cougar a puma

coulomb a unit of electricity

counter-intuitive contrary to intuition, to common sense or what one might expect

counterpane a bedspread

counterpoint playing a melody in conjunction with another

coup a successful, unexpected strategy or act

coup d'état Fr. a sudden, violent, or illegal seizure of government power

coup de foudre Fr. 1) a flash of lightning 2) a thunderbolt 3) a sudden unexpected event, a bolt from the blue 4) love at first sight

coup de grâce Fr. a final shot or blow that kills off a wounded person or animal to end their suffering

coup de théâtre Fr. an unexpected and sensational turn in a play

course to flow, to run – *blood coursing through her veins*

couth cultured, refined, well-mannered

couvade a custom in some cultures in which the husband also takes to his bed while his wife is in labour or giving birth

coven a group or gathering of witches

coverture 1) covering 2) the condition of a married woman considered to be under her husband's protection

covin a conspiracy to defraud or injure somebody

cowed intimidated into submission

cowl 1) a hood 2) a hood-shaped chimney cover

cox, coxswain the steersman of a boat, the helmsman of a racing eight or four

coxcomb a fop, a dandy

cozenage cheating

crabbed 1) crusty, bad tempered, irritable 2) (of handwriting) difficult to read or understand

craic Irish fun, enjoyment, entertainment

crane fly = harvestman = daddy-longlegs

crapulence drunkenness

crapulent, crapulous drunk

craven a coward, cowardly

creaturely obsequiously, subserviently

credence belief in, or acceptance of, as being true

credible believable

creditable praiseworthy, commendable

credo a formal statement of beliefs or principles, opinions; a creed

credulity a ready willingness to believe

credulous too believing, gullible

creed 1) a system of beliefs or principles 2) a formal statement of the essential parts of Christian belief

creel an angler's wicker basket for newly-caught fish

cremona a type of organ stop

crenellated having indented battlements

crepitate to crackle

crepitation a crackling sound from the lungs indicative of pneumonia

crepuscular to do with twilight

crescendo a gradual increase in loudness; a climax

crestfallen sad and disappointed; dejected, downhearted

cretaceous composed of or resembling chalk; chalky

cricoid ring-shaped

crimson deep, purplish red

crinal to do with hair

crinate(d) having hair

crinigerous, crinite, crinose hairy

crispate having a wavy, curled appearance

crispin a shoemaker

Crispin of Soissons the patron saint of shoemakers

criterion the basis on which a judgment or decision is made

critical mass 1) the minimum amount of fissile material needed to maintain a nuclear chain reaction 2) the minimum amount of resources required to start or maintain a venture

criticaster, critickin a second-rate critic

critique a detailed analysis and assessment

critter a creature

crocket an architectural ornament placed at regular intervals on the sides of spires, canopies, gables, pinnacles, etc.

Croesus a very rich king in ancient Greece; the last king of Lydia

cromlech 1) (in Wales) a dolmen; a megalithic tomb consisting of a large flat stone laid on upright ones 2) (in Brittany) a circle of standing stones

crone a cantankerous, withered, witch-like old woman

crosier, crozier a hooked staff carried by a bishop or abbot

crosspatch a bad-tempered person

crucible 1) a vessel in which metals or other substances can be melted or subjected to very high temperatures 2) a severe, intense trial or test

cruciform, cruciate cross-shaped

cruciverbalist somebody who sets/solves crossword puzzles; a crossword puzzle enthusiast

crural to do with the leg

crux decisive stage or point

cryogenics the branch of physics concerned with the production and effects of very low temperatures

cryonics deep-freezing the bodies of those who have died with a view to reviving them in the future

crypt an underground room or vault beneath a church

cryptic hidden, obscure in meaning

crypto – concealed, secret, hidden

cryptogam a plant with no flowers or seeds which reproduces by spores – ferns, liverworts, mosses, algae, fungi, and lichens

cryptogram a text written in code

cryptography writing/solving codes

crystalline *literary* very clear

crystallize to make or become definite in shape or form

ctenoid comb-shaped

ctenophore a type of jellyfish

cuckold a man whose wife has committed adultery

cucurbit a plant of the gourd family which includes melon, pumpkin, squash, and cucumber

cui bono? Lat. for whose benefit? who stands to gain?

culinary to do with cooking or the kitchen

culpable guilty

culvert drain or covered channel

cumbersome awkward

cumbrous cumbersome

cunctation delay

cunctator one who delays

cuneal, cuneate wedge-shaped

cuneiform 1) wedge-shaped 2) written in the wedge-shaped characters used in the ancient writing systems of Assyria, Babylonia, and Persia

cupidity greed

cupola a dome

cupreous of or containing copper; copper-coloured

cur a dog

curculio the fruit-weevil

curd the cheese part of milk

curlicue a fancy twist or curl, such as a flourish made with a pen e.g. in handwriting

curmudgeon a bad-tempered, surly or miserly person

curry favour to ingratiate oneself

cursive (of writing) joined up

cursory hasty and brief; not thorough

curtail to reduce or cut short

cushat woodpigeon, ring-dove

cusp a point where two curves meet

cutaneous to do with the skin

cutlass a kind of curved sword

cutlet a piece of best end of neck of pork or lamb

cut to the chase to cut out the chit-chat and get to the point

cut to the quick *fig.* deeply hurt

cyan greenish/blue

cyanide a poisonous salt

cybernetics the comparative study of communications and automatic control systems in machines and living things

cyberspace the notional environment in which on-line communication over computer networks take place

Cyclops *Gk. myth* a member of a race of one-eyed giants

cyclothymia manic depression – alternating periods of elation and depression

cynosure the centre of attention

Cynthia the moon personified

cy pres 'as near as possible'; the legal doctrine that when the intentions of the testator or donor cannot be followed precisely, they should be carried out as closely as possible

cyto- to do with a cell or cells

cytology the study of cells in plants and animals

D

Dada, Dadaism early 20th-century anarchic and nihilistic movement in the arts which mocked the traditional and conventional aesthetic criteria; its approach was wholly irreverent and based on the incongruous, the illogical, the irrational, and the absurd

daddy-longlegs = harvestman = crane fly

daedal skilful, inventive

dago *(offensive slang)* a member of a Latin race, esp. a Spaniard, Portuguese, or Italian

daguerreotype early (*1830s*) photographic process named after its French inventor L.J.M. Daguerre

dale a valley

Dalit = a **Harijan** an untouchable in the Hindu caste system

dalliance flirtation

dally 1) to waste time 2) to spend time in a casual, romantic or sexual relationship with someone

Damascene to do with or from Damascus

dander temper; **to get one's dander up** to lose one's temper; to become annoyed or angry

Dando (formerly) somebody who walked out of an establishment – a hotel, restaurant, etc. – without paying

Danegeld a land tax levied in Anglo-Saxon England to buy off Danish invaders, or to finance forces to oppose them

danse macabre Fr. dance of death

Dante Alighieri (*1265-1321*) Italian poet; born in Florence, the founding figure of Italian literature

Danton Georges Jacques (*1759-1794*) French revolutionary; lawyer and exceptional orator; originally an ally of Robespierre and the Jacobins but more moderate; he called for the end of the Reign of Terror and was guillotined on the orders of Robespierre.

dappled marked with spots or patches

darbies handcuffs

Dark Ages the period in European history between the break-up of the Roman Empire in the West (a.d.476) to about 1000 a.d.; a time that has been perceived as a period of relative cultural and economic decline following the collapse of the Roman Empire

dastard(ly) coward(ly)

daube stew of beef braised in wine

daunting intimidating, worrying, discouraging, disheartening, causing apprehension

dauntless = undaunted

dearth a scarcity, a lack of

debacle a disastrous failure, downfall or defeat

debauchery excessive drunkenness, sexual activity, or drug-taking

de bene esse *(legal) Lat.* ' good for the present', something which is accepted for the moment but may have to be reconsidered; conditional, provisional, pro tem.

decadence moral or spiritual decay

decadent in moral or cultural decline; degenerate; dissolute

decal, decalcomania transferring designs from transfer-paper onto glass, porcelain, etc.

Decalogue the Ten Commandments

decennial lasting for or recurring every ten years

decimate *lit.* to kill one in ten; *by ext.* to inflict heavy damage upon (short of totally destroying)

declaim to speak rhetorically or in an impassioned way

déclassé Fr. fallen in social status

decoct to extract the essence, flavour, or medicinal qualities of, by boiling

décolletage *Fr.* a plunging neckline

deconstruction a technique in literary theory initiated by the French philosopher Jacques Derrida (*1930-2004*). It involves dismantling, unpicking a text in order to bring out its supposed internal tensions, inconsistencies and contradictions

decorticate to remove an outer layer, the bark

decorum dignified, proper, correct behaviour appropriate to a prevailing social code

decoy a person or thing used to mislead or lure someone into a trap

decry to belittle, to denounce, to condemn

decumbent lying down, lying flat

decussate shaped like an X

deemster, **dempster** a judge esp. in the Isle of Man

de facto *Lat.* in fact, whether rightfully or not

defective faulty; not working properly

défi, un a challenge

defibrillation a controlled electric shock administered to stop quivering of the heart

deficient lacking something; missing a necessary part

defile a narrow passage or gorge through which troops can march in single file only

defile, to 1) to make foul or dirty 2) to make unfit for ceremonial use; to desecrate or profane (something sacred); to rape or sexually assault (a woman)

definite precise and unmistakable

definitive the most authoritative and conclusive

deflagrate (to cause) to burn with great heat and light

defray to provide money to pay

defrock to strip (a clergyman) of his status and rights in the church, to unfrock

defuse 1) to remove the fuse from (an explosive device) 2) to make less harmful, dangerous, tense, or hostile

dégagé Fr. unconcerned, free and easy, nonchalant

deglutition the act of swallowing

dégringolade Fr. a tumbling down, a collapse, a downfall

degust, degustate to taste

de haut en bas Fr. 'from top to bottom' contemptuously, condescendingly

dehisce to split or burst open, to gape

dehiscent opening spontaneously to release seeds or pollen; gaping, yawning

dehort to dissuade (from)

deictic, deixis 1) (in logic) proving something by direct argument 2) (in grammar and linguistics) dependent for meaning on context and something already mentioned **deictics** are pronouns and adverbs referring to person, place, and time **deixis** is the use of deictics

deification making a god of; apotheosis

deign to condescend to

deipnosophist a master of conversation at the dinner table

déjà voulu Fr. a feeling that your present desires are exactly the same as those you have had previously

déjà vu Fr. 'already seen', the feeling of having previously experienced the present situation

de jure *Lat.* rightful, rightfully, by right

delate to report (a crime); to inform against

delectable delicious, delightful

delegate 1) to give a job or responsibility to a junior 2) a person representing others esp. at a conference

deleterious harmful, injurious, damaging

delft the glazed earthenware usu. decorated in blue on a white background orig. from Delft in the Netherlands

delict a civil wrong, a tort which can be made the basis of a civil claim by A against B

deliquesce to become liquid esp. during decomposition

deliquescence a dissolving into liquid; a melting away

deliquescent *adj.* liquid, becoming liquid

dell a valley

delphic deliberately obscure or ambiguous, as if spoken by an oracle

deltiology collecting picture postcards

deluge a downpour, heavy rain, a flood

delusion a false belief

delusional having lost touch with reality; falsely believing in something despite strong evidence to the contrary

demagogue a political agitator who, with crude oratory, appeals to the popular prejudices and basest instincts of the mob in order to stir up social discontent; a rabble-rouser

dementia serious mental disorder or deterioration marked by memory failures, personality changes, impaired reasoning, loss of concentration or judgment *adj.* **demented**

de mal en pis *Fr.* from bad to worse

démarche *Fr.* a diplomatic, political step or move

demeanour behaviour

dementi *Fr.* a flat denial

demersal (of fish) living near the seabed

demijohn a type of large bottle encased in wickerwork

demi-mondaine Fr. a kept woman, a prostitute

demi-monde Fr. 1) the twilight world of women of doubtful morality 2) any group of dubious standing considered to be on the fringes of respectable society

demirep a woman of dubious sexual reputation

demise 1) death 2) lease

demiurge 1) the creator of the universe (Plato) 2) a secondary god (Gnosticism)

démodé Fr. dated, out of fashion

demography the study of human population statistics esp. with regard to births, deaths etc.

demonize to characterize as evil

demonstrative openly showing affection or other feelings

demos the ordinary people

Demosthenes (*384-322 b.c.*) Athenian statesman and renowned orator

demotic to do with the everyday language of ordinary people esp. modern Greeks; colloquial cf. **katharevousa**

demulcent soothing

demy 1) a standard size of paper 2) a standard book size

dendrochronology the dating of events and climate variations by comparative study involving the counting of the annual growth rings in the trunk of a tree

denizen an inhabitant

de nos jours Fr. these days, nowadays

dénouement *Fr.* the final unfolding of a plot

denounce to condemn openly

denude to make nude, bare; to strip

deontic concerning duty and moral obligation

deontology the study of the nature of duty and moral obligation

Deo volente Lat. God willing

deoppilate to free from obstruction

dependant a person who is dependent

dependence is the state or fact of being dependent

dependent is the adjective of dependant

deplore you can deplore a thing or a quality but not a person

deprecate to deplore

depreciate 1) to belittle 2) to decrease in value

depredation an act of plundering, pillage

de profundis Lat. from the depths

depurate to purify

depurative *n. & adj.* a purifying substance; a purgative, an aperient; purifying

deracinate to uproot

deranged with the order or normal condition disturbed or upset esp. one's mental order; insane

dereliction abandonment

de rigueur Fr. strictly required

derisive laughing at, mocking, jeering at, ridiculing, scoffing

derisory laughable, absurdly small, inadequate, or ridiculous

dermatitis inflammation of the skin

dermatology the treatment of skin disorders

dernier cri Fr. the latest fashion

derogate to detract (from)

derrick a crane

derring-do *(lit. or joc.)* a daring deed, heroic courage

dervish a member of a Muslim religious order, the Mevlevi, noted for their frenzied, ecstatic, whirling dance

descry to catch sight of, to espy, to spot

déshabillé, dishabille *Fr.* (a state of being) only partly clothed

desiccant 1) a drying agent 2) *adj.* drying

desiderate to long for

despoil to rob, to loot, to plunder

despoliation plundering, pillaging

despot a tyrannical ruler

desquamate *v.i.* to scale off, to peel, to come off in scales or flakes

destrier a war-horse

desuetude disuse, inactivity

desultory 1) flitting from one thing to another 2) half-hearted; lacking purpose or enthusiasm

determinism the notion that all events and actions are caused by external forces acting on the will so that freedom of choice is illusory: everything that happened had to happen; everything that did not happen could not have happened and no-one could have acted differently, so no-one is morally responsible for his actions

detriment harm, damage

detrimental causing harm, damage or loss

detritus debris esp. that resulting from erosion e.g. rock fragments

de trop Fr. too much, too many

detumescence the process of subsiding from a swollen state

deuteranopia colour blindness from insensitivity to green light

deuterogamy = digamy a second marriage contracted after the termination of the first by death or divorce

devastation widespread destruction

devil's advocate one who argues against a proposition to test its validity or to provoke discussion

dewlap a loose fold of skin below the throat in cattle, dogs, etc.

dexter on the right side

dexterity skill esp. with the hands

dexterous, dextrous adroit, skilful

dextral to do with the right side or the right hand; right-handed

diachronic to do with the historical development of (esp. a language)

diacritic a mark – an accent, umlaut, cedilla, tilde etc. – above or below a letter or syllable to signify a difference in pronunciation

diacritical serving to separate or distinguish, as a mark or sign; concerning marks used to distinguish the sounds of letters

diadem a crown or headband, typically light and jewelled, worn by royalty

diaeresis a mark consisting of two dots, placed over a vowel to indicate it is pronounced separately e.g. in naïve

dialectic the art of logical argument or debate to arrive at the truth by reconciling opposites. For Socrates this involved a process of question and answer probing the opponent's case. The German philosopher, Hegel (*1770-1831*), applied a dialectical triad of proposition (*thesis*), an opposing *antithesis*, and a reconciling *synthesis*.

dialectical materialism the combination of Hegel's dialectical triad and the materialist philosophy of Marx and Engels. Although it is the basis of both Marxism and Communism it was never used as a term by Marx or Engels.

dianoetic to do with reasoning; intellectual

dianoia 1) perception and experience considered as lower modes of knowledge 2) the faculty of discursive reasoning

diantre Fr. the devil

diaper 1) a baby's nappy 2) a linen or cotton fabric woven in a repeating pattern of small diamonds

diaphanous (of fabrics) light, delicate, and translucent; sheer and gauzy

diaphoretic causing sweating; sweating heavily

diaphragm membrane dividing the thorax from the abdomen

Diaspora the dispersion of the Jews beyond Israel

diaspora people *(esp. Jews)* dispersed beyond their native land

diastema a space between different types of teeth; a gap between a person's two upper front teeth

diatribe a bitter, strongly-worded, abusive verbal attack; a rant

dicastery 1) the court of the Athenians chosen annually to act as judges 2) an administrative subdivision of the papal court

dichotomy a split, a division, a schism

didactic instructive, teaching

diet a legislative assembly in some countries

different from which is acceptable in all contexts, is preferred to different to or different than

diffident shy, reserved

diffuse to spread, to disperse or disseminate *adj.* widely spread; lacking conciseness

digamy a second (lawful) marriage aka **deuterogamy**

diglossia two types of speech within the same language, e.g. Low German (rural) and High German (standard)

dihedral 1) having or contained by two plain faces 2) an angle formed by two plain faces 3) upward inclination of an aircraft's wing

dik-dik a dwarf African antelope

diktat a decree or order

dilapidated in a state of disrepair

dilatory delaying, slow to act, tardy; tending to or causing delay

dilemma a choice between two unsatisfactory alternatives

dilettante a dabbler esp. in the arts

diminished responsibility limitation of a person's criminal responsibility due to mental abnormality or instability

diminishing returns, law of after a certain point, further increases in production, expenditure, investment lead to successively smaller increases in output

diminuendo *mus.* let the sound die away gradually; a gradual decrease in loudness

diminutive *adj.* 1) small 2) designating certain affixes that denote smallness, youth, familiarity, affection, or contempt, such as *-let* in booklet, *-kins* in babykins

dimity light strong cotton fabric with woven stripes or squares

dineric relating to the interface between two immiscible liquids

Diocletian Roman Emperor (*284-305*) divided the Empire (twice); undertook vast administrative, military, judicial, and monetary reforms; a stickler for the old Roman ways, he launched the last great persecution of the Christians in 303. His rule tended to absolutism.

Dionysiac, Dionysian 1) relating to Dionysius, Gk. god of wine 2) to do with the sensual, spontaneous, emotional aspects of human nature

diorama a miniature three-dimensional film set

diphyodont having two successive sets of teeth

dipterous to do with two-winged flies

diptych a painting on two vertically hinged panels which can be closed like a book

dire dreadful, awful, disastrous, terrible; urgent, extremely serious

dirge a lament for the dead – a song or poem of mourning

dirk a dagger

dis, diss to speak disrespectfully to or about

disabuse to free (someone) from a mistake or misguided idea or belief

disambiguate to remove uncertainty of meaning, ambiguity from

disassemble to take apart, to strip

disavouch to disavow

disavow to deny knowledge of or responsibility for (something); to disown

discalced without shoes, barefoot

discern to recognize or perceive clearly; to recognize or perceive (differences)

discernment good taste or judgment

discerp to separate

discerptible capable of being separated

discombobulate to confuse, bamboozle

discomfit to discomfort

disconcerted flustered, unsettled, ruffled

discreet tactful

discrete separate, distinct

disdainful scornful and haughty

disenfranchise to deprive of the right to vote

dishevelled disordered and untidy (of appearance, hair, clothes); in a state of disarray

disingenuous not candid or sincere esp. in feigning ignorance, pretending to be naive

disinterested impartial, neutral cf. **uninterested**

disjecta membra Lat. scattered fragments of a literary work

disoblige to offend (someone) by disregarding their wishes

disobliging unaccommodating; uncooperative

disparate different, not comparable

dispathy, dyspathy dislike, antipathy – the opposite of sympathy

dispensation exemption from a rule or requirement

disport 1) *reflexive* to disport oneself to enjoy oneself 2) *intrans.* to frolic, to gambol

disquisition a dissertation, treatise, thesis

dissemble 1) to disguise 2) to feign; in each case by falsely appearing or pretending to have different feelings 3) to conceal

disseminate to spread widely, to scatter widely

dissimulate to dissemble

dissipation 1) a scattering or dispersing 2) *n.* indulging excessively in the pursuit of pleasure or debauchery

dissolute overindulgent in sensual pleasures; debauched

dissonant unharmonious; clashing

distaff the stick which holds the wool or flax for spinning; hence women's work

distaff side the female side or branch of a family

distich a two-line verse, a couplet

distil 1) to purify a liquid by vaporizing it with heat then condensing it with cold and collecting the resultant liquid 2) to extract the essence of

distinct 1) recognizably different in nature; individual or separate 2) readily distinguishable by the senses

distinctive individually characteristic; distinct from others of its kind

distrait distracted, absent-minded

distraught very worried and upset

dithyramb a passionately eloquent utterance or piece of writing in honour of someone, orig. Bacchus *adj.* **dithyrambic**

diuretic causing the increased discharge of urine

diurnal 1) during the daytime 2) daily

diva a famous songstress, a prima donna

divagate to digress, to deviate, to wander, to stray

divaricate to diverge, to part into two branches, to fork

divarication the act of spreading apart; divergence

Dives a rich man (Luke XV1: 19-31)

divest to deprive of; to dispossess of; to rid oneself of

divination discerning or discovering the future or the unknown by supernatural means

divisionism = pointillism a technique of neo-Impressionist painting using tiny dots of various pure colours, developed by the French painter Georges Seurat (1859-91); he preferred this term to **pointillism**

dizzard a blockhead

docent 1) a lecturer at a college or university just below the rank of someone in full-time qualified employment 2) a guide in a museum, art gallery etc.

docetism the belief that Christ had only the semblance of a human body and that therefore his sufferings and death were apparent rather than real

docimasy testing an ore or metal to determine its ingredients and quality

docimology a treatise on the testing of metals

dodecagon a plane figure of twelve straight sides and angles

dog days (about 3rd July to 11th August) the hottest weeks of the year in the Northern hemisphere

dogged obstinately determined; stubbornly persevering

doggerel crude, trivial verse often written for comic effect but lacking any poetic quality

dogma a principle or set of principles laid down by an authority as true and incontrovertible

dogmatic asserting as absolute truth what are merely principles, beliefs, ideas or opinions

dogmatist one who states his opinions in a forceful or arrogant manner

doit 1) a former small Dutch coin worth about half a farthing 2) a thing of little or no value

dolichocephalic long-headed – of a head longer than it is wide

dolmen a prehistoric megalithic tomb with a large flat horizontal stone laid across vertical ones; the French name for a cromlech

dolomite a type of limestone rock which gives its name to a range of mountains in northern Italy

dolorous feeling sorrow or grief, melancholy

dolour sorrow, grief

dolt a dimwit, a dope, a dullard, a dunce

doltishness stupidity

Dom (R.C. Church) a title given to certain dignitaries, monks and canons

dominie (*Sc.*) a schoolmaster

donnybrook a free-for-all

doozy *n.* something excellent, outstanding, stunning

doppelgänger *Ger.* a ghostly double of somebody

dorado 1) a brightly-coloured edible fish of warm seas 2) a golden-coloured South American freshwater fish

Doric 1) of the Dorians who invaded Greece from the north c.1100 b.c. and settled mainly in the Peloponnese 2) concerning the oldest and simplest style or order of classical Greek architecture

dormant inactive

doryphore one who delights in pointing out the small mistakes of others

dotage feebleness of mind due to old age; senility

dotard a person in his, her dotage

double jeopardy the prosecution of a person twice for the same offence

doublet a man's close-fitting jacket, with or without sleeves

doubt, doubtful I doubt *whether*… In ordinary positive statements the conjunction whether is preferred: 'I doubt whether he will come next week' In questions and negative statements that tends to be used: 'Do you doubt that he will come?' 'There's no doubt that he will come' The slightly informal *if* is an acceptable substitute for whether in most contexts

doughty dauntless, resolute and brave

douse to drench

dowager a widow with a title or property from her late husband; an elderly woman of high social standing

dower a widow's life interest in her husband's estate

dowry the property or money brought by a bride to her husband on their marriage

dowse to use the divining-rod to search for underground water, minerals etc.

doxology a hymn or liturgical expression of praise to God

doxy 1) a mistress 2) a prostitute 3) an opinion

doyen a dean; the most highly regarded person in a particular field, *female* **doyenne**

draconian harsh, very severe

dragoman an interpreter or guide in the Middle East

dragoon 1) v. to force, to coerce into doing something 2) *n.* a former mounted infantryman

Drambuie a sweet Scotch whisky liqueur

draught 1) the depth of water needed to float a ship 2) the amount of liquid that can be taken in by one act of swallowing; a gulp or swallow

dreamt not dreamed

drill to sow seeds by dropping them into a shallow trench or burrow

droit du seigneur = jus primae noctis the right of a feudal lord to have sexual intercourse with the bride of a vassal on her wedding night

droll amusing in an odd way

dromedary an Arabian camel with one hump

drone a non-working male bee with no sting whose only function is to mate with the queen; it lives off the labour of the worker bees, hence an idler

dropsy 1) oedema 2) a tip or bribe, a 'bung'

dross 1) waste material 2) rubbish

drudge a lowly employee who works hard at menial, dull tasks

drugget a type of coarse, long-lasting cloth

dryad a nymph of the trees

dualism any theory that draws a fundamental distinction between two different aspects of the same thing e.g. mind and body; good and evil; form and content

ductile (of a metal) capable of being drawn out into a thin wire

dudgeon deep resentment; **in high dudgeon** fuming

duenna an older woman acting as a governess and chaperone to girls in a Spanish or Portuguese family

due to is adjectival so you can have *'the cancellation of the match due to rain'* but not *'the match was cancelled due to rain'*; 'owing to' or 'because of' are unexceptionable in that context, or re-cast the wording

dugong 'sea cow' a whale-like coastal mammal found mainly in shallow tropical waters of E. Africa; the supposed original mermaid; now very rare

dulcet sounding sweet and soothing to the ear, melodious

dumdum a type of bullet that expands on impact

dun 1) a debt-collector/creditor 2) a demand for payment 3) to pester for payment; to importune

duplicity deception, deceitfulness

durance vile miserable, wretched imprisonment

durchkomponiert Ger. *adj.* concerning a song which has different music for each verse

durgan a dwarf

durian the fruit of the S.E. Asian tree of the same name; it has a foul smell but an agreeable taste

dusty answer a curt and unhelpful reply

dynamic *n.* driving force

dyne a unit of force

dysfunctional 1) not operating normally or properly 2) unable to cope with normal social relations

dyslogistic conveying censure; disapproving

dyspareunia painful or difficult sexual intercourse

dyspepsia indigestion

dyspeptic suffering from indigestion; grouchy, ill-tempered

dysphemism a disagreeable term used instead of one that is innocuous, inoffensive or neutral

dysphonia difficulty in speaking

dysphoria a feeling of being ill at ease

dysphoric painful

dyspnoea difficult breathing

dysteleology the denial of purpose in life

dystopia (opp. **Utopia**) an imaginary place where everything is as bad as possible

E

ear the head or spike of corn or cereal that contains the seeds

easel a support for an artist's canvas or for a blackboard

eatable reasonably palatable cf. **edible**

ebb to fall back, to recede, to go away

ebony a type of hard, dark wood

ebullient bubbling with excitement, enthusiasm; exuberant

ebullition 1) the action of boiling or bubbling up 2) a sudden violent or emotional outburst

eburnine of or like ivory

ecaudate tailless

eccaleobion an apparatus for the artificial hatching of eggs

ecchymosis discoloration of the skin after bruising has caused blood to escape into the tissues just under the skin

ecclesiastic a minister or priest

ecclesiastical to do with a church or churches

ecdemic not native or endemic; foreign

ecdysiast (*joc.*) a stripper, a striptease artist

ecdysis *n.* the sloughing, shedding of old skin; casting off the outer layer

echinate prickly like a hedgehog

echolalia the repetition of the spoken words of another person either 1) in a meaningless, pathological way usu. as a symptom of mental disorder or 2) by a child learning to talk

echt *Ger.* genuine, real, authentic and typical

éclat *Fr.* brilliant display, performance, achievement or effect

eclecsis a compilation from various sources

eclectic from various sources

eclipse total or partial obscuring of the sun or moon

ecliptic the plane of the earth's orbit around the sun

eclogue a short pastoral poem

écorché an anatomical figure in which the muscles are shown stripped of the skin

écrasé *Fr.* crushed

ecru the light fawn colour of unbleached linen

ectomorph a person of slim build

ectopic in an abnormal place or position

ectoplasm the substance supposedly emitted from the body of a spiritualistic medium during a trance or seance

ecumenical worldwide, universal; striving to promote unity among the world's Christian churches

edacious given to eating; gluttonous; voracious

edaphic to do with soil; produced by, or influenced by the soil

eddy a whirlpool

edentate 1) having no or few teeth 2) a mammal with no incisor or canine teeth e.g. anteater, sloth, armadillo

edentulous, edulate having no or few teeth

edible eatable in the sense of fit to eat, non-poisonous

edict an official order or proclamation; a declaration or decree

edify to improve the mind of; to instruct morally, intellectually, or sprirtually

educe to elicit, to extract, to draw out

effect to cause to occur

effective 1) producing a desired or intended result 2) existing in fact though not formally 3) (of a law or policy) operative

effectual answering its purpose

effendi a title of respect used in addressing an educated man or one of high social standing in Turkey and the Middle East

efferent carrying or conveying outwards or away from a part or organ of the body

effete 1) exhausted, worn out 2) (of men) effeminate, soft, decadent, over-refined, lacking vigour

efficacious having the potential to do the job in question; capable of producing the desired effect; potentially effective; doesn't refer to humans; usually applied to medical treatments

efficient producing results with little waste of effort or expense

efflorescence 1) bursting into flower, blooming, blossoming 2) the powder formed as a result of flowering 3) any skin rash or eruption

effluviate to give off an unpleasant smell

effluvium an unpleasant smell, fetor, mephitis, miasma

effulgent shining brilliantly

effusive unrestrained in expressing gratitude, pleasure, or approval; gushing

eft a newt

Egeria a female adviser; a woman who advises or inspires

egest to excrete, to discharge from the body

egesta excrement *n.* egestion *adj.* egestive

ego 1) excessive self-esteem 2) the part of the mind that is most in touch with external reality and adjusts responses to it

egocentric concerned only with oneself as the centre of the universe; an extreme egoist

egoism the philosophical doctrine that individual self-interest is the foundation of morality and the only real and proper motive for action

egoist one who believes in egoism; a person concerned only for his own interests and feelings

egomania obsessive concern with fulfilling one's own needs and desires, regardless of the effect on others; the result is a morbid obsession, a mania

egotist one who continually talks about himself

egregious outstandingly or exceptionally bad

egret a wading bird similar to a white heron

eident busy; diligent

eider sea duck of the N. hemisphere

eidetic having very strong visual recall that contains vivid detailed images

eidolon 1) an apparition; a spectre; a phantom 2) an image of an ideal

eirenicon, irenicon a proposal for peace

eke, eke out 1) to add to, to supplement in order to extend 2) to make something go further, last longer by economising, being frugal 3) to achieve something with difficulty, with great effort

ekphrasis the art of describing works of art; the verbal representation of visual representation

élan energy, style, enthusiasm

elapid a snake of the Elapidae, a family of venomous, mainly tropical snakes – the cobra, coral snake, mamba

eldritch weird; hideous; supernatural

elective 1) relating to election, voting 2) (of study, treatment) chosen by the student, the patient; optional not compulsory 3) tending towards certain things rather than others

Electra complex a girl's attraction towards her father with accompanying hostility towards her mother; the female counterpart of the Oedipus complex

electron a subatomic particle in all atoms that has a negative electrical charge; the movement of electrons in orbit around the nucleus of the atom constitutes electric current

electuary a medicine to be swallowed but taken with a sweetening accompaniment

eleemosynary charitable; contributing to or dependent on charity

elegant variation the deliberate practice of not using the same word, phrase or expression within close proximity in the same piece of writing

elegiac wistfully mournful, sad, plaintive

elegy 1) a mournful poem esp. a lament for the dead 2) a sorrowful musical composition

elemental 1) basic, fundamental, essential 2) concerning the primitive and powerful forces of nature 3) relating to (a) an element (b) an uncombined chemical element – see next entry

elements the more than 100 materials that cannot be broken down by chemical means into subsidiary materials; most occur in nature, a few have been made in the laboratory

elenchus a logical refutation esp. the Socratic way of getting at the truth by question and answer

elenctic *adj.* refuting an argument by proving the falsehood of its conclusion

elephant in the room an enormous problem obvious to everyone but which some pretend does not exist

eleutherian bountiful

elide to omit

elision the omission of a vowel or syllable in speech or writing

elixir 1) a potion supposedly able a) to change metals into gold b) to prolong life indefinitely 2) a cure-all, a panacea

elk a large deer *N. America* a wapiti

ellipse an oval

ellipsis 1) an omission 2) a set of dots indicating an omission

elliptic, elliptical 1) relating to an ellipse or an ellipsis 2) obscure, ambiguous, difficult to understand; with something left out

El Niño a warming of the eastern tropical Pacific; occurring every five to eight years, it alters the weather pattern of the tropics and can have effects on the weather in other parts of the world

elucidate to make clear (lucid); to explain

eluriate to wash out impurities

Elysium, Elysian Fields 1) *Gk.myth* the abode of the blessed after death 2) a place or state of ideal happiness; paradise; any delightful place

emaciated thin

emanation the act or process of originating (from a source)

emasculate 1) to deprive of (masculine) vigour; to weaken 2) to castrate

embargo *n.* a ban *v.* to ban

embellish 1) to adorn, to decorate 2) to make (a story) more interesting by adding details which may not be true

ember days special days for fasting and prayer

emblazon 1) to decorate with a coat of arms 2) to proclaim or publicize

emblem a symbol

emblematic symbolic

embolism obstruction of an artery by a clot of blood or an air bubble

embonpoint plumpness esp. a woman's large breasts

embourgeoisement *Fr.* the process of assimilating traditionally working-class people into the middle class

embrangle to confuse or entangle

embryo an organism in the earliest stage of its development esp. an unborn human in the first two months from conception

emcee a master of ceremonies

emend to restore a text to its original state; to remove errors or irregularities from (a text)

emery a hard rock used in powdered form for polishing, as an abrasive

emery-board a nail file

emery paper paper coated with crushed emery for polishing or cleaning metals etc.

emetic causing vomiting

emigrate to move abroad

eminence high ground **Eminence** form of address to a cardinal

éminence grise *Fr.* a person who wields power or

influence unofficially, behind the scenes and without holding office

eminent famous; well-known

emir a Muslim (usually an Arab) ruler

emollient softening or soothing the skin; a soothing or calming substance

emolument a salary, wages or fees from employment

emoticon a combination of symbols in e-mail and text messaging to indicate the state of mind of the writer such as :-) to express happiness

empathy the identifying with and sharing of the feelings of another

(the) emperor's new clothes the title of a story by Hans Christian Andersen (1835) in which an emperor was duped into wearing a new suit of clothes, invisible to unworthy people but which did not in fact exist. Nobody was prepared to tell the emperor that this meant that he was naked until a young boy pointed it out; hence a failure to draw attention to the absence of qualities in a person that are imagined but which are in fact fictitious

empirical based on practical experience, experiment, observation , the evidence of the senses – not theory or logic

emprise an enterprise, an undertaking esp. a hazardous or chivalrous one

emption the act of buying, a purchase

empyrean, empyreal of or concerning heaven, heavenly *n.* the high heavens, the sky

emulate 1) to strive to equal or excel 2) to rival

emulous striving to emulate

emunctory *n. &. adj.* an organ of the body (that carries off waste); an excretory duct

enantiosis the expression of an idea by negation of its contrary – 'he is no fool' = 'he is wise'

enceinte 1) pregnant 2) an enclosing wall 3) the area enclosed

enchilada a tortilla; **big enchilada** someone or something of great importance; **the whole enchilada** the whole situation, everything

enchiridion a handbook, a manual

enchorial, enchoric of or used by the people in a particular country; demotic, indigenous, native

encomiast one who expresses formal high praise; one who composes or delivers an encomium

encomium formal high praise, eulogy, panegyric

encumber to hinder, to impede; to burden

encyclical a letter in a set form sent round to many persons or places esp. one from the Pope to all Roman Catholic bishops

endeictic showing, exhibiting

endeixis an indication

endemic native; present within a particular area or group of people

endive a chicory-type plant used in salads

endlösung Ger. 'the final solution' euphemism for Hitler's plan to exterminate the Jews of Europe

endogamy marrying within one's own tribe or a designated group

endogenous from within; internal

endomorph a person with a soft, round, fat body

endoscope a medical instrument introduced into the body to view its internal parts

endue, indue to endow with a quality or ability

energumen 1) one who is possessed by the devil or an evil spirit 2) an enthusiast, fanatic, or zealot

enervate to deprive of strength or energy, to devitalize *adj.* drained of strength, devitalized

enervated listless, lethargic and inactive, exhausted, drained of energy

enfilade 1) gunfire directed along a line from end to end 2) rooms with doorways in line with each other

engorged filled to excess, crammed

engouement Fr. 1) a fad 2) a passion, infatuation

enharmonic *in music* having intervals smaller than a semitone (e.g. between G sharp and A flat); the notes sound the same on keyboard instruments such as the piano, but have a slight difference in pitch on string and wind instruments.

enigmatic puzzling, mysterious, difficult to understand or interpret

enjoin to command, to order

Enlightenment, the 18th-century intellectual and philosophical movement in Europe stressing the importance of reason, rather than tradition, and the need to reappraise existing ideas and social institutions

enmity hostility, hatred, ill-will

ennui *Fr.* tedium, boredom

enormity excessive evil; great wickedness; it is not uncommon for the word to be used neutrally to mean ' the great size or enormousness ' of but this is frowned upon

enosis the political union (desired by some) of Cyprus and Greece

en plein air Fr. outdoors

ensign a flag

entablature the upper part of a classical building supported by the columns or a colonnade; it comprises an architrave, frieze and cornice

entelechy 1) the realization of a potential 2) the supposed vital force that guides the development and functioning of an organism and generally directs its life

entellus = hanuman

enteric to do with the intestines

entomology the study of insects

entreat to ask (someone) earnestly to do something

entrepôt a port or other centre for import and export; a warehouse

entropy *(tech. term in physics)* used non-technically and loosely to mean lack of organisation, disorder or randomness in a system

enure = inure

enuresis unconscious or involuntary urination, esp. by children at night

envisage to form a mental picture of; to imagine; to visualise

envision (mainly North American) = envisage

envy the desire to have for oneself something possessed by somebody else cf. **jealousy**

eonism the practice by a man of dressing and behaving like a woman; transvestism

epact the number of days by which the solar year (365) exceeds the lunar year (354)

epalpebrate having no eyebrows

epeira a spider

epeiric to do with a continent or continents

epeolatry the worship of words

epexegesis the addition of a word, phrase, clause, or sentence to a text to make the meaning more clear

ephebe in ancient Greece, a young man of 18-20 doing military training

ephemera items of short-lived duration, interest, or use, esp. printed matter that become collectibles – postcards, posters, tickets, etc.

ephemeral living or lasting for only a day or a very short time

epicene 1) having characteristics of both sexes; hermaphrodite 2) having no characteristics of either sex; sexless 3) effeminate

epicentre, epicenter the point on the surface of the earth directly above the focus of an earthquake

epicure, epicurean a person with refined taste in food and wine

epideictic done for effect or display esp. to show off the rhetorical skill of a speaker

epidemic a widespread occurrence of a disease

epidemiology the study of epidemics and diseases

epidermis the outermost layer of the skin

epidural (anaesthetic) injected round the nerves of the spine esp. in childbirth

epigeal, epigean, epigeous above ground

epigone an inferior follower or imitator

epigram 1) a concise and witty remark or saying 2) a short witty poem

epigraph 1) an inscription (on a coin, statue, monument, building etc) 2) wording at the beginning of a book or a chapter suggesting its content

epinephrine adrenalin

epinician in celebration of victory

epiphany any sudden, important revelation or manifestation – orig. of Christ to the Magi

epiphenomenon 1) a secondary phenomenon or effect; a by-product 2) an unrelated or unexpected, atypical symptom occurring during the course of a disease 3) a mental state regarded as a by-product of brain activity

epiphyte one of the so-called 'airplants', not rooted in the ground; it grows on other plants or trees but is not parasitic on them e.g. mistletoe, moss, and tropical orchids, *adj.* **epiphytic**

episcopal 1) to do with bishops 2) governed by bishops

Episcopal Church an autonomous branch of the Anglican Church in Scotland and the U.S.

epistaxis bleeding from the nose, a nosebleed

epistemology the study, science or theory of knowledge – justified belief not opinion; what do we mean when we say we know something?

epistrophe the repetition of the same word or phrase at the end of successive clauses, sentences or lines

epithalamium a song or poem celebrating a marriage

epithesis = paragoge

epithet an adjective; descriptive word(s)

epithymetic to do with desire, lust

epitome 1) a perfect example of; an embodiment 2) a summary

epitonic overstrained

epizeuxis the immediate repetition of a word for emphasis

eponym a word derived from the name of a person e.g. a cardigan, named after the woollen jacket worn by the troops of the Earl of Cardigan in the Crimean war

eponymous bearing the name of the person with whom something is associated

epoxy an adhesive plastic paint

epulation feasting

epyllion a miniature epic

equestrian to do with horse-riding

equine to do with horses, horse-like

equipoise balance

equipollent equivalent; equal in power, effect or significance

equivocate to use evasive, vague, ambiguous language; to make a statement with one or more possible interpretations often with the intention of misleading

equivoque, equivoke an ambiguous expression, a pun

eradicate to uproot, to deracinate, to extirpate, to get rid of

Erastianism the theory that the state should have authority over the church in ecclesiastical matters

eremite a Christian hermit or recluse

erethism 1) abnormally high irritability 2) an abnormal tendency to become quickly aroused sexually

ergative descriptive of either 1) a verb that can take the same noun as direct object or subject or 2) a case of nouns that can be used interchangeably as direct object of a transitive verb or subject of an intransitive verb e.g. 'I stalled the car' and 'the car stalled'

ergonomics the study of the efficiency of people at work

ergotocracy government by the workers

ericaceous relating to a family of plants with typically bell-shaped flowers including heather, rhododendron and azalea that come from heathland and like an acid soil

Erin Ireland

erinaceous to do with or resembling hedgehogs

Erinys *pl.* **Erinyes** a Fury

eristic to do with debate or argument, esp. with winning the debate employing subtle and usu. specious argument

erlang a big jam in a telephone system caused by the overwhelming number of simultaneous calls

erl-king *Ger – myth.* evil spirit who carries off children

ermine (white winter fur of) the stoat

erne a sea eagle

erogenous responsive to sexual stimulation

erostrate having no beak

erotema, eroteme, erotesis a rhetorical question

erotetic to do with a rhetorical question

erotology the study of erotic stimuli and sexual behaviour

ersatz an inferior substitute or imitation *adj.* being an artificial and inferior substitute or imitation

Erse Irish Gaelic

erubescent turning red; blushing

eruciform caterpillar-like

eruct, eructate to belch

eructation belching, a belch

erudite learned, scholarly

erudition learning

erumpent (as though) bursting out through an overlying structure

eruv *Judaism* an area within which activities forbidden to Jews on the Sabbath are permitted

escamotage Fr. a conjuring or disappearing trick

escarole a type of endive used in salads

escarpment a long steep slope

eschatology the branch of theology concerned with the last or final things – death, final destiny of humankind, the end of the world etc.

escheat the reverting of property to a higher owner in terms of legal status

eschew to shun, avoid, abstain from

escritoire *Fr.* a writing-desk

escrow money, contract, or other document held by a third party and taking effect only when a specified condition has been fulfilled

esculent (something) edible, eatable

escutcheon 1) a shield with a coat of arms 2) reputation

esemplastic shaping into one

esoteric intended for or understood by the few with specialised knowledge

esprit *Fr.* liveliness and spirit eps. in wit

esprit de corps *Fr.* a unifying feeling of pride and mutual loyalty amongst the members of a group

esprit de l'escalier Fr. the repartee or remark that comes to mind too late e.g. on the stairs (l'escalier) on the way out

espy to catch sight of; to glimpse something partially hidden

essoin an excuse for not appearing in court

estimable worthy of great respect; esteemed

estop to stop or prevent by estoppel

estoppel a legal rule that stops somebody from acting in a way that is at variance with something they have previously said or done or with something in an earlier relevant legal decision

estovers the right to take wood for fuel, repairs, or some other necessary purpose from land which one does not own

estrange to alienate

estranged separated and living apart

estreat 1) *n.* a copy or extract from a court record 2) *v.* to enforce the forfeiture of (a surety for bail or other recognizance)

esurient hungry; greedy

estoppel
*a legal rule that stops somebody from acting
in a way that is at variance with something
they have previously said or done or with
something in an earlier relevant legal decision.*

etesian annual, seasonal, periodical

Etesian winds north-west winds that blow each summer in the Mediterranean

ethereal heavenly or spiritual; delicate, insubstantial, light, seeming not to be of this world but 'of the air', of the ether

ethmoid resembling a sieve

ethnography the scientific description of individual human societies

ethnology the study of different races and peoples, their relations to one another, their origins, and their distinctive characteristics

ethology the study of animal behaviour

ethos the distinctive character, spirit or attitudes of a people, culture, era or community

etiolate to become or cause to become pale through lack of light

etiology, aetiology the study of causation esp. the causes of disease

étrier a short rope ladder used in mountaineering

Etruria 1) ancient territory of west central Italy between rivers Arno and Tiber (*modern Tuscany and parts of Umbria*); home of the Etruscans 2) the place in Staffordshire where Josiah Wedgwood (*1730-1795*) and his successors made and developed their ceramics and in particular the trademark powder-blue porcelain with white embossed cameos

Etruscans the earliest inhabitants of Etruria; their civilization influenced the Romans who had conquered them by about 200 b.c.

etymology the study of the origin and development of words

etypic, etypical uncomformable to type

Eucharist Holy Communion

euchre a North American card game *v.* to deceive or outwit

eudemonism the doctrine that the basis of moral and rational action should be its capacity to bring about happiness and personal well-being

euge *Latin* Well done! Well!

eugenics race improvement by selective breeding

euharmonic producing perfectly concordant sounds

euhemerism the theory which explains mythology as growing out of real history, its gods being former kings and heroes deified after death – Euhemerus, 4th- century b.c. Greek philosopher

eulogy words of praise esp. at a funeral concerning a person who has recently died

Eumenides euphemistic name for the Erinyes or Furies

eunomy equal, righteous law

euonym a fitting name for anything

eupatrid a member of the Athenian aristocracy

eupepsy good digestion, opp. of **dyspepsia**

eupeptic having good digestion

euphemism an inoffensive, milder or softer word or phrase used instead of one considered to be unpleasant, offensive or embarrassing e.g. 'to pass away'

euphonious sounding pleasant, harmonious

euphony 1) sound which is pleasing to the ear 2) the changing of speech sounds to ease pronunciation

euphoric intensely happy and elated

euphuism an exaggeratedly elaborate style of writing or speaking; the language used is affected, artificial, high-flown, ornate and generally 'over the top'

eurhythmic having harmonious rhythmic movement

eurhythmics a system of rhythmical physical movements to music

eutaxy good order *adj.* **eutaxitic**

Euterpean relating to music – Euterpe the muse who presided over music

eutrophic (of lakes and water habitats) rich in nutrients

eutrophy healthy nutrition

evanescent fleeting; vanishing; quickly fading away from sight, memory , or existence

evangelical 1) adhering to and upholding the Christian gospel 2) having an ardent and crusading enthusiasm for something

evangelistic militant, zealous in preaching the Christian gospel to produce converts

evert to turn inside out, to turn outwards

evince to show, to indicate

eviscerate to disembowel

evzone a soldier in an elite Greek infantry regiment

ewer a large pitcher or jug with a wide mouth

ewigkeit Ger. eternity

exacerbate to make worse, to aggravate

exalt *v.tr.* 1) to raise (someone) in rank, position or dignity 2) to praise highly

exalted 1) raised to a higher level 2) noble, lofty, sublime 3) elated

exasperate to irritate, to annoy; to cause to feel frustrated

Excalibur King Arthur's magic sword; ensured his immunity in battle

ex cathedra Lat. from the chair and with the full authority of office esp. the pope's throne or a professor's chair, hence with infallibility

exceptionable open to objection

exceptional out of the ordinary

exceptis excipiendis *Lat.* with proper exceptions, excepting whatever is to be excepted

excise an internal tax on goods for the home market, especially spirits and on certain licences

excoriate 1) to skin, to strip the skin from 2) to criticize severely, to berate

excrescence an outgrowth – a bunion, tumour, wart

exculpate to free from blame, to absolve from wrongdoing, to exonerate

exculpatory blameless

execrable accursed, appalling, detestable

execrate to curse, to feel and express loathing and hatred of

exegesis an explanation, interpretation esp. of scripture

exegete one who explains, interprets texts esp. the Bible

exequies funeral rites

exercitation exercise

exergue the small space (or inscription) below the principal emblem on a coin or medal on the reverse side, often filled up by the date

exhilarating making joyful or lively

exhort to urge strongly

ex hypothesi *Lat.* on the basis of the hypothesis proposed

exigencies demands (of the situation)

exigency emergency

exigent 1) *(of people)* demanding 2) *(of situations)* urgent

exiguous small, scanty, meagre

eximious excellent, eminent, select and distinguished

existentialism has two basic tenets 1) your life is what you make it and 2) life itself is meaningless

ex nihilo Lat. out of nothing

exobiology the science of possible life on other planets or in space

exogamy marrying only outside one's own tribe

exogenous from outside; external

exonerate to free from responsibility or blame

exonym a name foreigners use for a place instead of the name used by the locals – *Londres for London, Florence for Firenza*

exophagy the custom of cannibals not to eat persons of their own tribe

exophoric concerning pronouns ('I', 'you' etc.) the meaning of which is found outside a text rather than from references within the text itself, cf. **anaphora**

exophthalmic having bulging eyes

exorbitant (of a price or charge) unreasonably high, extortionate

exorcize to drive out (an evil spirit)

exordium the beginning or introductory part of a discourse

exoteric intended for the general public, popular, untechnical

exotic 1) foreign, from a distant part of the world 2) strikingly different or colourful; strange and fascinating through being unfamiliar or foreign

ex parte *Lat.* (in legal proceedings) of an application to the court, by one party only

expatiate to speak or write at length or in detail; to elaborate

expectorate to expel phlegm from the lungs; used loosely to mean 'to spit'

expedient *adj. & n.* convenient and practical, but possibly improper, (means to an end)

expendable not absolutely essential, that can be done away with, sacrificeable

expiate to atone for; to make amends for a sin or wrongdoing

expletive a swear word

exponential increasingly rapid; ever more rapid

exposition 1) an explanation 2) an exhibition

expostulate to express disapproval, to remonstrate, to reason with esp. in order to dissuade

Expressionism a broad term in the (mainly) visual arts describing the movement which sought to represent the inner world of emotion rather than external reality; conventional notions of beauty or harmony gave way to distortion, symbolism and exaggeration

expurgate to remove anything obscene or offensive from a text before publication

exsanguinate to drain of blood

extant still in existence; surviving

extemporaneous, extemporary without planning or preparation

extempore without preparation or the benefit of notes

extemporize to perform or speak without preparation or the benefit of notes

extirpate to uproot; to take out by the roots; to eradicate; to deracinate

extol to praise highly

extortionate (of a price) far too high, exorbitant

extraneous coming from the outside; irrelevant, unimportant

extrapolate to infer from a limited number of known facts

extravasate *v.tr.* to force out a fluid esp. blood from its proper vessel; *intr.* to flow out or escape; *of lava,* to pour out

extravasation an escape of fluid from the vessels or passages which ought to contain it

extreme unction *R.C. Church* the former name for the sacrament of anointing the seriously ill or dying with consecrated oil in their last hours

extrorse, extrorsal turned outwards

extrovert an outgoing, uninhibited, social person

extrude to thrust out, to force out

exult to rejoice

exultant joyful; jubilant; triumphant

exurbia, exurbs the prosperous, semirural, residential areas beyond the suburbs of a city

exuviae *Lat.* cast-off coverings – skins, shells etc.

exuviate to lay aside an old covering for a new one; to shed (a skin or similar outer covering)

eyelet a small hole for string or cord to pass through

eyot, ait a small island in a river

eyrie the nest of an eagle or other bird of prey built on a crag or in some other high, inaccessible place

F

fabaceous descriptive of plants having seeds in pods, leguminous, bean-like

Fabian adopting a delaying, cautious approach esp. in order to wear down an opponent, in the manner of the Roman general Quintus Fabius Maximus Verrucosus 'the Cunctator' ('delayer'), died 203 b.c.

facet, faceted 1) one side of something with a number of sides esp. a cut gem 2) one aspect or feature

facetiae 1) humorous sayings or writings 2) (in bookselling) pornography

facetious using inappropriate humour

facile 1) easy, easily achieved 2) overly simple and showing lack of real thought; ignoring the complexities of an issue; superficial

facile princeps Lat. an obvious leader

facilitate to make easy or easier

facinerous dreadfully wicked

facticity the essential quality and nature of being factual

faction 1) a small dissenting group within a larger one 2) strife or dissension within a group

factious relating to dissension

factitious artificial; sham; contrived; lacking in authenticity

factoid something repeated so often it becomes accepted as fact

factotum an employee who does all kinds of work

facture the act, process or manner of making something esp. the way in which an artistic work is made

facula a bright area on the surface of the sun

facultative 1) pertaining to a mental faculty 2) not bound to occur; optional 3) *bio.* able to live under more than one set of conditions e.g. bacteria can live with or without oxygen

facundity fluency, flow of words, eloquence

fadaises Fr. silly things, nonsense

faïence pottery orig. from Faenza, Italy

fain willingly; gladly

fainéant 1) idle 2) an idler

fairing 1) streamlining on a plane, vehicle etc. to reduce drag or air resistance 2) a present acquired at a fair 3) a type of biscuit

faisandé Fr. (of game) well hung, high, gamy

fait accompli Fr. something done and completed and consequently irreversible

faitour an impostor

fakir a Hindu/Muslim ascetic holy man

falaise Fr. a cliff

falcate curved like a sickle e.g. the crescent moon

falciform in the shape of a sickle

falcon a hawk

falconer 1) a breeder and trainer of hawks 2) a person who hunts with hawks

fallow 1) *(of land)* lying idle; ploughed but left untilled or unsown 2) dormant or inactive 3) *(of a sow)* not pregnant 4) light yellowish-brown

fallow deer in summer its coat is reddish-brown with white spots

Falstaffian like Shakespeare's Falstaff – fat and jolly, humorous, and dissolute

famous is often otiose: if something is famous is it necessary to say so?

fanatic a person with excessive zeal for an extreme religious or political cause

fanatical possessed by enthusiasm to the point of being irrational

fanfaronade bragging, boasting

fardel 1) a burden 2) a bundle

farci *Fr.* stuffed

farina flour *adj.* **farinaceous**

farouche 1) feral 2) sullen; shy; socially inept – feral animals have a tendency to shy away when approached

farrago a hotchpotch, a hodgepodge, a confused mixture, a gallimaufry

farrier a person who shoes horses

farrow 1) a litter of pigs 2) *of a sow* to give birth to piglets

farthingale a hooped petticoat

fascide 1) a bundle 2) a section of a book published in parts

fash *n.* worry, trouble, bother *v.* to trouble, bother, annoy

fashed worried, annoyed

fastidious fussy, finicky, meticulous esp. with regard to accuracy, detail, and cleanliness

fastigiate (of a tree or plant) having erect branches more or less parallel to the main stem

fastness a fortress

Fata Morgana *It.* a mirage

fatidic, fatidical having the power to foretell future events; gifted with prophetic power

Fátima village in Portugal which claims a sighting of the Virgin Mary in 1917

Fatima youngest daughter of Muhammad

Fatimids descendants of Fatima, an Arab dynasty that ruled in and around Egypt (*909-1171*)

fatiscent gaping *n.* **fatiscence**

fatuous foolish, silly

faucet a tap on a barrel; *N.Amer.* a tap

fauna the animal life of a region or time

faute de mieux Fr. for want of anything better

Fauvism an art movement starting in Paris in 1905 as a reaction against Impressionism; it favoured a simplified form and the use of vivid colours; prominent members included Matisse and Dufy

faux Fr. false

faux amis Fr. (false friends) words in one language which are the same as or similar to words in another language but which have a different meaning

faux-naïf Fr. pretending to be simple and naive

faux pas Fr. a socially embarrassing blunder, a gaffe

favela a shanty town in Brazil

fawn 1) a baby deer 2) a light brown colour 3) to behave in a servile manner, to display exaggerated flattery or affection

fawning flattering, grovelling

fazed disconcerted, perturbed, put out

fealty loyalty

feasible capable of being done; practicable

febrifuge medicine for combating fever

febrile feverish

feckless feeble; lacking character and determination

feculent filthy

fecund fertile, fruitful

feisty spirited, sparky, spunky

felafel (falafel) a spicy Middle Eastern dish of mashed chick-peas formed into balls and deep-fried

feldspar an important group of minerals, pale or colourless, from which a great many rocks are formed

felicitations congratulations

felicitous well-chosen, apt

felicity 1) happiness 2) a happy knack 3) the ability to express oneself appropriately

feline to do with a cat; cat-like

fell an animal skin

fellah (*pl.* **fellahin**) a peasant or farm worker in Arab countries

fellic, fellinic obtained from bile

fellifluous flowing with gall

felo de se 1) suicide 2) person who commits suicide, 'felon of oneself '

felony (formerly) a serious crime

felucca a small Mediterranean boat with oars or lateen sails or both; now used on the Nile

femme fatale *Fr.* a dangerously attractive or seductive woman

Fenians 19th-century Irish Republican revolutionaries, precursors of the IRA

feral wild, savage

Fermat Pierre de *(1601-65)* French mathematician

Fermat's last theorem if n is greater than 2, then there is no whole number whose nth power can be expressed as the sum of two smaller nth powers, i.e. $3^2+4^2=5^2$ but for any higher powers this does not work

ferment, foment have different core meanings but both tend to be used mainly figuratively and mean 'to stir up'

ferruginous 1) of or containing iron 2) rust-coloured

ferrule 1) a ring or cap strengthening the end of a walking stick, umbrella or the like 2) a short length of tube for strengthening or forming a joint between pipes

fervent ardent, passionate (with impartial or favourable connotations)

fervid means the same as fervent but, arguably, has disapproving undertones and is rarely used to describe people

fervour intense and passionate feeling

Fescennine scurrilous, obscene

fess up to confess

festina lente Lat. hasten slowly or gently

festinate to accelerate

festination an involuntary quickening of gait occurring in some nervous diseases

festoon 1) a decorative chain or garland hung between two points 2) to adorn with garlands

festschrift a collection of writings contributed to honour a scholar esp. a colleague

fetid, foetid stinking

fetish 1) an object supposed to have magical powers 2) a fixation, mania, obsession 3) something which, improbably, stimulates sexual desire

fetor a horrible smell, miasma, effluvium, mephitis

fettle condition– *in fine fettle*

feuilleton 1) the part of a newspaper esp. French or European, that covers non-news items – the arts, criticism, letters, reviews, serialized features etc. 2) (an instalment of) a serialized novel

fey 1) magical or fairy-like, otherworldly, as if under a spell; somewhat unreal 2) clairvoyant, supernatural

fiacre a type of taxi cab, four-wheeled, horse-drawn usually with a folding roof, originally hired out from the Hôtel de St. Fiacre in Paris

fiançailles Fr. betrothal; engagement

fiasco a ludicrous or humiliating failure

fiat an official order or authorization

Fibonacci sequence a series of numbers in which each number is the sum of the two preceding numbers (1,1,2,3,5,8 etc.); significant in various fields esp. botany, it has further possible applications in art, architecture and music; named after the Italian mathematician Leonardo Fibonacci (*c.1170-1250*)

fibrillation quivering of a muscle esp. in the heart

fibrous 1) consisting of fibres 2) of strong character

fickle changeable, not loyal

fictive to do with fiction, the writing of fiction, the imagination

fideism the theological notion that religious truth is a matter of faith and cannot be demonstrated by reason cf. **natural theology**

fidibus a paper spill for lighting a candle or pipe

fiducial *adj. tech.* (of a point or line) used as a standard of reference or measurement

fiduciary involving trust or having the nature of a trust

fiduciary issue an issue of banknotes not backed by gold

fieldfare a type of thrush

fifth amendment in the United States the right guaranteed by the Constitution of not having to answer questions which might lead to incriminating oneself

fifth column those inside a country at war who are sympathetic to or working for the enemy

fifth estate (in jest) certain 'authorities' or establishment bodies e.g. the Trade Unions, the B.B.C.

Figaro an artful rogue who features initially in plays by Beaumarchais and later in operas by Mozart, Paisiello, and Rossini; it is also the name of a leading Paris newspaper founded in 1854

figural = figurative

figurative metaphorical, not literal use of words

figurine a statuette

filament 1) a slender thread or fibre 2) a thin wire in a light bulb

filial relating to a son or daughter

filibuster 1) obstructing legislation by long speeches and other delaying tactics 2) a military adventurer

filigree ornamental lace-like work of twisted fine gold, silver, or copper wire formed into a delicate, intricate design or tracery

fille de joie *Fr.* a prostitute (*lit.* 'daughter of joy')

fillip boost, stimulus

film noir *Fr*. a film of a type or genre characterized by menace, pessimism, fatalism

filth 1) a jokey acronym for a struggling barrister or other professional trying to revive their career: failed in London, try Hong Kong 2) a slang term for the police

fimbriate, fimbriated having a fringe or border

fimetarious growing on dung

fimicolous of *fungi* growing on dung

finagle to achieve by craftiness or trickery; to wangle

fin de siècle Fr. end of the 19th century; decadence; decadent

finesse *n*. 1) elegant and delicate skill 2) refinements and subtlety in handling or manipulating people or situations *v*. to do (something) in a subtle and delicate manner esp. to try to avoid blame in a tricky situation

fingerspitzengefuëhl Ger. 'fingertip feeling' instinctive feeling, flair, touch; tact

finial 1) the ornament finishing off and crowning the top of pinnacles, gables, spires of esp. a Gothic building 2) a crowning ornament

finical finicky

firmament the heavens; the expanse of the sky

first-day cover an envelope with a stamp or stamps postmarked with the date of their first issue

fiscal 1) relating to taxes, government revenue 2) *N. Amer.* relating to finance generally; a financial year

fishplate a type of metal plate used to strengthen a joint

fishwife a coarse, abusive, nagging woman

fissile 1) tending to split 2) capable of being split and, in the case of an atomic nucleus, producing a nuclear explosion

fissiparous 1) reproducing by splitting 2) tending to split

fistula an abnormal or surgically made passage or duct between an organ and the body surface or between two organs

fitch, fitchet, fitchew a polecat

fitful irregular

fitz (a prefix) son of; used, as a prefix, in relation to the illegitimate sons of kings and princes e.g. Fitzroy 'son (*fils*) of the King' (*roi*)

fizgig 1) a flighty young woman 2) a kind of firework 3) a police informer

flabellate, flabelliform fan-shaped **flabellation** *n.* the action of fanning

flaccid flabby, hanging loose, drooping, soft and limp

flagellate to whip, to flog

flagitious shamefully and criminally wicked

flagrant blatant, conspicuously offensive

flailing swinging wildly, threshing about

flair 1) natural ability or talent 2) distinctive style, elegance, originality

flak heavy criticism

flambé *Fr.* to cook or serve food in flaming brandy; cooked in that way

flamboyant behaving in a very noticeable, extravagant way; very brightly coloured and showy

flamenco a vigorous gypsy dance

flammable, inflammable both mean liable to catch fire – **flammable** is preferred because **inflammable** could be mistaken for non-flammable

Flanders an area of north-west Belgium and north-east France on the North Sea; it also extends into the Netherlands

flâneur Fr. 1) a stroller; an idler 2) a man about town; one who saunters around closely observing society

flapdoodle foolish talk; nonsense

flatulence build-up of gas in the digestive tract

flaunt to show off (something)

flavescent turning yellow; yellowish

flaxen pale yellow

flay 1) to strip the skin from by whipping 2) to criticize savagely

Fleming a native of Flanders

Flemish 1) the language of Flanders 2) to do with Flanders, its people or language

flibbertigibbet a gossip, a quidnunc

flippant not showing appropriate gravity or respect

flitch a side of bacon

floccinaucinihilipilification the action of contemptuously dismissing something, or treating it, as worthless

flocculent like tufts of wool

flora the plant life of a region or time

florilegium an anthology

flotsam wreckage found floating on the sea

flotsam and jetsam 1) odd and ends; useless or discarded objects; rubbish 2) vagrants

flounce 1) to walk exagerratedly 2) to express anger, annoyance or impatience 3) a strip of fabric attached to the hem of a skirt

flounder to move clumsily, to struggle to keep one's balance; to go forward clumsily and in confusion, to press on or struggle hopelessly

flout disregard

flume 1) a sloping water channel 2) a water slide at a swimming pool

flummery meaningless flattery; nonsense; humbug

floccinaucinihilipilification
*the action of contemptuously dismissing something,
or treating it, as worthless*

fluting *archit.* decorative, vertical, parallel grooves on the shaft of a classical column

fly smart, knowing

flyting 1) a scolding, rebuke 2) a heated dispute, a noisy argument

fodient digging

foetus, fetus an unborn mammal, esp. an unborn human more than eight weeks after conception

fogey an old-fashioned or aged person

foible a small weakness of character

foil a type of fencing sword

fold a pen or enclosure for animals

folderol a piece of nonsense

folie à deux *Fr.* delusion or mental illness shared by two people in close association

folie de grandeur *Fr.* delusions of grandeur

folio a sheet of paper folded in half to form two leaves (four pages) of a book, called a folio (book)

foment see **ferment, foment**

foolhardy recklessly bold or rash

footling trivial, silly, petty and irritating

fop a man preoccupied with his appearance; a dandy

foray a sudden attack, raid

forbear to refrain from doing something

forbidding unfriendly, threatening, hostile

force majeure unforeseeable circumstances beyond human control that prevent someone from fulfilling a contract

forebear an ancestor

forebode to act as an advance warning of (something bad)

forego to go before

forfeiture the loss of the right to something

forgo to do without

forlorn sad, lonely, and uncared for

forlorn hope a desperate or final undertaking or attempt

formication a feeling as of insects crawling over the skin

formidable 1) frightening, fearsome 2) impressive; inspiring admiration

fornicate to have sexual intercourse without being married

forswink to exhaust by work

forswonk overworked

forte *n.* something at which a person excels *mus.* loud and forceful

fortitude courage in adversity; strength of mind

fortuitous happening by chance, unplanned

fossick to search for, to rummage

foster 1) to promote the development of; to nurture 2) to bring up (a child that is not one's own by birth)

foudre Fr. lightning; *ce fut le coup de foudre* – it was love at first sight

foudroyant of lightning speed

founder (of ships) to sink; to collapse; to stumble; to fail, weaken, or give way

fount a complete set of printing type

fourth estate journalists; the press

foxed (of the paper of old books or prints) discoloured with brownish marks, spots

fractal an irregular geometric shape that can be successively subdivided into parts which are smaller copies of the whole

fractious 1) badly behaved, unruly, given to fighting 2) peevish, irritable, cranky

frampold peevish, cross-grained, quarrelsome

francophile a lover of France, the French, or anything French

Frank a member of one of the Germanic tribes who conquered Gaul in the 6th century

Frankenstein is not the monster but the scientist who created him

frankish 1) the language of the Franks 2) *adj.* to do with the Franks or their language

frappant Fr. striking

frappé *Fr.* iced

fratricide the killing of a brother

fraught, fraught with filled with, involving; loaded with something ominous

frazzled completely exhausted

fremescent raging, roaring, riotous

French leave 1) absence from work or duty without permission 2) abrupt or unauthorized departure

frenetic frenzied, wild, excited, and uncontrolled

frescade a cool walk

fresco painting in watercolours on fresh moist plaster

freshet 1) a flood of a river caused by melting snow or heavy rain 2) a rush of fresh water flowing into the sea

friable crumbly

fribble a person or thing of no consequence

fricative 1) referring to the sound made by forcing the breath through a narrow opening 2) a consonant (*f.th.*) produced in this way

fricatively challenged describing the mispronunciation of a word containing a fricative consonant e.g. saying 'wif' or 'wiv' instead of 'with' or 'norf' for 'north'

frieze 1) *archit.* the horizontal band of sculpture between the architrave and cornice of an entablature 2) a band of decoration along a wall near the ceiling 3) heavy fabric used for carpets

frippery cheap and showy clothing, showy or unnecessary ornament

frisson Fr. a thrill; an excited shiver or shudder

fritillary 1) a plant of the lily family 2) a butterfly with spotted wings

frond the leaf of a fern, palm, or similar plant

frottage 1) rubbing against somebody's clothed body for sexual gratification 2) creating an image of something by putting paper over its uneven surface and rubbing on it with a pencil or similar

froward difficult to deal with; contrary

frowsty (of an atmosphere) stale, stuffy, lacking fresh air / ventilation

frugal thrifty

fruition fulfilment, realization of a plan or project

frutescent shrubby

frutex a shrub

fruticose, fruticous shrub-like

fubsy short, fat and squat

fucivorous eating seaweed

fucus seaweed

fug a warm, stuffy, stale atmosphere

fugacious fleeting

fugleman a soldier who acts as a drill leader; a leader or exemplar of soldiers at drill

fugue 1) a composition in which a short melody or phrase is successively taken up by different parts and developed by a continuous inter-weaving 2) loss of awareness of one's identity and disappearance from home

fulcrum the pivot for a lever

fulgent shining brightly

fulgurant flashing like lightning

fuliginous sooty, dusky, soot-like

fulminate to 'thunder' or inveigh explosively, loudly and fiercely against; to denounce

fulsome overabundant, excessively lavish, offensively insincere; the old objection to fulsome as denoting 'full, abundant' is now in doubt so that the word can, apparently, bear that positive meaning

fulvous reddish-yellow, tawny

fumigate to smoke out a room or building to disinfect or decontaminate it

funambulate to walk on a tightrope

funambulist a tightrope walker

fundamentalism belief in the strict and literal interpretation of the Bible

fungible(s) replaceable(s), interchangeable(s); not unique

funicular a railway on the side of a mountain with ascending and descending cable cars counterbalanced

funiform having the form of a rope or cord

furcate to divide into two parts; forked

Furies *classical myth* the three goddesses of vengeance and punishment; also called Erinyes or Eumenides

furlong an eighth of a mile, 220 yards

furlough leave of absence from the military

furtive stealthy, surreptitious, sly; sneaky, shifty

fuscous dark, brownish grey

fused participle the bête noire of H.W.Fowler and his brother who insisted that 'Women having the vote reduces men's political power' was 'indefensible' and that the only acceptable construction was 'Women's having the vote…'

fustian turgid language; inflated or pompous talk or writing

fustigate to flay, to thrash esp. with a stick

fusty 1) smelling of damp or mould; musty 2) old-fashioned

futon a Japanese quilted mattress laid on the floor or on a frame for use as a bed

fuzzy logic allows degrees of imprecision in reasoning and knowledge to be represented in such a way that the information can be processed by computer; a classical set might be persons aged over 70 whereas a fuzzy set might refer to 'elderly' persons

fynbos the indigenous plant life of S. Africa's Cape region

G

gad to go from place to place, to move about, to travel

gadabout a habitual pleasure-seeker

Gadarene *in the Bible* describing the pigs of Gadara that rushed suicidally 'down a steep place into the sea' and to their death; *hence* involving a headlong or precipitate, disastrous rush

gadfly 1) a fly that bites or annoys livestock 2) an irritating, annoying person 3) a goad, one who prods or urges to action, one who is a provocative stimulus or catalyst to action 4) an irritating critic

Gaelic any of the three Goidelic languages – Scottish Gaelic, Irish, and Manx or all of these

gaffe an embarrassing blunder, a faux pas

galactagogue *n. & adj.* (a drug) inducing the flow of milk from a mother's breast

Galen 2nd- century Greek physician, regarded as the founder of experimental physiology

galère Fr. a gallery

galimatias gibberish

gall 1) bile 2) impudence 3) bitterness

gallant *(meaning depends on the context or pronunciation)* 1) brave, heroic *(stress on the first syllable)* 2) attentive to women, chivalrous *(stress on the second)*

Gallicanism a movement for the freedom from Papal control of the R.C. Church in France

Gallicism a word or phrase borrowed from French – has pejorative overtones

gallimaufry a heterogeneous mixture, a hotchpotch, a mishmash, a jumble

gallivant to go from place to place in pursuit of pleasure

galumph to go prancing in triumph – coined by Lewis Carroll – from gallop and triumph?

galvanize to spur or stimulate into thought or action

gambit an opening move (esp. in chess) involving some strategic sacrifice or concession but calculated to gain a subsequent advantage

gamboge a gum resin from certain Asian trees, used as a yellow pigment and as a laxative

gambol to frolic

gamete a sperm or egg able to participate in fertilisation

gamic involving sexual reproduction

gamin a street urchin

gamine a female gamin; a young woman or girl, slim and attractive in a boyish way

gammon 1) deceitful nonsense; humbug 2) to deceive (somebody)

gamut the entire range of something

gander 1) a look, a glance 2) a male goose

ganglion a mass of nerve cells; a swelling

gangrene death of body tissues, necrosis

gangue the valueless earth/stone matrix in which ore is found

Ganymede a catamite; orig. a beautiful Trojan youth in Greek mythology

garble to confuse, distort or mutilate (a message), so that it becomes unintelligible

gargantuan gigantic, huge, enormous

gargoyle a waterspout in the form of a grotesque face or figure projecting from the guttering just below the roof of a building to carry rainwater clear of the wall

garish gaudy; bright and showy

garner to gather, store up, collect

garnet a deep red, semi-precious stone

garnishee where A owes money to B who owes money to C, garnishee proceedings by C against A (often a bank) would seek an order for A to pay the debt (or part of it) not to B but to C

garret a (poor) attic

garrulous talkative

gasconade from Freud 1) boasting 2) to boast

gastric concerning the stomach

gastronome a food expert

gastronomic 1) choosing, cooking, and eating good food 2) any particular regional style of cooking

gauche awkward in manner; lacking social graces

gaucherie awkward and unsophisticated ways

gaucho a cowboy of the South American pampas, i.e. from the Argentine

gaudy garish; tastelessly showy; flashy, having overly bright colours

gauleiter 1) an official in charge of a district in Nazi Germany 2) an overbearing official

gauntlet an armoured glove

gavage forced feeding

gavial, gharial large fish-eating Indian crocodile with the longest and thinnest jaw and more pointed teeth than other types of crocodile

gazebo a summerhouse

gazelle a small, graceful and very swift African or Asian antelope

gazump to raise the previously agreed price for a property

geek 1) a social misfit 2) an obsessive enthusiast esp. a computer buff

gehenna hell

geist spirit; thought and feeling; attitude

gem, gemstone a precious or semi-precious stone esp. when cut and polished

gemütlich Ger. good-natured; cosy, snug

gemütlichkeit Ger. good-nature; cosiness; comfort

gene a unit of heredity in a chromosome which is transferred from a parent to offspring

generic 1) to do with a group or class 2) not having a brand name

genial 1) friendly and cheerful 2) pleasantly mild and warm (weather)

genocide the killing of a nation or an ethnic group

genre 1) a kind, a type, a category 2) a type of painting depicting scenes from ordinary life

Gentile a non-Jew

genuflect to bend the knee and lower the body in worship or as a sign of respect

genus a kind, a type

geo earth

geocentric considering the earth as the centre of the universe

geomancy divination involving earth in various guises e.g. observing the pattern after throwing a handful into the air; the configuration of dots drawn at random and connected with lines etc.

geometer a specialist in geometry

geophagist a person who eats earth

George Dandin comedy by Molière (1668). G.D. marries above himself but has to endure the extravagances of his wife: *'Tu l'as voulu, George Dandin, tu l'as voulu'*

georgic 1) rural, agricultural 2) a poem or book about rural or agricultural matters

geratology the branch of medicine concerned with the elderly

gerbil a type of rodent often kept as a pet

germane relevant

Geronimo 1) a shout given out by U.S. paratroopers as they jump into battle 2) an exclamation expressing exhilaration when jumping from a great height, after *Geronimo (1829-1909)* the Apache Indian chieftain

gerontocracy government by old men, a council of elders

gerontology the study of old age and ageing

gerontophile a person sexually obsessed with the elderly esp. a man with a fetish for old women

gerrymander to manipulate the boundaries of (a constituency) so as to give an unfair advantage to one party

gerund an English verbal noun ending in *–ing* e.g. singing

gesamtkunstwerk Ger. the concept of a total integration of music, drama, and spectacle – the notion of the German composer Richard Wagner (*1813 – 83*)

gesso plaster of Paris or gypsum used in painting or sculpture

Gestalt a whole, an overall impression that is created and is considered to be more than the sum of its parts

gestalt psychology a movement in psychology founded in Germany in 1912; it attempted to explain human perception in terms of gestalts

gesundheit Ger. Good Health! – said to someone who has just sneezed

gewgaw a gaudy, showy trinket that is worthless, useless

geyser a natural spring that spouts hot water or steam

gherkin a small cucumber

ghoul 1) an evil spirit or demon that robs graves and eats corpses 2) a person morbidly interested in death

gibbet 1) an upright post with an arm on which the bodies of executed criminals were left hanging 2) the gallows

gibbon a small arborial ape from S.E. Asia

gibbous 1) (of the moon) more than half but less than fully illuminated 2) hunchbacked; convex, protuberant

gesamtkunstwerk
*Ger. the concept of a total integration of music, drama,
and spectacle – the notion of the German composer
Richard Wagner (1813 – 83)*

Gibeonite a slave's slave (Joshua IX: 27)

gift of tongues see **glossolalia**

gig a light, two-wheeled carriage pulled by one horse

gigmanity Thomas Carlyle (*1795-1881*) nonce-word for a narrow philistinism based on having a little more money than others; from gigman, one who drives or keeps a gig

gimcrack 1) showy, cheap 2) a showy, cheap trinket

gimlet 1) a small hand tool for boring holes 2) a gin or vodka and lime juice cocktail 3) **gimlet-eyed** with a piercing, penetrating look

gin 1) a snare, a trap 2) a kind of crane 3) a machine for separating cotton from its seeds

gingerly in a careful, cautious, delicate manner

gingham plain-woven cotton cloth in stripes or checks

ginkgo an ornamental Chinese/Japanese tree, aka the maidenhair tree

Gioconda, La another name for the Mona Lisa

girasol 1) a type of opal with a reddish glow 2) a Jerusalem artichoke

Girondins, Girondists the moderate French republican party at the time of the Revolution; their leaders were deputies from the département of the Gironde; aka Brissotins

gittern a medieval guitar

gizmo a gadget

gizzard the muscular stomach of a bird

glabrate, glabrous having no hairs or projections; smooth-skinned

gladsome glad; joyous; gay

glandiferous bearing acorns or nuts

glasnost *Rus.* openness

glaucous smoky-blue, dull greyish-green

glaze a shiny coating

glean to gather

gleanings things gathered

glebe church land belonging to a parish church and benefiting the local clergyman

gleichschaltung Ger. the standardisation within an authoritarian state of political, economic, social and cultural attitudes and approaches and the elimination of all opposition

glib articulate and fluent but insincere and shallow

glissando a continuous sliding of adjacent notes up or down

glitch a fault that stops something working; a hitch

gloaming, the dusk, twilight

glockenspiel a xylophone-like percussion instrument of tuned metal plates played with a pair of small hammers

gloop *N.Amer.* **glop** a gooey, sticky, messy, semi-fluid substance or matter

Gloriana the nickname of Queen Elizabeth 1 of England and Ireland

gloss a misleading explanation

glossolalia the phenomenon of appearing to speak in an unknown language esp. during worship in some evangelical Christian churches or as part of a psychological or psychiatric disorder aka **gift of tongues**

glossologist one who defines technical terms, who is versed in the science of language; a philologist

glottal of the glottis e.g. using the glottal stop instead of 't' in the cockney bu'er for butter

glow-worm a larva or wingless female beetle that emits light

gloze to explain away; to minimize the effect or importance of

glut an excessive supply

glutinous sticky, like glue

gluttony excessive eating or drinking

glyph 1) *archit* . an ornamental vertical groove as on a frieze 2) a symbol on a road sign or in computer graphics that informs without using words

glyptic to do with carving or engraving

gnathic relating to the jaws

gnathonic deceitfully flattering; sycophantic

gneiss a type of rock

gnomic in the form of short, pithy maxims or aphorisms often in an enigmatic, ambiguous way

gnomon the fixed piece on a sundial that shows the time by its shadow

Gnosticism a body of early heterodox Christian teaching which was denounced as heretical by the orthodox church but which lasted until about 300 a.d.

Gnothi seauton *Know Thyself* inscription on the temple of the oracle of Apollo at Delphi

gnu a large African antelope aka **wildebeest**

goatling a young goat esp. one between one and two years old

goatsucker = whippoorwill = nightjar

gobemouche *Fr.* a simpleton *lit. a swallower of flies*

Gödel's theorem (1931) the proof of the Austrian-born American mathematician that the truth or falsity of propositions formulated within a system cannot be tested without reference to criteria outside the system

godparent the person who, at baptism, guarantees a child's religious education and spiritual welfare

godwit a long-legged migrant wading bird of the sandpiper family

Goidelic Scottish Gaelic, Irish, and Manx, the northern group of Celtic languages

goitre a swelling of the neck caused by enlargement of the thyroid gland

golem 1) (in Hebrew legend) a clay figure brought to life by magic 2) an automaton, a robot

Golgotha Calvary

golpe Spanish equivalent of a coup d'état

gonad an animal organ that produces gametes e.g. a testis, an ovary

Gondwanaland a hypothetical southern portion of the earth's original land mass, Pangaea. Some 200 million years ago, Africa, South America, India, Arabia, Australia, Madagascar, New Guinea, the Malay Peninsular, Indonesia and Antarctica are thought to have begun drifting apart out of Gondwanaland

Gongoristic (of a literary style) cluttered, affected, florid and artificial – in the manner of the Spanish lyric poet Luis de Góngora y Argote (*1561-1627*), noted for his exaggerated pedantic style

gonorrhoea a venereal disease involving inflammation and a discharge from the genital organs

goodself, goodselves 'I'm very well, thank you, And your goodself?' 'We have previously written to your goodselves about this matter'. 'Goodself' and 'goodselves' are not English words

Gordian knot, cut the Gordian knot solve a difficult problem in a direct or forceful way

Gorgons *in Gk. myth* three monstrous sisters of hideous appearance and with snakes for hair who could turn anyone who looked at them to stone

gormandize to eat greedily like a glutton

Gormenghast an ancient, crumbling castle peopled by weird and bizarre figures; the abode of the Earl of Groan in the Gothic novels (*1946-59*) of Mervyn Peake

Goshen 1) a region of Ancient Egypt, east of the Nile delta 2) a place of comfort and plenty

gosling a young goose

Gotham New York City

Gothic 1) barbaric, barbarous 2) (of literature esp. novels) involving ghoulish, grotesque, macabre, supernatural events in remote, gloomy and desolate settings 3) of the predominant style of architecture in western Europe from 12th – 16th cent. characterized by pointed arches, rib vaults, flying buttresses, and large windows 4) *in printing* (with regard to type) old-fashioned German, black letter, or sanserif

Götterdämmerung *Ger.* 'the twilight of the gods'; their complete downfall; the end of the world

gouache opaque, watercolour paint, bound with glue

gourmand a glutton

gourmet a connoisseur of fine food and drink

gowan a daisy

gracile thin or slender in a graceful way; graceful

graminiverous feeding on grass

Gramsci Antonio (*1891-1937*) a founder and leader of the Italian Communist Party

grandee 1) a nobleman of the highest rank in Spain or Portugal 2) a person who has a high rank or position

Grand Guignol a series of short plays involving macabre and gruesome incidents intended to shock; the theatre in which such plays were performed

grandiloquence pompous speech

grandiloquent using pompous, extravagant language

grangerize to illustrate a book by inserting portraits, prints, drawings and any other matter bearing on the subject

graphic highly descriptive in a vivid, detailed way

graphology analysis of handwriting to deduce a person's character

gratuitous unnecessary, unwarranted, unjustified, uncalled for, unprovoked, unwelcome; without charge or obligation, free

gravamen the main thrust

grave 1) to engrave or carve on a surface; to cut, sculpt 2) to fix firmly in the mind

graven image a carved figure of a god used as an idol

gravid pregnant

gravitas dignity, solemnity, seriousness

gravitate to move or to be drawn towards something

gravlax, gravadlax dry-cured salmon, marinated in herbs, as served in Scandinavia

grayling a silvery edible freshwater fish that resembles the trout

Greats (at Oxford University) the informal name of the final school of *Literae Humaniores*, the honours course in classics, philosophy and ancient history

gregarious enjoying the company of others; sociable

Gregorian calendar introduced by Pope Gregory XIII in 1582 is now in general use

gremlin a mischievous sprite, the cause of unexplained failures in machinery or equipment

Greystoke, Lord the fictional, infant son of an English aristocratic family was abandoned as a child in the African jungle and brought up by apes to become known as Tarzan in the novels of Edgar Rice Burroughs (*1875-1950*)

grice a little pig

gricer a railway enthusiast, a trainspotter

gride 1) intr. to grate or scrape harshly 2) a harsh or piercing sound

griffin a mythical monster with an eagle's head and wings and a lion's body

Grimaldi Joseph (*1779-1837*) the original English circus clown

gringo an English – speaking foreigner in Spain or Latin America

grisaille painting in shades of grey to give a three-dimensional effect or to imitate sculpture

griseous streaked or mixed with grey; somewhat grey

grog-blossom redness of the nose or face from excessive drinking

grommet a rubber, plastic or metal ring or eyelet

grosso modo *Lat.* roughly speaking

grove a small wood

grovel 1) to lie or crawl face downwards 2) to humble oneself

grub the larva of an insect, esp. a beetle

grudging felt or done unwillingly

gruelling exhausting

Grundyism narrow-minded propriety and prudery – from the frequently-repeated question 'What will Mrs Grundy say?' in Thomas Morton's play *Speed the Plough* (*1798*)

guaiacum = lignum vitae

gubernatorial to do with a governor

guerdon a reward; to reward

guerrilla an irregular soldier in a small group, typically a liberation movement, carrying out sabotage and harassment operations against larger regular forces

Guignol a popular French glove puppet

guild an association of people, typically craftsmen, with similar interests

guile craftiness, skilful cunning

guileless simple, artless, unscheming

guillemot an auk with a long narrow bill

Gulag the penal system of harsh labour camps in the former Soviet Union (*1930-1955*)

gulch a ravine

gules red (*in heraldry*)

gull to trick

gullible easily deceived; believing things too readily

gummous consisting of, or of the nature of gum, gum-like

gumption common sense

gung-ho vigorously, aggressively enthusiastic

gunnel 1) an eel-shaped marine fish 2) variant spelling of gunwale, the top of the side of a ship

gunny coarse sacking

gunwale = gunnel sense 2

Gurkha 1) a native of Gurkha, Nepal 2) a member of one of the Gurkha regiments in the British army

gurning pulling a face esp. for a competition

guru a teacher, a mentor

gussied up smartened up, dressed up

gustation tasting

gustatory relating to the sense of taste

gusto vitality, enthusiastic enjoyment

guttate speckled or spotted

guttural throaty, pronounced in the throat

guy to make fun of; to ridicule

gymkhana a children's horse riding contest

gymno- *combining form* naked, bare, or exposed

gynaecologist a doctor who specializes in the treatment of diseases and conditions specific to women

gynandromorphic having male and female characteristics

gyrate to revolve or spin

gyve a fetter or shackle

H

haberdasher a dealer in 1) dress-making accessories and small articles used for sewing 2) *N. Amer.* men's clothing

habile skilful with the hands, adroit, deft

habituate to make (somebody, esp. oneself) used to something

habitué a frequent visitor, a frequenter

haboob a sandstorm in North Africa

Habsburg, Hapsburg one of the principal dynasties of central Europe; sometime ruling house of Hungary, Austria, Bohemia, and Spain

hachuring the drawing of short parallel lines on a map to represent high ground or sloping land

hacienda 1) a ranch or large estate with a house on it 2) the main house itself

hackneyed overused; unoriginal and trite

Hades 1) the underworld home of the spirits of the dead – grim and gloomy rather than a place of punishment and torture because Gk. myth has no Satan 2) hell *(informal)*

haecceity the individual quality that makes something unique

haematite an iron ore

haft the handle of a weapon or tool

hag 1) a frightful, ugly, old woman 2) a witch

haggard drawn and weary in appearance; looking exhausted and unwell

haggis a Scottish dish made from sheep's or calf's offal, oatmeal, suet, and seasonings boiled in a skin made from the animal's stomach

hagiography writing the lives of saints – uncritical, biographical accounts

hagiolatry the worship of saints

ha-ha a ditch serving as a boundary

haiku a Japanese poem of seventeen syllables

hair shirt a penitent's or ascetic's shirt of coarse haircloth (horsehair and wool or cotton)

hajj the annual Muslim pilgrimage to Mecca

haka Maori war dance

halal food, esp. meat, lawful under Muslim law (Arabic = lawful)

halcyon idyllically happy and peaceful

halitosis bad breath

hallmark stamped mark on a gold, silver or platinum object to indicate the purity of the metal

hallow 1) to make holy, to consecrate 2) a saint or holy person

hallux the big toe

halyard a rope on a ship for raising and lowering a flag, a sail or a yard

hamartia (in Greek tragedy) the error of judgment that leads to the tragic hero's downfall

hangdog dejected or guilty in appearance or manner; shamefaced

hanged people are hanged; pheasants and pictures are hung

hanker to feel a desire, a longing for or to do something

Hanukkah 'rededication'- an eight-day Jewish festival of lights held in December

hanuman a pale-coloured Indian monkey, venerated by Hindus aka **entellus**

haplography accidentally writing only one letter or syllable where there should be two or more – 'oviparous' instead of 'oviviparous'

haplology missing out a similar sound or syllable in pronunciation – saying 'libry' for 'library'

haptic relating to the sense of touch

hara-kiri Japanese ritual suicide by disembowelment

harangue 1) a forceful or angry speech 2) to lecture (someone) at length in an aggressive and hectoring manner

harbinger 1) (historical) one who goes ahead to arrange lodgings or prepare the way for others 2) a person or thing that announces or signals the approach of something

hard-wired 1) inbuilt, innate 2) permanently wired into a computer, replacing separate software

Harijan = a **Dalit** or untouchable in the Hindu caste system

harlequin 1) a mute, stock, comic character in traditional pantomime wearing a mask and a diamond-patterned, multicoloured costume 2) a buffoon 3) brightly coloured; variegated

harlot a prostitiute

harpy a shrew

harquebus an early type of shotgun or rifle

harridan a belligerent old woman, a battle-axe

harrier a kind of hawk

harrow 1) to plunder 2) to inflict great distress on; to torment

harrowing distressing

harrumph to clear the throat

hart the stag or male red deer

hartebeest a large African antelope

harum-scarum reckless; impetuous

haruspex (in ancient Rome) a diviner who foretold events from the inspection of the entrails of animals offered in sacrifice

harvestman = crane fly = daddy-longlegs

Hasidism a Jewish mystical movement which began in Poland in the 18th century; its present-day followers are ultra-conservative Jews mainly in Israel and New York

hassock 1) a cushion for kneeling on in church 2) a clump of grass

hastate spear-shaped

hatchet a small axe

hatching the drawing of fine lines to give an effect of shading

hatchment a large diamond-shaped tablet bearing the coat of arms of someone who has died, displayed in their honour

haulm a stalk or stem of a plant

hausfrau a German housewife

hauteur haughtiness

havelock a cover for an army cap with a flap hanging down at the back to protect the neck from the sun

hawker a pedlar

hawser a thick rope or cable used in warping esp. for mooring or towing a ship

Hayek F.A. von (*1899-1992*) Austrian-born British economist, free marketeer, the 'father of monetarism', anti-Keynes, a strong influence on Thatcherite monetary policy; shared Nobel Prize for Economics, 1974

hazchem hazardous chemicals

headlong headfirst

hearsay evidence which is usually disallowed in a court because it is based on what somebody said took place and not what was directly observed by a witness

heather mixture a fabric of interwoven yarns of mixed colours resembling heather

Heaviside layer aka the **E layer**. A region of the ionosphere between 55 miles and 95 miles above the earth able to reflect medium-frequency radio waves

hebdomadal weekly

hebetate to make dull or blunt

hebetude dullness, lethargy

hecatomb a great public sacrifice orig. among the Greeks and Romans, of a hundred oxen

hectare a land measurement of almost 2.5 acres

hector to bully esp. to address someone in a bullying manner

hedonism (the doctrine of) the pursuit of pleasure

hedonist a person bent on having a good time

heft 1) weight, heaviness; ability or influence 2) to lift something esp. to assess its weight 3) to heave

Hegel G.W.F. (*1770-1831*) German philosopher who developed the notion of a dialectical scheme in which ideas grow and gradually move towards a better grasp of reality: an idea or thesis takes shape in relation to its opposite or antithesis; eventually the interaction of the two leads to a resolution in the form of a synthesis.

hegemony dominance, esp. by one state or social group over others

hegira departure, flight, exodus orig. of Muhammad from Mecca to Medina in a.d.622

heinous hatefully wicked, evil, abominable

heir apparent has a claim that cannot be set aside by the birth of another heir

heir presumptive the birth of another heir may set aside his/her claim

heist a robbery

Heldentenor Ger. (a singer with) a strong tenor voice

heliacal to do with or near the sun

helical spiral

heliosis sunstroke, insolation

heliotrope bluish-violet to purple in colour

heliotropism the growth of a plant in response to sunlight

helix a spiral

hell-bent determined at all costs

Hellenic Greek

Hellenism ancient Greek culture

Hellenistic concerning post-classical Greek culture, from about 323 b.c. (death of Alexander the Great) to 27 b.c. (the start of the Roman Empire)

hell for leather at great speed

helot a serf or slave

helve the handle of a weapon or tool

Helvetia *Latin* for Switzerland

Helvetian 1) Swiss 2) a person from Switzerland

henbane a poisonous, foul-smelling plant with sticky, hairy leaves

henchman a supporter, an aide, esp. one prepared to be unscrupulous

hendiadys the joining of two words by 'and' instead of using one word to modify the other – 'nice and warm', instead of 'nicely warm'

henge a prehistoric monument of a circle of stones or wooden uprights

hen harrier a kind of hawk that attacks poultry

henna 1) a reddish dye for the hair 2) the tropical shrub from which the dye is obtained

hepatic to do with the liver

heraldry 1) the devising, describing and regulating of coats of arms and other armorial bearings 2) the armorial bearings themselves

herbivore an animal that feeds on grass and other plants

herculean requiring or having great strength or effort

heresiarch the founder of a heresy; a leader of a heretical movement

heresy unorthodox belief or doctrine

heretic one who has unorthodox beliefs or opinions in matters of religion

hermaphrodite a person or animal having both male and female sex organs or characteristics

hermeneutics the interpretation and explanation of (originally) the Bible and now literary or other texts; **exegesis**

hermetic sealed so as to be airtight

hermitage the retreat of a recluse; the abode of one who lives alone

Herodotus 5th- cent. b.c. Greek historian; magnum opus is 'History of the Persian Wars'; known in the West as 'the Father of History'

herpetology the study of reptiles and amphibians

hetaera a courtesan in ancient Greece

hetaerism concubinage in ancient Greece

heteroclite 1) abnormal 2) an abnormal thing or person 3) an irregularly declined Greek or Latin noun

heterodont having different kinds of teeth

heterodox not orthodox

heterogeneous composed of different, dissimilar kinds or parts

heterological (of an adjective) not descriptive of itself e.g. 'monosyllabic' cf. **autological**

heterosis = hybrid vigour

heurige 1) Austrian new wine 2) the tavern where it is drunk

heuristic 1) enabling people to find out things for themselves 2) searching for a solution by trial and error

hew *N. Amer.* to adhere to, to conform to (a code, principle, etc.)

hex *v.* to cast an evil spell on, to curse *n.* 1) an evil spell, curse or jinx 2) a witch

heyday the period of one's greatest success, activity or vigour

hiatus a gap, a space, a lacuna

hibernal relating to winter

Hibernia (_Iverna_) Latin for Ireland

hic jacet 'here lies' – an epitaph on tombstones

hickory 1) N. American hardwood tree (bears edible nuts – pecan nuts) 2) its hard wood

hidalgo a minor nobleman in Spain; a Spaniard of aristocratic bearing

hidebound restricted; held back; narrow-minded, rigidly conventional, inflexible, unimaginative

hidrosis excessive sweating

hie to hasten

hieratic 1) to do with priests; sacerdotal 2) (of a style or language) formal, associated with priests or other educated elite

hieroglyphics writing in pictures as used in ancient Egypt

hierophant (in ancient Greece) a priest / interpreter of sacred or esoteric mysteries

high-falutin pompous or pretentious

high relief standing out from a surface to a greater extent

hilt the handle of a sword, dagger, or knife

Hindustan the Hindu region of northern India

hinny offspring of a male horse and a female donkey

hinterland 1) an area behind a coast or river-bank 2) a remote region 3) the area around or beyond a port or major town

hippocampus 1) sea horse – a small (15cm./6") upright marine fish resembling the head and neck of a horse; swims vertically and has a forward-curled prehensile tail; when breeding the males carry the eggs until they hatch 2) part of the brain

Hippocratic oath an oath taken by doctors to observe a code of medical ethics

hippodrome 1) originally (in ancient Greece or Rome) a racecourse for horses/chariots 2) a music hall

hippophagy the eating of horseflesh

hippophile a person who is fond of horses

hircine goat-like; to do with a goat or goats; caprine

hirsute hairy

hirundine concerning a swallow

Hispanic Spanish

hispid covered with strong hairs or bristles; bristly

histogenesis, histogeny the formation and development of tissues

histoid resembling normal tissue

histology the study of the microscopic structure of tissues

histopathology the branch of medicine concerned with the changes in tissues caused by disease

historic famous or important in history

historical to do with history or the past

histrion an actor

histrionic excessively emotional or theatrical, melodramatic; orig. to do with actors or acting

histrionics over-acting to attract attention

hoard a store of money or valued objects

hoary 1) ancient, venerable by reason of age 2) greyish white 3) overused and trite

hobble *N. Amer.* to hamper, to impede

hobbledehoy a clumsy, awkward youth

hobgoblin a mischievous imp

Hobson's choice the choice of taking what is offered or nothing at all

hock German white wine from the Rhineland

hoedown 1) a square dance 2) a gathering for lively folk dancing

hoi polloi the ordinary people; the rabble

hold storage cavity below a ship's deck

holistic dealing with the whole rather than a part or parts

hologram a three-dimensional image of an object

holograph a manuscript handwritten by its author

holophrastic making utterances in single words – stop!, more!; polysynthetic

holothurian a sea cucumber

Holy Grail 1) a dish, supposedly used by Christ at the Last Supper, regarded as a symbol of perfection and sought by the knights of the Round Table 2) any desired ambition or goal

homage a public expression of respect or tribute

homeopathy treated with minute doses of substances that in large doses produce symptoms of the disease in healthy persons; a controversial therapy, it is based on the theory that 'like cures like' – either because the drug induces a condition which displaces the disease or that it stimulates the body's protective responses

Homeric 1) epic 2) to do with Homer, Greek epic poet, 8th century b.c.

homiletic relating to a homily or sermon

homily a sermon

homodont having teeth all alike

homogeneous consistent, uniform, of the same kind

homogenize to make or become the same, uniform

homogenous *bio.* (of organisms) having the same ancestry

homograph a word spelt the same as another but having another meaning – e.g. bear ('carry' and a large heavy animal)

homological (of an adjective) descriptive of itself e.g. 'English', 'polysyllabic'; autological

homologous sharing a similar structure or evolutionary history with something else – *used now to describe a variety of situations far removed from the word's original context in biology*

homology the relationship between corresponding parts of different organisms e.g. arms and wings, or the limb of a dog and the limb of a wolf

homophile a homosexual

homophobia an aversion to homosexuals

homophone a word having the same sound as another but a different meaning – e.g. try (an attempt; a score at rugby) or a different spelling e.g. lite; light or both a different meaning and a different spelling e.g. pair; pear

homunculus, homunculi a little man, manikin, dwarf; a very small human

honcho a leader, boss

hone 1) to sharpen 2) to develop and improve (a quality or ability)

honorand a person receiving an honorary degree

honorarium a voluntary payment made to a professional person in recognition of services rendered without charge

honorific 1) a respected title or form of address – *Your Excellency* 2) showing or conferring honour or respect

hooey nonsense, humbug

hoof, on the 1) (of cattle) not yet slaughtered, alive 2) without great forethought or preparation; in an impromptu manner

hookah the oriental tobacco pipe with a long, flexible tube which draws the smoke through water in a bowl

hoon a hooligan, a lout

hooper a cooper; a maker or repairer of barrels, casks

hoopoe a salmon-pink bird with a distinctive down-curving bill and long crest

hoplite a heavily armed foot soldier of ancient Greece

hoplology the study of weapons or armour

horde a large group of people

horologe a clock, a timepiece

horometry the measuring of time

horripilation the medical term for pimply skin with hairs raised, caused by cold, fright, etc. aka goose-flesh

hors de combat *Fr.* disabled, out of action

hortatory, hortative exhorting, encouraging, urging

hostage to fortune a potentially unwise act, remark or commitment that could prove to be problematic because of unforeseen circumstances

hotspur a hothead, a rash person

Hottentot (offensive) former name of a dwindling, nomadic, pastoral, pale-brown race of S.W. Africa; now referred to as **Khoikhoi** or **Nama**

houri 1) a female virgin attendant of the blessed in the Muslim paradise 2) a beautiful young woman

housecarl a member of a king's or nobleman's bodyguard

howitzer a short, squat gun, used for shelling at a steep angle in siege and trench warfare

hoyden a boisterous girl, a tomboy

hubble-bubble = hookah

hubris arrogant pride (leading to nemesis)

huckster 1) a hawker, a pedlar 2) a person who uses aggressive selling or promotional methods

hudibrastic (of verse) mock-heroic, of inferior quality, bordering on doggerel; in the style of the three-part Hudibras (1663, 1664, and 1678) by Samuel Butler

Huguenots French protestants of the 16th – 17th centuries

humanism doctrine or philosophy that emphasises the human capacity for self-fulfilment without the need for religion

humanities the study of literature, philosophy, the arts, history, music and human culture generally

humectant holding moisture

humgruffin a terrible person

hummock a hillock, a knoll

humongous, humungous enormous, huge

humoresque lively, playful musical composition

humours the four chief fluids of the body – blood, melancholy, phlegm, choler – which in the Middle Ages were believed to determine a person's physical and mental disposition

hung see **hanged**

hunker to squat or crouch down low so that the haunches nearly touch the heels

hunker down to apply oneself seriously to a task

husbandry farming

husk the dry outer covering of certain fruits and seeds, esp. nuts

hustings (place of) political campaigning

huzzah hurrah

hyaline 1) to do with glass, vitreous 2) *literary* a clear sky, a smooth sea

hybrid a cross; an animal or plant resulting from cross-breeding *adj.* formed from different elements or sources

hybrid vigour the increased size, strength etc. of a hybrid as compared to either of its parents; aka **heterosis**

Hydra *Gk. myth* a many-headed water snake of the marshes whose heads grew again after they were cut off

hydra-headed increasingly difficult to kill off, springing up again and again

hydrocyanic acid a particularly poisonous liquid with a smell of bitter almonds aka *hydrogen cyanide, prussic acid*

hydropathy medical treatment involving the use of water

hydrophobia rabies

hygienic sanitary

hygrometer an instrument for measuring humidity

hymen a membrane which partially closes the opening of the vagina; its presence is traditionally taken to be a mark of virginity but it usually ruptures spontaneously before puberty

hymeneal nuptial, relating to marriage or weddings

hymenoptera insects – ants, bees, wasps etc. – with four membranous wings and frequently a sting

hypaethral roofless; open to the sky

hypalgesia diminished susceptibility or sensitivity to pain

hypallage the transferring of an epithet from its natural to a less natural position for rhetorical effect – ' he raised his questioning hand'; everyday speech provides many examples – 'a successful day'; 'a bad hair day' or 'uncomfortable shoes' – the shoes are not per se uncomfortable but may be for a person wearing them

hyperbaton an inversion, for emphatic effect, of the normal order of words – *bad manners I deplore*

hyperbole exaggeration

hyperborean relating to the far north or Arctic; freezing cold

Hyperion 1) *Gk. myth* a Titan 2) a satellite of Saturn

hypermetropia, hypermetropy longsightedness

hypernym a superordinate or word of more general meaning that includes the meaning of another word or words e.g. animal is a hypernym of lion and horse – cf. **hyponym**

hyperopia = hypermetropia

hypnagogia the state just before one is fully asleep

hypnagogic image an image experienced by a person just before falling asleep which often resembles a hallucination

hypnopaedia the learning of lessons heard during sleep

hypochondria neurotic belief that one is ill

hypocoristic to do with a pet name, term of endearment

hypodermic concerning the area under the skin

hypogeal, hypogean underground

hyponym a word of narrower, more specific meaning, that can be subsumed under a wider, more general term – vermilion is a hyponym of red; schooner is a hyponym of sailing ship cf. **hypernym**

hypostasis the essential nature of a substance as opposed to its attributes

hypotaxis, hypotactic the use of connecting words between clauses or sentences showing the relationships between them – opp. is **parataxis, paratactic**

hypothecated 1) mortgaged 2) earmarked

hypothesis supposition put forward as a basis for discussion

hypothetical supposed but not necessarily true

hyrax a type of hamster or rabbit from Africa and Arabia

hysteron proteron a figure of speech in which the natural order of words is reversed e.g. *kin and kith*

I

ianthine violet-coloured

iatric, iatrical to do with medicine or physicians; medical

iatrogenic (of a disease, illness) doctor-induced, caused by medical intervention

iatrology a treatise on medicine

Iberia Spain and Portugal

ibex a goat

ibidem in the same place

ibis a wading bird- a type of stork or heron – worshipped by ancient Egyptians

ichor 1) a fetid discharge from a wound or ulcer 2) the fluid said to flow like blood in the veins of the gods

ichthyology the study of fishes

icon I) a religious image 2) an idol, a cult figure

iconoclasm the breaking of images; the attacking of cherished beliefs

iconoclastic destroying religious images, cherished beliefs; seeking to overthrow popular ideas, institutions or traditions

icterus jaundice

ictus a stroke (in medicine)

id the unconscious part of the mind that gives free rein to primitive impulses; it clashes with the **ego** and **superego**

ideogram, ideograph a symbol representing a thing or idea, e.g. (%) or (+) without indicating how to say it

ideography the use of ideograms to communicate ideas

ideology the body of ideas and beliefs of a person, group, or nation

idiograph a person's private mark or signature

idiolect the form of language, speech pattern or speech habits peculiar to a particular individual; the way a particular person speaks

idiom an expression which has acquired a certain, non-literal, meaning in a language and which is understood by users of that language but which, if translated word for word, into another language would not make sense – *raining cats and dogs, top-drawer*

idiopathy, idiopathic a disease or condition the cause of which is unknown

idiosyncrasy a characteristic of behaviour or way of thought specific to an individual

idiot savant a person with learning difficulties who has considerable ability in a specific area esp. one involving memory

idyll 1) a short poem or prose work describing a picturesque pastoral scene 2) a peaceful or blissful period or situation

idyllic ideally picturesque and peaceful in a charming, pastoral or rustic setting

igneous 1) to do with fire 2) (of rock) having solidified from lava or molten rock

ignicolist a fire-worshipper

ignis fatuus glowing light above marshy ground at night; will-o'-the-wisp

ignoble 1) of humble origins 2) dishonourable

ignominious shameful, humiliating, disgraceful

ignominy shame, disgrace, dishonour

ignoratio elenchi a purported refutation of a proposition that does not prove it false – if required to prove an act is legal, to show it ought to be, is ignoratio elenchi aka the fallacy of irrelevant conclusion

ignotum per ignotius *Lat.* an explanation that is more obscure than the thing explained: the unknown by means of the still more unknown

ikebana Japanese flower arranging

Île-de-France the area around Paris, by far the most populous part of France

illicit illegal, unlawful

illocution an action performed by saying or writing something, e.g. promising or ordering

illuminati people who are exceptionally enlightened

imago the final and fully developed adult stage of an insect, e.g. the butterfly

imam 1) the leader of prayers in a mosque 2) a Muslim leader

imbibe to drink

imbricate to lay (tiles) so that they overlap; overlapping

imbroglio a confused and complicated situation; an entanglement, predicament

imbrue to stain, soak, drench esp. with blood

imbue to instil or inspire, to fill with ideals or principles, feelings, etc.

immaculate 1) completely clean and tidy 2) completely without flaws or spots (maculae)

immanent 1) existing within, inherent 2) (of God) present throughout the universe

immasculation the process whereby women are taught to think as men, to identify with a male point of view, and to accept as normal and legitimate a male system of values, one of whose central principles is misogyny

immigrate to come to live in a foreign country

imminent about to occur

immiscible that cannot be mixed so as to form a homogeneous mixture – e.g. oil and water

immolate to kill or offer as a sacrifice, esp. by burning

immotile incapable of moving spontaneously and independently

immund dirty

immure to confine or imprison; to shut up within walls

immutable unchangeable

impacted wedged

impala an antelope of southern and East Africa capable of enormous leaps; the male has lyre-shaped horns

impale to thrust a stake through

impalpable 1) not able to be sensed by touch; intangible 2) hard to understand

impanation = **transubstantiation** or **consubstantiation**

impart to give; to make (information etc.) known

impartial even-handed, unbiased, fair

impasto the application of thick layers of paint or pigment

impavid fearless, intrepid

impayable priceless; pricelessly funny

impecunious habitually short of money

impediment a hindrance

impending about to happen

imperative 1) expressing a command 2) essential

imperious high and mighty; domineering; arrogant; commanding, bossy, used to being obeyed

impermeable not allowing fluid to pass through

impervious 1) not able to be influenced by; not receptive to 2) not able to be penetrated

impetrate 1) to supplicate or entreat for, esp. by prayer 2) to obtain by prayer

impetuous impulsive, rash, hasty, precipitate

impetus moving force

impious not showing reverence; ungodly

implacable not capable of being appeased

implicit implied or understood

implode to collapse inwards, to crumple

implore to beg earnestly

imply to suggest: speakers or writers *imply*

imponderable that cannot be predicted, evaluated, or analysed

importunate making persistent, pressing requests, demanding

importune 1) to harass with persistent requests 2) to approach to offer one's services as a prostitute

importunity a persistent, pressing demand

impost a tax

impostume an abscess

imposture the act of an impostor – one who assumes a false identity in order to deceive or defraud

impound to confiscate; to take (property) into legal custody

impracticable that cannot be done at all, incapable of being put into practice

impractical that can be done but is not worth doing

imprecation a curse

impregnable 1) unable to be broken into or taken by force 2) unable to be overcome

impresario a director or producer of shows or concerts

imprescriptible (of rights) that cannot be taken away by prescription or lapse of time

Impressionism 1) an artistic style originating in France in the late 19th century; it was concerned with capturing the visual impression of the moment rather than precise academic draughtsmanship esp. with regard to the transient effects of light on colour and texture in mainly landscape subject-matter 2) in music or writing, a style that seeks to capture a feeling or experience rather than achieve accurate depiction.

imprimatur official approval, orig. of R.C. Church for a book to be printed or published

impromptu improvised, makeshift

impropriate to transfer Church property into lay hands

improvident not providing for the future

impudicity impudence, shameless immodesty

impugn to challenge

impunity exemption from punishment

impute to attribute to

imputrescible rot -proof

inadvertently unintentionally

in aeternum Lat. forever, eternally

inalienable that cannot be given or taken away

inamorata a female lover; a woman who is loved

inamorato a man with whom one is in love; a male lover

inane senseless, meaningless, foolish

inanition exhaustion, weakness esp. from lack of nourishment

inaugurate to introduce; to open; to begin

inauspicious suggesting an unfavourable outcome; unpromising

incalescent increasing in warmth

in camera *Lat.* in the chamber; in secret; in private

incandescent 1) glowing with white heat; white-hot 2) extremely angry

incantation words chanted as a magic spell or charm

incarcerate to imprison

incarnadine rosy-pink, flesh-coloured, carnation-coloured

incarnation the putting into a living, human, bodily form of a deity, spirit or abstract quality *adj.* **incarnate**

Incas the short-lived dynasty of Peru, centred on Cuzco, began c.1100 a.d.; conquered by invading Spaniards in early 1530s

inceptive to do with the beginning; initial

incendiary 1) designed to cause or capable of causing fires 2) tending to stir up or inflame anger, conflict, or violence; inflammatory

incense to infuriate

inchoate only begun, incomplete; incoherent, confused

incidence occurrence, or the rate of frequency of occurrence

incipient just starting

incisive quick, direct and forceful; clear and decisive; intelligently analytical and concise

incognito with one's identity kept secret; under an assumed name or appearance

incoherent 1) disordered; unconnected 2) unable to think or express thoughts in a clear or orderly manner

incommensurable lacking a common basis of comparison; incapable of being compared

incommensurate disproportionate

incommode to inconvenience, trouble, disturb

incommunicado out of communication with others

incondite not well put together, poorly constructed or composed

incongruous out of place, inappropriate, incompatible

inconsequential unimportant

incontinent unable to control one's 1) bladder 2) bowels 3) sex drive

incorporeal having no physical existence

incorrigible incapable of being corrected or reformed

incrassate to make thick

incredulous disbelieving

increment increase

incubus 1) a male demon who supposedly has sex with sleeping women 2) a nightmare – type of oppressive burden that torments somebody

inculcate to instil something indelibly into someone's mind

inculpate to incriminate

incult uncultivated

incumbent 1) a person currently holding an office 2) having an obligation or duty

incunabula books produced in the very early days of printing (in the cradle) i.e. before 1501; hence the early stages of something

incuse 1) a design stamped or hammered onto a coin 2) to impress (a design) onto a coin or to impress (a coin) with a design by hammering or stamping

indefatigable tireless, unflagging

indehiscent not splitting open to release seeds or pollen

indelible unable to be removed

indemnity protection, insurance against, or compensation for, loss or damage

indeterminate not fixed in extent or character

Indian summer dry sunny weather in Autumn

indict to accuse; to charge

indigence a lack of funds; reduced circumstances

indigene a native

indigenous *adj.* native to an area

indigent needy, poor

indign unworthy

indigo (tropical plant producing) dark blue dye

indiscriminate at random, without careful judgment

indispensable impossible to do without

indite to put (something) down in writing; to compose

indolence laziness

indolent idle, lazy

indomitable unconquerable

indubitably unquestionably

induce to persuade, produce, cause

inductive (in logic) characterised by the inference of general laws from particular instances; an inductive argument involves a generalisation based on a certain number of specific observations

indulgent yielding to the wishes of others; willing to gratify; lenient

indurate to make or become hard, to harden

inebriated drunk

inedible not fit for eating

ineffable 1) too great, intense or sacred to be expressed in words; unutterable 2) unspeakable, indescribable

ineluctable that cannot be struggled against; unavoidable; inescapable

inept incompetent; awkward or clumsy

inertia a tendency to do nothing or to remain unchanged; motionless sluggishness

inesculent inedible

in esse *Lat.* in actual existence, in being, in fact

inexorable 1) that cannot be moved or persuaded by request or entreaty 2) relentless

in extremis Lat. 1) in considerable difficulties 2) at the point of death

infamy a bad reputation; great notoriety

infangthief the right of the lord of the manor to hang one of his feudal tenants or serfs caught in the act of crime cf. **outfangthief**

infarct a localised area of dead tissue resulting from failure of blood supply

infelicitous inappropriate; unfortunate; unsuitable

infer to deduce; listeners or readers *infer*

infibulation the sewing together of parts of the labia, often after excision of the clitoris, to prevent sexual intercourse; the practice is still carried out in parts of Africa

in flagrante delicto *Lat.* in the very act of committing the offence, red-handed

inflammable catching fire easily

inflammatory arousing strong feeling or anger; rabble-rousing

infra dig beneath one

infraction an infringement

infrangible that cannot be broken or infringed

infrastructure the basic foundations of a society – transport, education, public utilities, health care etc.

infundibular funnel-shaped

infuscate tinged or clouded with brown

infuse 1) to fill with (a quality or emotion) 2) to soak or be soaked to extract flavour

infusible very difficult or impossible to dissolve or melt

infusion 1) a liquid or drink obtained by infusing 2) the introduction of a new quality or element

ingenious inventive, clever, and original

ingénue *Fr.* an innocent, inexperienced, unsophisticated young woman

ingenuous innocent, naïve and trusting

ingest to swallow

ingot an oblong block of gold, silver, steel or other metal

ingrate ungrateful; an ungrateful person

ingress entry

inguinal to do with the groin

inhere to exist (in)

inherent existing in something as an inseparable part, integral to its being; intrinsic

inhume to bury, to inter

inimical hostile

iniquitous very unfair, unjust

injudicious unwise; showing poor judgment

inkhorn pretentiously learned; affectedly pedantic; ostentatiously recondite

inlay to embed one thing into another so that the surfaces are smooth and flat

in medias res Lat. straight to the point, into the plot, without preamble

innate inborn; natural; existing from birth rather than acquired

innervate to supply with nerves, nervous energy; to stimulate the nerves in (a part of the body)

Innisfail poetical and literary name for Ireland

innocuous harmless, doing no harm

innominate nameless, unnamed

innuendo an indirect remark implying or insinuating something derogatory

inoculate to protect against disease by injecting with a vaccine; same as **vaccinate**

inopportune inconvenient, inappropriate, badly timed

inordinate excessive

inosculate to join by intertwining

in pari materia *Lat.* upon the same matter or subject

in petto *Lat.* 'in the breast', secretly

in posse *Lat.* possible; potential; in potential existence; in possibility

in propria persona *Lat.* personally, in person, 'live'

inquiline (an animal) living in or using the abode of another species, e.g. the cuckoo

in retrospect when looking back; with hindsight

insatiable, insatiate never satisfied

inscape the essential inner nature or unique quality of a person or thing

inscrutable mysterious, hard to fathom or penetrate, puzzling, enigmatic

insectivora shrews, moles, hedgehogs – eaters of insects, worms, etc.

insensate 1) lacking physical sensation 2) lacking sympathy; unfeeling 3) completely lacking sense; foolish

inshallah if Allah wills it

inside of although fairly common is considered to be incorrect or non-standard

insidious proceeding stealthily, imperceptibly but with harmful effect

insignia symbols of authority or office; identifying badge

insinuate to hint or imply slyly

insipid tasteless, bland, dull; unstimulating; lacking excitement, flavour or zest

insolation sunstroke, heliosis

insolvent bankrupt, unable to meet one's debts

insouciant carefree, unconcerned

inspissate to thicken by evaporation, by condensation

instigate to initiate; to incite

instil to implant (a concept) into someone's mind gradually

insufferable unbearable

insufflate to blow (a powdered medicine or vapour) into a cavity to treat a disease

insular 1) to do with an island 2) not open to change or new ideas; lacking contact with other people

insulin hormone controlling the body's absorption of sugar

intagliated carved on the surface

intangible that cannot be touched; difficult for the mind to grasp

integer a whole number or zero without fractions or decimals

integrity complete honesty

integument the outer protective covering of an animal or plant, e.g. skin or husk

intension the internal content of a concept; the set of characteristics that belong to the thing a word refers to; a connotation

intentional fallacy the understandable but widely challenged view that the author is the best judge of the meaning of a work; the better view, it is claimed, is that once the work is published and in the public domain, it has an independent existence of its own; it belongs to the public at large which is the best judge of its meaning and worth

inter alia *Lat.* among other things

intercalate 1) to insert (an intercalary day etc. e.g. 29 Feb.) in the calendar (in a leap year) to harmonise it with the solar year 2) to insert (something) between or among existing items, elements, or layers

intercession the saying of a prayer on behalf of another

interface a point where two things meet and interact

interjacent lying between; intervening

interlard (with) diversify or provide with things scattered at intervals, intersperse esp. embellish (writing or speech) with foreign or technical words

interlocutor a person who takes part in a conversation, dialogue or discussion

interloper an intruder

interminable never ending and boring

internecine 1) to do with slaughter, carnage 2) concerning costly, self-destructive in-fighting – purists object to this second meaning mainly on etymological grounds

interpleader a legal procedure enabling somebody finding himself in possession of goods or property to which third parties have asserted competing claims to ask the court to adjudicate

interpolate 1) to insert or introduce (usu. spurious words) into a text 2) to interject (a remark) in a conversation 3) to insert (intermediate estimated values) into a series of known values

interregnum the time between sovereigns' reigns; a period when activity is suspended

interstice a chink, crevice, crack

interstitial to do with a narrow opening; between the cracks

intertextual descriptive of the relationship texts have with other texts or discourses, whether consciously or unconsciously

intestate without leaving a (valid) will

intimate *v.* to make (something) known in an indirect way; to imply or hint

intone to speak, recite or chant in a flat, solemn, monotonous pitch of the voice

intractable 1) hard to handle 2) stubborn 3) unmanageable 4) (of a problem or illness) difficult to solve or cure

intransigent refusing to compromise, to change one's views; stubbornly uncompromising

intrepid fearlessly brave, often describing an adventurer

intrinsic belonging naturally; belonging to the essential nature of a thing; inherent; innate

introspection examination of one's own thoughts and feelings

introvert one who is concerned more with inner feelings than with external reality; a reserved, unsociable person

intumescence a swelling

inturbidate to make turbid, cloudy, muddy

intuse a bruise

intussusception obstruction of the bowel caused by one portion of the intestine entering or telescoping into the lower portion immediately adjacent to it

Inuit Eskimo

inure, enure 1) to accustom (someone) to something unpleasant 2) to take effect

inurn 1) to place in an urn 2) to bury, to inter

invagination the turning back or unfolding into itself of a tubular organ so that it becomes ensheathed; intussusception

invective strongly attacking language; abusive criticism or accusation

inveigh (against) to speak or write strongly (against)

inveigle to get someone to do something; to get something out of someone – in each case by using some form of guile

invertebrate (an animal) without a backbone

inveterate of long standing and unlikely to change, habitual

invidious unfair and likely to cause ill-will, resentment or anger in others; offensive

inviolable that must not be transgressed

inviolate free from injury or violation

involute, involuted complicated

involution 1) the shrinkage of an organ in old age or when it is not being used 2) a complication

invulnerable that cannot be harmed or damaged; easily fending off attack, criticism

invultuation that part of witchcraft which involves sticking pins or similar objects into an effigy or image of a person on the basis that pain or injury will thereby be caused to the person

ion an atom or molecule that has lost one or more electrons (a cation) or gained one or more (an anion)

iota 1) the Greek equivalent of the letter 'i', the ninth and smallest letter in the Greek alphabet 2) a very small amount; a jot

ipecacuanha South American shrub and a drug prepared from its dried roots used as a purgative and emetic

ipse dixit **Lat.** 'he himself said it' an arbitrary and unsupported assertion

ipsissima verba *Lat.* the very words, verbatim

ipso facto *Lat.* by that very fact or act

iracund angry

irascible easily angered

irenic (irenical, eirenic, eirenical) aimed at promoting peace; conciliatory

iridescent shimmering and coloured like the rainbow; glittering with changing colours

Iris (goddess of) the rainbow

irrational 1) not logical 2) not capable of reasoning

irrational number *maths.* not expressible as a ratio of two integers i.e. as a fraction

irrecusable not able to be rejected or challenged as evidence

irredeemable not able to be saved, improved or reformed; beyond remedy

irredentism late 19th-century Italian nationalist movement seeking the return to Italy of Italian-speaking territories in neighbouring states; policy of regaining territory that is historically, culturally connected to one's nation but now under foreign control

irreducible not able to be reduced or simplified

irrefragable indisputable

irrefrangible inviolable

irrefutable incontrovertible

irremeable not allowing any possibility of return

irremediable not able to be remedied

irremissable unpardonable; inexcusable

irreparable impossible to make reparations for, not able to be repaired, or put right

irrepleviable not able to be replevied

irreverent not respectful

irrevocable impossible to change or take back; unalterable

irruption a forcible or sudden entry; an invasion; a breaking in

isagoge an academic introduction to a specialized subject

isagogic introductory

isagogics an introductory study to the Bible

ischiadic (ischiatic, ischial) concerning the area of the hip

isinglass a type of gelatine made from fish bladders

Isis the local name for the River Thames at Oxford

isogenic having essentially identical genes

isogeny the same genetic structure

isometric of equal measurements, dimensions

isomorphic similar or equivalent in form or structure

isonomy equal law, rights or privileges

isonym a paronym, a word derived from the same root

isotropic having physical properties which are identical in all directions

isthmus a narrow neck of land connecting two larger areas

iterate to state again or do again

ithyphallic having an erect penis; obscene

itinerant *adj.* travelling from place to place *n.* one who travels around

itinerary a planned route or journey

its is the possessive form of *it*: 'the cat licked its paw'

it's is short for *it is*: 'it's time to go'

ixnay 1) *v. imperative* do not do or talk about (something) 2) *n.* No

izzard the letter Z

J

jabberwocky nonsense language

jacinth a reddish-orange transparent zircon used as a gemstone

jackal 1) a wild dog native to Africa and parts of Asia and Europe; it hunts in packs and is aka a lion's provider because it reputedly found prey for the lion 2) hence one who does menial work for another

jackanapes a conceited, impertinent type; an upstart

jackstraw 1) a spillikin 2) a game of spillikins

Jacobean 1) concerning the reign of James 1 of England (*1603-1625*) 2) *of furniture*, dark brown, carved oak 3) *of architecture*, a combination of late Gothic and classical features

Jacobites adherents of the Catholic James II and his descendants; after he was deposed in 1688, they made a number of unsuccessful attempts to regain the British throne

jactation 1) bragging, boasting 2) extreme restlessness or tossing in bed, often associated with a high fever aka **jactitation**

jactitation 1) a false boast or claim of being married to another 2) jactation, sense 2

jade 1) a green, hard gemstone 2) bluish-green 3) a clapped-out old horse

jaded tired from overwork; bored or lacking enthusiasm from overindulgence

jaeger = skua

jaggery a coarse brown sugar from the East Indies

jalousie a type of venetian blind or shutter

jankers *slang* for punishment for committing a military offence in the British armed services

Janus-faced two-faced, hypocritical

japan a black, glossy varnish orig. from Japan

jaspé randomly coloured like jasper

jasper semi-precious stone, often carrot-coloured

jaundice yellowing of the skin

jaundiced 1) affected by jaundice 2) bitter, resentful

jealous(y) *n.& adj.* suspicion or fear of being displaced by a rival; possessive and watchful in keeping something one already has

jejune 1) dull, bland, uninteresting, lacking in worthwhile content 2) juvenile, puerile, childish

je ne sais quoi Fr. distinctive but undefinable feature

jeopardy danger

jeremiad a long, mournful complaint or lamentation, a tale of woe

jerry-built badly or hastily constructed

jetsam discarded items washed ashore esp. those thrown overboard to lighten a ship in difficulty

Jew's harp a small lyre-shaped musical instrument held between the teeth and struck with a finger

jibbings the last milk drawn from a cow

jibe *n.* a scornful, taunting, or insulting remark *v. N. Amer.* + with – to be in accord, to agree

jillion an extremely large number

jingoism belligerent patriotism, chauvinism

Job (in scripture) the personification of patience

Job's comforter one who purports to sympathize with another but whose efforts serve only to exacerbate the situation

jocose that involves joking

jocoserious half jocular, half serious

John Dory an edible fish of the eastern Atlantic and Mediterranean

joie de vivre *Fr.* exuberance, ebullience, hearty or carefree enjoyment of life

jolie laide = belle laide *Fr.* an intriguingly plain or ugly woman, whose manner and charm make her attractive

jongleur *Fr.* an itinerant minstrel

jonquil a narcissus with small fragrant white or yellow flowers

joshing joking, teasing

journeyman 1) a skilled worker who is employed by another 2) a reliable but not outstanding worker

Judaism the religion of the Jews

judicial to do with a court of law or a judge

judicious of sound judgment

juggernaut 1) a huge and overpowering force 2) a large heavy vehicle, esp. an articulated lorry

jumart the offspring of a bull and a mare, or a horse and a cow

jumentous resembling (the strong smell of) a horse's urine

jumping bean a seed of certain Mexican shrubs; it contains the lava of a moth whose movements cause the seed to jerk or roll

Junoesque tall and shapely, like the goddess Juno

junta a military or political group that seizes power in a country

jurisdiction official power or authority over something

jus primae noctis = droit du seigneur

jussive commanding; expressing a command, an order; imperative

juxtapose to place next to or side by side

K

Kafkaesque nightmarish – characteristic of the works of the Czech writer Franz Kafka (*1883-1924*)

Kali terrifying Hindu goddess of death and destruction

kalian = hookah

Kant, Immanuel (*1724-1804*) German philosopher. In his *Critique of Pure Reason (1781)* argues that any affirmation or denial regarding the ultimate nature of reality makes no sense. His *Critique of Practical Reason (1788)* affirms the existence of an absolute moral law.

kaput broken and useless

karma (*Hinduism & Buddhism*) a person's destiny is decided by his or her actions in previous existences

katharevousa the traditional, literary and official form of modern Greek

keen 1) an Irish funeral song with wailing 2) to lament, mourn the dead in this way

ken one's range of knowledge or understanding

kenning a metaphorical phrase in Old English and Old Norse poetry such as *oar-steed* = ship

kerosene, kerosine paraffin

ketch a type of sailing boat

Keynes, John Maynard (*1883-1946*), English economist; Keynesian theory holds that full employment is not a natural condition. It believes in government stimulus programmes to assist an economy facing a recession/depression

khan the title given to certain rulers in Central Asia

Khoikhoi see **Hottentot**

killick, killock an anchor

kilter proper working order or alignment

kine cows, cattle

kinetic to do with motion

kismet destiny, fate

kitsch worthless, trashy art, literature etc. usu. with popular or sentimental appeal

kiwi a nocturnal, flightless, bird from New Zealand

klaxon a horn, hooter

kloof a deep, narrow valley in South Africa

klutz a gauche, stupid, socially inept person

knell the sound, toll of a bell

knoll a small rounded hill; a mound

koan a verbal puzzle used as a mental stimulus

Koh-i-noor famous Indian diamond now part of the British crown jewels

kohl black powder used as eye make-up

kosher in accordance with Jewish law (Heb. = proper)

kowtow (Chinese custom) to kneel and touch the ground with the forehead as an expression of submission or respect

kraken a fabled sea monster supposedly seen off the coast of Norway

kremlin a citadel esp. the one in Moscow

kris a Malayan dagger with a wavy-edged blade

kudos praise, glory, honour, prestige

Ku Klux Klan American anti-black secret society

kulaks property-owning Russian peasants persecuted out of existence by Stalin

kylie a boomerang

kyphotic hunchbacked

L

laager *S. Afr.* a camp defended by a circle of wagons

labefaction, labefactation a weakening, deterioration or downfall

labile liable to change, unstable; temperamental, moody

labium *pl.* **labia** *Lat.* one of the four lip-shaped folds of skin that enclose the vulva

laboured showing signs of great effort; not spontaneous

labret lip-ring or ornament in the lip

labrose thick-lipped

labyrinth a complex, maze-like network of passages or paths

labyrinthine complicated, twisted like a labyrinth

lac resin secreted by the lac insect, a source of lacquer, shellac, varnish, etc.

lacerate to tear (the flesh or skin)

lacertilian *n.& adj.* a lizard; lizard-like, saurian

laches delay

lachrymose tearful, weeping

lac insect a scale insect of India and S.E. Asia; lives in trees

lackerdaisical 1) lacking vitality and purpose 2) lazy and careless in a dreamy way

lackey a footman, a servant, a servile follower

lacklustre 1) lacking in vitality, force or conviction 2) dull

Laconia ancient region and present-day department of Lakonia in Greece in the S. E. Peloponnese – capital, Sparta

laconic terse and meaningful; of few words, from *Lakon* Spartan, the Spartans being known for terse speech

lactic relating to milk

lactiferous producing milk

lactifluous flowing with milk

lacuna a gap

lacustrine relating to lakes

lagan goods or wreckage lying on the sea bed sometimes tied to a marker buoy or float for later recovery

laggard one who lags behind, a dawdler

La Gioconda another name for the Mona Lisa

lagniappe 1) a small gift to a customer who makes a purchase 2) a gratuity or bonus

laicize to take out the religious element; to secularize

laissez-aller Fr. absence of restraint

laissez-faire Fr. non-interference in the workings of the free market

laissez-passer Fr. a pass, a permit allowing passage

laity 1) people who are not members of the clergy 2) people who do not belong to a specific profession

lallation the pronouncing of *r* as *l*

lama a Buddhist monk in Tibet or Mongolia

Lamarckism the theory that acquired characteristics can be inherited

lambada an erotic dance from Brazil

lambast(e) 1) to criticise severely 2) to thrash; to beat

lambative (a medicine) to be taken by licking

lambda the Greek letter '*l*'

lambent 1) flickering over as if touching lightly 2) softly radiant 3) (of wit or humour) lightly or effortlessly brilliant

lamé fabric interwoven with gold or silver threads

lamella a thin layer

lameter, lamiter a cripple

lamia a bloodsucking female demon or vampire

laminate involving layers, sheets

lampoon to ridicule

lamprey eel-like fish with a round sucking mouth and horny teeth

lanate woolly

lancinating piercing, stabbing

landfall approach to land after a journey by sea or air

langlauf cross-country skiing by contrast with downhill

languid 1) lethargic, lacking vigour, listless 2) laid-back

languish 1) grow weak or feeble 2) to live under miserable conditions

languorous 1) languid 2) elegantly slow-moving

lanolin fatty substance derived from wool and used in cosmetics and ointments

lanuginous downy

lanugo fine, soft hair

lanyard a rope for fastening sails; a cord for hanging a whistle, key, etc. around the neck or shoulder

laodicean (a person who is) lukewarm, indifferent with regard to religion, politics etc.

lapidary 1) to do with stone(s) 2) (of writing) elegant, dignified, exact, and succinct – suitable for inscriptions in stone 3) a cutter, polisher, engraver of gemstones; one who sets the stones or deals in them

lapidate to stone to death

lapis lazuli 1) a bright blue semi-precious stone 2) ultramarine, bright blue

lappet 1) a flap or fold on a garment or headdress 2) a hanging or loose piece of flesh or membrane, e.g. the wattle on a bird's head 3) a type of moth

la propriété c'est le vol Fr. property is theft (**Proudhon** *1809-1865*)

lapsus calami Lat. a slip of the pen

lapsus linguae Lat. a slip of the tongue

lapsus memoriae Lat. a slip of the memory

lapwing a large crested plover, noted for its slow, erratic flapping flight

larboard the port or left side of a ship

larceny theft

lares and penates 1) valued household belongings 2) the home (orig. ancient Roman guardian gods worshipped by households)

largesse the generous giving of gifts, favours, or money

largo 1) in a slow and stately manner 2) a piece of music performed in that way

lariat a lasso

larva 1) an insect in active immature form between egg and pupa – a caterpillar is the larva of a butterfly or moth 2) the early form of an animal that undergoes change before adulthood, e.g. a tadpole

larynx the upper part of the windpipe and the cavity in the throat holding the vocal chords

lascar a sailor from the East Indies

lasciviously lecherously, lustily

lashings a copious amount of

lassitude physical or mental weariness; lack of energy

lateen (of a ship's sail) triangular

latent existing and potential but not active, developed, or visible

lateral on the side

laterite a reddish clay sometimes used for making roads in the tropics

laths thin flat strips of wood forming the framework/support for plaster

latifoliate, latifolious broad-leafed, having broad leaves

latitudinarian liberal esp. in matters of religion

laudable praiseworthy

laudanum 1) a tincture of opium 2) a solution prepared from opium, formerly used as a narcotic painkiller

laudatory expressing praise

launder to cause money obtained dubiously or illegally to appear from an apparently respectable source i.e. a bank

Laurasia ancient supercontinent which formed the northern landmass of the world when Pangea split into two sections at the end of the Palaeozoic era

laurels symbols of victories or honours gained

Lavoisier A.L. (*1743-1794*) Fr. scientist, regarded as the father of modern chemistry

lawn linen

Law of the Medes and Persians, The something that cannot be altered – see Daniel VI:8

lay 1) a short narrative poem meant to be sung; a ballad; a song 2) not having professional qualifications

layette a set of clothing and bedclothes for a newborn child

lay figure a dummy or jointed manikin of a human body used by artists

lea a meadow

leach 1) to cause a liquid, esp. water, to pass through matter 2) to subject something to such treatment 3) to remove (a soluble substance) from soil or other matter by the treatment

leading question one that suggests the answer being sought

league a former measurement of distance by land, equivalent to about 3 miles (5 km)

leal true-hearted, faithful

leaven *n.* 1) any substance such as yeast that produces fermentation in dough and makes it rise 2) a pervasive influence that modifies something or transforms it for the better *v.* to lighten 3) to permeate and modify or transform for the better

lebensraum Ger. living-space, breathing space

lederhosen Ger. traditional leather Tyrolean or Bavarian men's shorts with braces

lee 1) shelter 2) the sheltered side, away from the wind or weather

leech 1) bloodsucking worm 2) clinging or dependent person; parasite 3) former term for a doctor or physician

lees sediment; dregs

leeway room for manoeuvre

legation diplomatic mission ranking below an embassy

legato *mus.* in a smooth, slowish, flowing manner

legerdemain 1) conjuring skill; sleight of hand 2) deception; trickery

leghorn a breed of chicken

legion numerous

legumes 1) plants which have seeds in pods e.g. those of the pea or bean family 2) the usu. edible pods, peas or beans themselves

leguminous to do with plants which have seeds in pods

lei a Polynesian garland of flowers, esp. in Hawaii

Leibniz G.W. (*1646-1716*) German rationalist philosopher, exponent of optimism, satirized by Voltaire in *Candide*

leiotrichous of the smooth-haired races

leister fishing spear with three or more prongs for catching salmon

leitmotif, leitmotiv orig. a recurring musical theme associated with a particular person or thing; used also of recurring themes in literary works and in relation to human existence itself – see **Sisyphus**

leman a lover, a sweetheart

lemma 1) a subsidiary proposition 2) the citation or core form of a word as it appears in a dictionary together with its various inflections 3) a heading or title indicating the subject of a literary composition

lemming 1) a type of vole; many drown in the sea during mass migrations 2) a suicidal, self-destructive person

lemniscate the shape of a figure 8 lying on its side

lemur arboreal intermediate between insectivore and monkey with a snout and long tail, found in Madagascar

lenient merciful or tolerant; forgiving

lenitive palliative, soothing, alleviating

Lenten relating to Lent

Le Nôtre 17th- century French landscape gardener, designed gardens at Versailles, Tuileries, Vaux-le-Vicomte, Sceaux, etc.

lenticular 1) shaped like a lentil seed or a double convex lens 2) to do with a lens or lenses

lentigo freckle or mole

lentitude slowness, sluggishness

lento at a slow pace

leonine lion-like

leotard a close-fitting garment worn by dancers and some gymnasts

lepidoptera butterflies and moths

lepidopterous relating to butterflies and moths

leporine of or resembling a hare, hare-like

lepto- thin

leptocephalic, leptocephalous having a narrow skull

leptodactyl(ous) having slender digits

leptology *n.* minute description

leptorrhine having a thin or narrow nose, aka **catarrhine**

leptosome a person with a small bodily frame and a slender physique

lèse-majesté *Fr.* 1) treason 2) presumptuous conduct, disrespect

lesion injury, damage

less, fewer less relates to quantity and singular nouns – *less food* fewer applies to numbers and plural nouns – *fewer meals*

lethe forgetfulness, oblivion *adj.* **lethean**

lethological unable to recall a particular word or phrase

leuco-, leuko- white, colourless

leucotomy = lobotomy

Levant the eastern region of the Mediterranean

levee a natural or artificial river embankment

leveret a young hare

leviathan 1) a sea monster 2) anything huge or powerful 3) an absolute state or monarch

levin lightning

levitation to rise or cause to rise and hover (as if) suspended in the air

levity frivolity

lexical to do with words, a lexicon or dictionary

lexicographer one who compiles dictionaries

lex talionis the law of retaliation

libation 1) the pouring out of a drink as an offering to a deity 2) the drink poured out 3) a humorous term for an alcoholic drink

libertine 1) one who leads a dissolute life, who acts without moral restraint; a debauchee 2) a freethinker in religious matters 3) one who follows his or her own inclinations

libidinous having a strong sexual drive

librettist the writer of the words of an opera or other musical composition

licentious sexually promiscuous

lickspittle a toady, a sycophant; a flattering, obsequious person

lied (*pl.* **lieder**) a German song for solo voice and piano

lien a legal right to hold on to a debtor's property until he settles the debt

ligament a band of tough tissue that connects a bone to a joint

lightning conductor a metal rod attached to the highest part of a building to divert lightning safely to earth

lightning rod = lightning conductor

ligneous to do with wood, woody

lignum vitae a hard, heavy, resinous wood aka **guaiacum**

like may be used as a preposition, 'you make me feel like an idiot' but not as a conjunction 'you make me feel like I was an idiot'

liliaceous relatng to the lily, tulip, and bluebell family of plants

Lilliputian 1) very small 2) a very small person or thing

limaceous to do with a slug; slug-like

limation *n.* filing or polishing

limax a slug

limbic to do with a system in the brain concerned with basic emotion, hunger and sex

limbo 1) the abode of the souls of pre-Christian good people and unbaptized infants 2) an intermediate, transitional condition in a period of uncertainty awaiting a decision

limbus *anatomy* the edge or border of any of various parts or structures

limerick a humorous poem of 5 lines

Limerick a county in the west of Ireland and its county town on the River Shannon

limicolous living in mud

liminal 1) relating to a boundary or threshold beyond which a sensation is too faint to be experienced 2) to do with a transitional or initial stage 3) at a boundary or threshold, on the edge

limivorous feeding on mud

limn to paint or draw, to portray, to depict

limnetic (of open water or lakes) down as far as the light penetrates

limosis an abnormal and unhealthy ravenous appetite

limpet a marine conical mollusc that clings to rocks

limpid clear

lineage a line of ancestors or descendants

lineament a distinctive facial feature

linear of or to do with a line or lines; consisting of, having the form of lines; straight; one-dimensional

lingua franca a common language used by people who have different native tongues

lingual titubation stuttering, stammering

linguistic relativism = Sapir – Whorf hypothesis

linguistics the study of language

links a seaside golf course

Linnear, Linnean relating to Carolus Linnaeus (*1707 – 78*), Swedish botanist, who established the binomial system of biological nomenclature

lintel a horizontal beam across the top of a door or window

lionize to treat someone as a celebrity or hero

lipoid, lipoidal relating to or resembling fat

lip-sync, lip-synch to mime

liquidate 1) to pay off a debt or claim 2) to dissolve a company and divide its assets among creditors 3) to convert assets into cash 4) to kill or eliminate

lissom(e) slim, graceful, agile, supple

listless sluggish, tired, or lazy

litany 1) a form of prayer in church services consisting of a series of appeals to God by the clergy and unvarying responses by the congregation 2) a long and boring, repetitive recital

literae humaniores (at Oxford University) the honours course in classics, philosophy, ancient history; the formal name for Greats (*Latin.* – the more humane studies)

literati educated, bookish people with an interest in literature

lithemia an excess of uric acid in the blood; gout

lithe supple, agile

lithic to do with stone

lithify to transform into stone

lithium a soft silver-white metallic chemical element of the alkali metal group; it is the lightest known alkali metal and is used in alloys, lubricating greases and batteries

lithoid resembling stone

lithotomy surgical removal of a stone

litmus paper unsized white paper impregnated with litmus and used as an acid-base indicator

litmus test 1) using litmus paper in different solutions, a test to determine alkalinity (paper turns blue) or acidity (paper turns red) 2) a decisive test

litotes a type of understatement made by denying the opposite of what is being asserted – not a bad player

Little Britain = Armorica = Brittany

littoral relating to the shore or coast

liturgy the prescribed form of worship in church esp. in the celebration of Communion

Litvak a Jew from Lithuania

livid 1) of the colour of lead, bluish-grey 2) extremely angry

livraison Fr. 1) delivery 2) one of the numbers of a book published in parts

lixiviate to separate out the soluble from the insoluble parts of a substance by the percolation of liquid; to leach

llama the South American beast of burden

loam rich soil

loan translation an expression adopted by one language from another in a more or less literally translated form such as *superman* from German *Übermensch* aka **calque**

loath reluctant; unwilling

loblolly sailor's gruel or thick porridge

lobotomy a surgical operation on the brain

locket a little ornamental case containing a memento – a lock of hair, a photo, a portrait – usu. hung from the neck

locus classicus Lat. the most authoritative or best-known piece of writing on a particular topic

Locusta a woman who murders those she is supposed to be nursing

locus standii Lat. officially recognized legal status

lodestar a guiding star – esp. the Pole Star or North Star

lodestone 1) a magnetic stone 2) a magnet 3) a person or thing that is the centre or focus of attention or attraction

logan, logan-stone a boulder that can be easily rocked

loggia an open-sided gallery, room or extension on the side of a building

locus classicus
Lat. the most authoritative or best-known piece of
writing on a particular topic

logic the section of pure philosophy concerned with the study of reasoning

logical atomism all statements or propositions can be analysed into simple independent or atomic statements which correspond directly to facts about our experience of the world

logical positivism, logical empiricism a statement has meaning only if its truth or falsity can be tested empirically

logical types, theory of a class must always be of a higher type than the members and thus to say of a class that it either is or is not one of its own members is meaningless

logistics 1) transporting goods to customers 2) moving, lodging and supplying troops and equipment 3) the detailed organisation and implementation of a large and complex operation

logocentric, logocentrism treating words and language as a fundamental expression of an external reality

logodaedaly verbal legerdemain

logomachy a dispute about words

logomania disease of the faculty of language

logorrhoea, logorrhea an excessive flow of words in mental illness

Logos the Word of God

loimic to do with the plague

longueur *Fr.* 1) a tediously prolonged passage of literature or music 2) a tedious period of time

longshoreman *N. Amer.* a docker

loom 1) to appear in a vague and often threatening form 2) to seem ominously close

loophole 1) an arrow slit in a wall 2) an ambiguity or inadequacy in the law or a set of rules

loot goods stolen in wartime or during riots; plunder

loquacious talkative

lordosis forward curvature of the spine tending to concavity of the back

lore a body of collective, traditional, learning or wisdom on a particular subject

lorimer, loriner a maker of metal accessories for horses e.g. spurs and bits

losel a worthless person

Lothario a womanizer

lotus a name given to several different plants, e.g. to various types of water lily

lotus-eater a person living in indolent luxury

louche shifty, disreputable, seedy (*Fr.* = cross-eyed, squinting)

loup-garou a werewolf (*Fr.*)

louring scowling; looking dark and menacing (often of the sky)

louvre a slatted window or door

lowering = louring

lowest common denominator the smallest number that can be divided evenly into two other numbers; it is often used to mean a dumbing down of quality; paradoxically it can be a relatively high number: the l.c.d. of 2,3,4, and 6 is 12 whereas the highest common factor is a relatively low number – the h.c.f. of 12 and 18 is 6

low relief standing out from a surface to a lesser extent

lox *N. Amer.* smoked salmon

loxodrome an (imaginary) line on the surface of a sphere esp. the earth cutting all meridians at the same angle, aka **rhumb line**

lubber a big clumsy person

lubricious lewd, lascivious, rude

lucent shining

lucerne = alfalfa

lucid clear and intelligible

Lucifer 1) Satan – the devil 2) the planet Venus when it appears as the morning star 3) a match

lucifugal, lucifugous shunning daylight

lucrative profitable

lucre money, wealth (usu. in a facetious sense)

luctation a struggle

lucubrate to write, study, esp. at night

lucubration laborious study, esp. at night

lucubrations learned writings; pompous, pedantic, or pretentious views expressed on some particular subject

luculent lucid, clear

Lucullan luxurious, lavish esp. of food

Lucy Stoner a North American sobriquet for a married woman who continues to use her maiden name

Luddite 1) one of the early 19th-century English textile workers who smashed labour-saving machinery which they thought threatened their jobs 2) somebody opposed to technological progress or innovations

ludic playful; to do with games

lug a lout

luge a toboggan

lugubrious glum, mournful; sad and dismal; gloomy

lumbrical worm -like

luminary a well-known person of considerable achievements who inspires or influences others

lumpen unthinking, unenlightened, stupid

lumpenproletariat the lowest people in society, the underclass, who are not interested in political advancement or revolution – the homeless, the urban poor, criminals, tramps etc. (Marx)

lunge 1) a sudden forward movement of the body 2) a thrust in fencing

lupine wolf-like; rapacious, ravenous

lurch a sudden pitch to one side, like that of a drunken man

lurcher a type of hunting dog

lurid 1) garish, gaudy, unpleasantly vivid in colour 2) sensational, shocking

Lusitania 1) ancient Roman province corresponding to present-day Portugal 2) Cunard liner sunk by German submarine in the Atlantic in May 1915, loss of 1,200 civilian lives, inc. more than 100 Americans

lustre a sheen; a glow of reflected light

lusus naturae *Lat.* freak of nature

Lutetia the Roman or Latin name for Paris

luthier a maker of stringed instruments – lutes, violins etc.

luxate to put out of joint, dislocate

luxation dislocation

luxuriant rich and abundant; lush; growing thickly and abundantly

luxurious characterized by luxury

lycanthrope a werewolf – a person who could change into a wolf

lycanthropy the mythical transformation of a person into a wolf; the delusion of being a wolf

Lyceum the place near Athens where Aristotle taught philosophy; a lecture hall

lymphatic 1) to do with the lymph or the lymphatic system 2) lacking energy, physical or mental; sluggish

lynch to hang somebody for an alleged offence without a legal trial

lyonnaise cooked with onions

lyre U-shaped stringed musical instrument like a small harp, used by ancient Greeks

lyrical emotional, effusive, carried away

lysis gradual dissolution, disintegration

M

macabre gruesome; ghastly; grim; it has an association with death – *danse macabre*, dance of death

macaque a monkey

macaw a parrot

macerate to soak

MacGuffin, McGuffin an object or device which serves merely as a trigger for the plot in a film or book – a coinage of Alfred Hitchcock in the 1930s

Machiavellian scheming, cunning, unscrupulous, devious esp. in politics – after the Florentine political theorist Niccolò Machiavelli (*1469-1527*)

machinate to plot, to scheme

macramé 1) the craft of knotting cord, string or thread in patterns to make coarse lace for use in furnishings often as a fringe or trimming 2) the ornamental lacework so produced

macrobiotics Buddhist diet of organic wholefoods to prolong life based on balance of yin and yang

macrology much talk with little to say

macrosmatic having a highly developed sense of smell

macrotous having large ears

macula a dark brownish spot on the skin *adj.* **macular**

maculate to mark with a spot or spots; to stain; *adj.* spotted or stained

madrigal a 16th- / 17th- century part-song for several unaccompanied voices

maelstrom a whirlpool

maenad a frenzied woman

maffick to celebrate exuberantly

Maghreb Morocco, Algeria, Tunisia and sometimes Libya

magenta reddish-purple

magister dixit *Lat.* thus spoke the master

magisterial having or showing great authority; domineering; dictatorial

magnanimous generous and forgiving; high-minded and noble

magnum a bottle of wine twice the normal size

magnum opus a great work of art, literature or music – the best the artist, writer or composer has produced

mahout an elephant driver/keeper

maidenhead virginity

maieutic concerning Socrates' method of eliciting latent knowledge by means of a series of questions

maigre (R.C. Church) denoting a day on which abstinence from meat is ordered

majolica decorative, enamelled, Italian pottery from 15th – 17th centuries; first made in Majorca

major-domo the principal steward of a great household, the head of staff

malacology the study of molluscs

maladroit clumsy, awkward, tactless

malaise feeling of illness, uneasiness, discomfort

malapert impudent, cheeky

malapropism the mistaken use of a word for another which sounds similar e.g. living in abstract (instead of abject) poverty – in the manner of Mrs Malaprop in Sheridan's play 'The Rivals' (1775); a confusion of similar-sounding words

malapropos out of place; inappropriate

malaxate to soften by kneading, mixing or stirring with a thinner or more liquid substance

malcontent a complaining, discontented person

mal de mer Fr. sea-sickness

malediction a curse, an imprecation; a slander

malefactor a criminal; a wrongdoer

malefic, maleficent evil, baleful; harmful, baneful

malevolent wishing evil to others; malicious

malice the desire to do evil; ill-will

malicious being deliberately harmful or spiteful

malign *adj.* evil *v.* to speak ill of; to slander

malignant showing considerable ill-will; life-threatening; cancerous

malinger to pretend to be ill in order to escape duty or work

malison a curse

malleable bendable

malleate to hammer

malm soft, chalky rock; soil from it

malocclusion a misalignment of the upper and lower teeth when the mouth is closed

malodorous foul-smelling

Malthus T.R. (*1766-1834*) English economist and clergyman who warned of the dangers of overpopulation

Mameluke one of the former rulers in Egypt and the Middle East; descended originally from Circassian slaves, they were eventually defeated in 1811 by Muhammad Ali

Mammon the earthly god of material wealth and greed, the worship of whom is considered a source of evil and corruption

mañana *Spanish* tomorrow

manatee an aquatic mammal with two front flippers, which resembles the dugong but is somewhat larger and has a rounded tail; it is found in the warm Atlantic coastal waters and adjacent rivers of W. Africa, Florida, and W. Indies

manciple an officer who buys provisions for a college, a monastery or an Inn of Court etc.

mandarin 1) a Chinese official 2) a colloquial term for an important government official or senior civil servant 3) a small kind of orange 4) porcelain decorated with figures representing Chinese mandarins

Mandarin standard Chinese, the official language of China

mandate an official order to do something; the political authority given to a government by an electoral victory

mandatory compulsory, obligatory

mandible the lower jaw

mandorla an almond-shaped area of light surrounding the head of a holy person; an aureole; a vesica piscis

mandragora the mandrake when used as a narcotic

mandrake a Mediterranean/south Asian plant whose forked root was once thought to resemble the human form; it was rumoured to have special properties and to shriek when plucked

manducate to chew, to eat

mangel-wurzel, mangold, a variety of beet used as food

mangonel a large medieval war engine or catapult for hurling stones or other projectiles

mania 1) an obsession 2) a mental disorder marked by periods of excitement, delusions, and hyperactivity

maniac a wild, violent person; one who has an uncontrollable enthusiasm for something

maniacal to do with madness, ungovernable frenzy

manic 1) extremely excited or energetic; frenzied 2) to do with mania

Manichaeism dualist religion founded in 3rd-century Persia by the prophet, Mani, based on the theory of the primordial struggle between the forces of good and evil, hence a Manichaean view of something that polarises everything into good and bad or other opposing, dualistic elements – light and darkness, for example – with nothing in between

manifold many and varied

manikin a small man, a dwarf

mannered affected, artificial, contrived

manoeuvre a movement or way of doing something requiring skill and dexterity

manqué (postpositive) failed or unfulfilled, would-be

mansuetude meekness, mildness, gentleness

mantic prophetic

mantis = **praying mantis**

mantra 1) *in Hinduism & Buddhism*, a word or formula repeated aloud or internally to aid concentration in meditation 2) a Vedic (Hindu) hymn

Mantua city in N. Italy (Lombardy), surrounded by lakes; birthplace of Virgil; ruled by Gonzaga family who in 16th cent. made it the most magnificent court in Europe; annexed by Austria in 1708

manumit to release from slavery

maquette a small preliminary model of a larger structure – e.g. a sculpture

maquillage make-up, cosmetics

Marat (*1743-1793*) Fr. Revolutionary leader, hard line opponent of Girondists during the Revolution; stabbed to death in his bath by Charlotte Corday

marcato *mus.* played with emphasis

marcel a deep, artificial wave in the hair

marcher an inhabitant of a frontier or border district

marches boundary regions

marcid withered, wasted

Mardi Gras Shrove Tuesday in areas under French cultural influence

mare's nest something which at first seems to be a great discovery but which proves to be nothing at all

margaric, margaritic concerning a pearl

margrave a German nobleman – the equivalent of a British marquess

mariachi 1) a group of strolling Mexican musicians who play at weddings, festivals and in the street 2) one of the group 3) the music they play

mariage blanc Fr. unconsummated marriage

marimba a Latin American xylophone

marinade a mixture of vinegar, oil, wine, and spices in which food is soaked (marinated) before cooking

mariolatry exaggerated veneration of the Virgin Mary

marionette a puppet

marivaudage Fr. language which is refined, delicate and precious, reminiscent of the French 18th-century playwright, Marivaux, known for his nuanced feeling and clever wordplay

marl crumbly, earthy, rock or soil consisting of clay and lime used as a fertilizer for lime-deficient soils

marmoraceous, marmoreal, marmorean *adj.*
1) marble, to do with, or like, marble 2) (of a literary style) cold, hard, smooth, impenetrable

marmoset a small tropical American monkey

marque the make of a product esp. a car, not a specific model – the Bentley marque

marquetry inlaid work in wood used in decorating furniture

marsupial a kangaroo / opossum / bandicoot / koala / wombat, the female of which carries her young in a pouch

marten a tree-living type of weasel valued for its fur

Martial (*c.40-104 a.d.*) Latin poet, born Spain; his books of epigrams provide a sharp picture of Roman life

martial to do with war; warlike

martinet a strict disciplinarian

Mary Celeste American brigantine en route from New York to Genoa found abandoned in the North Atlantic in Dec. 1872; the boat was in good condition but the fate of the crew has never been discovered

Masada an ancient mountaintop Jewish fortress besieged by the Romans for nearly two years. On the S.W. shore of the Dead Sea it was the scene in a.d. 73 of a mass suicide by almost all the inhabitants when the Romans eventually took the citadel; a symbol of Jewish national heroism

masterful
*strong, powerful, tending to take control
and dominate others*

masterly
*showing the skill of a master, demonstrating exceptional
expertise and performing with the utmost skill*

masochist one who derives pleasure or sexual arousal from undergoing pain

masque a play in which the performers wear masks

masquerade a false show or pretence; a masked ball

masterful strong, powerful, tending to take control and dominate others

masterly showing the skill of a master, demonstrating exceptional expertise and performing with the utmost skill

masticate to chew

mastodon a large, extinct, type of elephant

mastoid shaped like a woman's breast or nipple

Matignon 1) the office of the French Prime Minister in the seventh arrondissement (Rue de Varenne) in Paris 2) a metonymic reference to the job of the Prime Minister of France

matinée an afternoon performance in the theatre or cinema

matriarch a female head of a family or tribe; a dominant woman

matrix *the Latin word for 'womb' has, by association and extension, many different meanings including numerous technical ones in mathematics, the sciences, computing, linguistics and other disciplines, which cannot be incorporated here* 1) a mould 2) a cavity, substance, environment in which something is formed, develops 3) the earthy or stony material in which minerals, fossils, gems are embedded 4) the substance between cells of a tissue that holds them together

matutinal to do with the morning

maudlin weakly, effusively, tearfully sentimental and possibly slightly drunk

maunder to move, talk or act aimlessly, idly, or in a rambling manner

mausoleum a large stately tomb and monument

mauvais quart d'heure Fr. a brief unpleasant experience

maverick an unorthodox or independent-minded person

mavis a song thrush

maw the stomach, mouth, jaws or gullet of an animal

mawkish sickly sentimental

maximalist one who favours direct action, rejects compromise and expects full accedence to his often extreme, radical demands

Mayas a pre-Columban central American civilization of native American Indian peoples inhabiting the Yucatan peninsular, southern Mexico, Guatemala, Honduras, and Belize; recognised from as early as 2,000 b.c. the Golden Age lasted from about 250 a.d. to 900 a.d.

Mazda the supreme god of Zoroastrianism

mazuma money

mea culpa *Lat.* '(by) my fault' , an exclamation acknowledging one's guilt

meagre lacking in quality or quantity

mealy-mouthed not speaking frankly, openly, but so as to avoid giving offence

mean 1) unwilling to part with money 2) common or poor in appearance; shabby 3) unkind or spiteful

meconium the dark, greenish, semi-fluid material forming the first faeces of a newborn child

médaillon *Fr.* a small round or oval cut of meat or fish

medallion 1) a large medal 2) a pendant in the shape of a medal 3) an oval or circular decorative device resembling a medal, often bearing a figure or portrait in relief, used to decorate a building or in textile design

mediatize to annex (a small state) to a large one, leaving the ruler of the smaller power with his title and some authority

Medici wealthy, powerful and influential Italian family of bankers and merchants; rulers of Florence (15th – 18th centuries) and patrons of the Renaissance, they provided four popes and two queens of France

medina the old quarter of a North African town

medusa a jelly-fish, a quarl

Medusa the best known of the three **Gorgons**

meerschaum a white type of clay from Turkey used to make tobacco-pipes

meet suitable, proper, appropriate

megalith a large prehistoric stone forming a monument or part of it

megalopolis a large city

megillah a long, tedious or complicated story **the whole megillah** something in its entirety

meiosis understatement

Meissen a city near Dresden in Saxony (now Germany) where high quality porcelain (Dresden china) has been made since 1710

mélange a mixture

meld to mix, merge, combine

mêlée a brawl

meliorism the belief that the world can be made better by human effort

mellifluous flowing smoothly and as sweetly as honey

melodrama an emotionally charged, action-packed play or narrative involving, inter alia, suspense, sensation, improbable events, romance and frequently a happy ending

membrum virile Lat. the penis

meme a cultural or behavioural trait passed on by imitation or copying – habits, skills, games, etc.

memento mori (*Latin* remember you must die) – a reminder of death e.g. a skull

Memphis an ancient capital of Egypt on the western bank of the Nile just south of modern Cairo

Memphis city and port in south-west Tennessee on the Mississippi

mendacious lying, untruthful

mendacity untruthfulness, dishonesty

mendicant 1) begging 2) a beggar

menhir a tall, single, upright stone erected as a monument in prehistoric times

meniscus 1) the curved upper surface of a liquid in a tube – concave when the sides are wetted, and convex when they are dry 2) a lens, convex on one side and concave on the other

Mennonite a member of a protestant sect originating in Friesland in the 16th century; tenets similar to those of the Anabaptists

Mensheviks a minority party of the Russian Revolution; 'softer' than the Bolsheviks to whom they eventually lost out

mens rea *Lat.* criminal intent

mensuration measuring, measurement

menticultural improving the mind

Mephistopheles the name of the devil in Marlowe's Dr. Faustus and Goethe's Faust

mephitis (mephitic) 1) a horrible smell esp. from the earth 2) a putrid or foul-smelling, poisonous stench; a miasma, effluvium, fetor

mercenary 1) a professional soldier who will fight for any country willing to pay him 2) *adj.* concerned primarily with making money

mercer a dealer in expensive textiles and other such materials esp. silk

mercerize to treat cotton with sodium hydroxide and drying under tension to give greater strength and a lustrous appearance

Mercers Company a livery company in the City of London, one of the twelve 'great' companies and the first in order of precedence

mercurial prone to sudden changes of mood or mind, volatile, unpredictable

mereology the question of part-whole relationships in philosophy arising from issues such as 'is a whole something more than the sum of its parts?' The answer depends upon the nature of the entities involved.

meretricious superficially but falsely attractive, insincere, vulgarly conspicuous, tasteless

merganser a diving, fish-eating duck

merino a type of sheep with long, fine wool

merkin an artificial hairpiece for the pudendum; a pubic wig

meronym(y) the use of a term denoting a part of something to refer to the whole, e.g. head-hunting to mean searching for high-level executives often from rival companies

mésalliance Fr. marriage beneath oneself – to a person of a lower class

mescal a globe-shaped cactus from Mexico

mescaline, mescalin a hallucinatory drug derived from the mescal cactus

mesmerize to fascinate and hold spellbound, to enthral, to transfix

mesocephalic having a medium-sized head

mesomorph a person with a compact, athletic and muscular body

Mesopotamia ancient region of S. W. Asia and cradle of the world's earliest civilisations; in present-day Iraq it corresponds roughly with the area between the Tigris and Euphrates

mesothelioma a cancer often resulting from exposure to asbestos

Messiah the saviour of 1) the Jews 2) the world 3) any oppressed people or country *adj.* **messianic** referring to zealous or overzealous belief in a cause or a leader

mestizo a person of mixed race esp. the offspring of a Spanish American and a native American Indian

metabolism the chemical processes that occur in living organisms to maintain life, i.e. growth, the production of energy, and elimination of waste

metagrobolize to puzzle or mystify, to puzzle out

metalanguage 1) language about another language 2) a system of propositions about propositions

metamorphosis 1) a complete change in form or nature, character or appearance 2) *zoo.* the rapid change from larva into adulthood e. g. the change from a tadpole into a frog; a caterpillar into a butterfly or moth

metanarrative an overarching explanation or belief that underpins Western civilisation and purports to be universally valid – Christianity, a free market, the Enlightenment etc. all of which have, it is claimed, contributed to the West's oppression of a large part of the world

metanoia a change in one's way of life resulting from penitence or spiritual conversion

metaphor a trope or figurative, not literal, use of a word or expression e.g. a *branch office*; a resemblance to or a symbol of something else: *spaghetti junction*

metaphysics the branch of philosophy that enquires into the nature of reality i.e. what actually exists and what precisely existence is; it is concerned also with the aspects of reality that cannot be observed or measured, such as god and virtue.

metastasis the spreading of a disease esp. cancer, from one part of the body to another and the secondary tumours resulting from this process.

metastasize to spread from one part of the body to another

metathesis the transposition or switching of letters or sounds within a word – e.g. old English *bridd*, modern English *bird*

metempsychosis the supposed transmigration at death of the soul into a new body or cycle of existence

methuselah 1) a very old man 2) a wine bottle of eight times the normal size

meticulous very careful, thorough, and precise about details

métier a trade, profession, or occupation

métis a person of mixed race esp. in Canada, the offspring of a native American Indian and a French Canadian

metonymy a figure of speech in which the usual name for something is replaced by the name of something closely associated with it, e.g. *the bottle* for alcoholic drink

metopic concerning the forehead

metronome a mechanism which indicates the speed at which music should be played by producing a regular (and adjustable) tick

metropolitan 1) to do with a metropolis, a very large and busy city 2) (in the Orthodox Church), the head of an ecclesiastical province, ranking between archbishop and patriarch

Metternich (*1773-1859*) Austrian statesman who pursued policies of repressive conservatism at home and abroad

mettle 1) inherent character and temperament 2) courage, spirit, resilience 3) **on one's mettle** ready to put one's best efforts to the test

meunière coated lightly with flour, sautéed in butter and served typically with a lemon-and-butter sauce

mewl (of a baby) to cry weakly; to whimper

mezzanine an extra storey set between two others esp. between ground floor and first floor

mezzo-giorno an economically under-developed area of the southern Italian mainland, plus Sicily and Sardinia so called because of the intensity of the midday (mezzo-giorno) sun

mezuzah a religious text attached, in a bullet-like case, to a doorpost in a Jewish house

miasma an unpleasant or unhealthy smell or vapour; an unpleasant, unhealthy foreboding atmosphere

Micawber an idler who trusts to fortune; an eternal optimist whose schemes for making money never materialize, from the character, Mr. Wilkins Micawber, in Dickens's novel *David Copperfield* (1850)

Mickey Finn a drink drugged or doctored surreptitiously

microbe a micro organism, esp. a disease-causing bacterium, too small to be seen except under a microscope

microcosm something resembling something else but on a very much smaller scale

micturate to urinate

midrash (*pl.* **midrashim**) a Hebrew commentary on the Old Testament

mien the manner, bearing or look of a person

miff a small quarrel

miffed annoyed, irritated

migrate 1) to move from one country to settle in another 2) (of birds) to journey between different habitats at specific times of the year

miles gloriosus *Lat.* the soldier who boasts of his brave deeds as a warrior but is actually a coward – a stock character in comedy

milieu a person's social environment

militate (against) to serve as strong evidence or as a powerful influence

millenarianism a belief that the second coming of Christ will coincide with the beginning of the one thousand-year period of the millennium or the end of it

millet a cereal which bears a large crop of small seeds used to make flour or alcoholic drinks

milliner one who makes, designs, or sells hats for women; a modiste

millipede a small worm-like animal with a body of 20/100 segments, each with 2 pairs of legs

milquetoast a meek, submissive, or timid person

mimesis (mimetic) mimicry, imitation; in nature the problem for predators when an esculent or harmless animal resembles one that is not – the viceroy butterfly is not poisonous to birds but the almost identical monarch butterfly is.

minacious threatening, menacing

minaret the tower of a mosque from which the muezzin calls the faithful to prayer

minatory threatening

mince 1) to speak or walk with an affected daintiness 2) to soften, moderate, restrain (one's words etc.): *I didn't mince my words*

mind-set a habitual way of thinking

Minerva Roman goddess of wisdom

minger an ugly or unattractive person esp. a woman

minion a hanger-on, a servile dependant, an underling, a 'yes-man'

minister to attend to

ministration(s) the providing of assistance or care

miniver white fur used in ceremonial costumes

mink a type of weasel valued for its fur; emits a disagreeable odour

minnow 1) a small freshwater fish 2) someone or something small or insignificant

Minoan relating to Crete

Minotaur *Gk. myth* a monster with the head of a bull and the body of a man

minuend a number or quantity from which another (the subtrahend) is to be subtracted

minutiae very small details

minx a bitch

miosis excessive contraction of the pupil of the eye

mirabelle 1) a small, sweet, yellow type of plum 2) the tree from which it comes 3) a liqueur distilled from mirabelles

mirabile dictu Latin wonderful to relate; amazing to say

mirador a turret or tower on a building providing an extensive view

mirandize (U.S.) to formally notify a suspect of his legal rights

mire 1) a bog 2) a state of difficulty from which it is hard to extricate oneself *v.* to cause to become stuck in mud or entangled in something; to soil with mud or filth

Miró, Joan (*1893-1983*) Spanish painter; with Dali he was an originator of the surrealist movement

misalliance an unsuitable marriage or alliance

misandrist one who hates men

misandry hatred of men

misanthrope, misanthropist a person who hates humankind, people in general

misanthropy hatred of other people

misbegotten 1) born out of wedlock, illegitimate 2) ill-conceived 3) improperly obtained

miscegenation interbreeding of different races esp. those of different colour

miscible capable of mixing, of being mixed

miscreant a wrongdoer; one who behaves badly, unlawfully

mise-en-abyme Fr. 'putting into the abyss', infinite regression; a device which involves internal reduplication ad infinitum esp. in a literary or artistic work; well-known examples occur when somebody stands between two mirrors facing each other which create an infinite reproduction of the person's image; and in *Hamlet* the play within the play refers to and explains the plot of the larger play within which it is staged. A more homely illustration is provided by the traditional Quaker Oats emblem of the Quaker holding up a packet of Quaker Oats on which there is a Quaker holding up a packet of Quaker Oats and so on

mise en place Fr. (in a commercial kitchen) the preparation of dishes and ingredients before the beginning of service

mise en scène *Fr.* 1) the arrangement of scenery and the stage setting of a play 2) the setting of an event 3) the staging, producing, directing, presenting of a play etc.

misericord 1) a ledge on the underside of a hinged seat in a choir stall which, when the seat is turned up, supports a person standing 2) a dagger for applying the coup de grâce

misnomer a wrong, inaccurate, or inappropriate name for a person or thing

misocapric hating (tobacco) smoke

misoclere hating the clergy

misogamist one who hates marriage

misogamy hatred of marriage

misogynist a woman-hater

misogyny hatred of women

misologist one who hates reason

misology hatred of reason

misotheism hatred of god

misprision the deliberate concealment of one's knowledge of a crime

missal a book containing the services at mass for the year

missive a letter

mithridate a former concoction believed to be an antidote to every poison and a cure for every disease

mithridatism tolerance to a poison acquired by taking gradually increased doses of it

mitigate to soften, or reduce the severity of; to alleviate; to make less severe, serious, or painful

mitre the headdress of a bishop or abbot

mixed metaphor a combination of metaphors that are incompatible, incongruous, or inconsistent

mnemonic an aid to memory, esp. an acronym; aiding the memory

Mnemosyne the greek goddess of memory; the mother of the Muses

möbius strip a one-sided surface made by forming a twisted strip into a ring

mocha high quality Arabian coffee

modality 1) a form 2) a means to an end; a method

modicum a small amount

modernism the upheaval in the arts in the first half of the 20th century

modiste a milliner

modulate to modify; to regulate; to moderate; to measure

modus operandi *Lat.* a way of operating or working

modus vivendi *Lat.* a way of living

mogigraphia writer's cramp

mogul an important, powerful, or wealthy person

mohair the hair of the angora goat

moidore a former Portuguese gold coin

moiety a half

moire silk with a wavy, watery finish or effect

moiré having a wavy watered appearance

moke a donkey

mole 1) a small burrowing mammal 2) a spy 3) a breakwater, pier, causeway

molecule a group of atoms bonded together making the simplest unit of a chemical compound that can exist

mollify to pacify; to calm; to soothe hostile feelings

mollusc an invertebrate with a soft body and often a hard shell – a snail, oyster, etc.

monad a single unit; the number one

monandry mating in which the female has only one mate at a time

mondegreen a word or phrase that is misheard and misinterpreted as another word or phrase, usually with an amusing result

Monégasque concerning Monaco; a native or inhabitant of Monaco

monetarism (opp. of Keynes) the view that control of the money supply is the only way to beat inflation and stabilize the economy

monetary policy regulating economic activity by controlling interest rates and the amount of money in the economy

moniker a name

monism 1) mind and matter are not separate but a single common substance 2) there is only one supreme being

monition a warning of danger

monitor *v.* to keep a close watch over; to observe and keep a check on over a period; to maintain regular surveillance over

monitory *adj.* warning

monochrome in black and white or one colour only

monocle a single eyeglass held in position by the muscles around the eye

monocular, monoculous one-eyed

monogamy having only one spouse or one mate at a time

monoglot using only one language

monograph a detailed written study on a single specialized subject

monolith a large single (block of) stone

monologue a long speech by one person usu. when alone; a soliloquy

monoptote a noun with one case-form i.e. it is not declined

monorchid having only one testicle

monotheism the belief that there is only one God

monotreme a small order of egg-laying mammals (includes the platypus and echidna) which have a single opening for the genital and digestive organs

monoxylon a canoe made from one log

monoxylous made of a single piece of wood

monozygotic twins identical twins

montage a picture or composition made by combining several separate elements

mood a form of a verb: *indicative* expresses a simple statement of fact *subjunctive* a possibility or a wish, God help you, *imperative* a command, sit down *infinitive* to sit

moolah money

Moonie a member of a religious sect, the Unification Church

mooning bending down and exposing one's buttocks to someone as an insult; a traditional insult among the Maoris in New Zealand

moose 1) a large North American deer 2) the North American term for an elk

moot 1) debatable 2) a mock judicial proceeding in which law students argue hypothetical cases

moratorium temporary agreed ban on or prohibition of an activity

moray an eel

morbid diseased; having an abnormal and unhealthy interest in unpleasant subjects esp. death and disease

mordacious, mordant *adj.* 1) biting, given to biting 2) bitingly sarcastic, caustic

morel a type of mushroom

mores the customs and conventions embodying the fundamental values of a community esp. regarding moral conduct

morganatic descriptive of a marriage in which the spouse of lower rank and any children have no claim to the property or title of the spouse of higher rank

moribund about to die, at death's door

morkin a beast that has died accidentally

morose gloomy and unsociable, sullen and bad-tempered

morpheme the smallest meaningful unit of a language that cannot be further divided, existing either on its own- *'dug'* or as part of another word – *'dugout'*

Morpheus sleep personified

morphing a computer graphics technique whereby one image is gradually and imperceptibly transformed into another image

morphology the study of the form and structure of things esp. 1) organisms 2) words 3) language

morse 1) a clasp or fastening on a cope or cloak 2) a walrus

mortadella a large spiced Italian sausage

mortician *N. Amer.* an undertaker

mortify to cause to feel very embarrassed or ashamed

mosaic an arrangement of small coloured pieces of tile, glass or stone, used mainly on floors and walls

motet a short religious composition for a choir

mother-of-pearl the hard, smooth, shining, iridescent inner layer of shells of certain molluscs, e.g. oysters, abalones; aka **nacre**

motif recurring design, feature or melody

motile capable of motion

mot juste *Fr.* exactly the right word or verbal expression

motley 1) composed of a variety of sources; heterogeneous 2) multicoloured

moue a pout

mountebank 1) a charlatan, an imposter 2) a person who sold quack medicines in public 3) an unscrupulous salesman

mucedinous like mould or mildew

mucilage 1) a sticky gum extracted from plants 2) a sticky substance such as gum or glue, used as an adhesive *adj.* **mucilaginous**

muezzin Muslim crier who calls the faithful to prayer from the minaret

mufti 1) off-duty civilian clothes worn by a person who is normally in uniform 2) a Muslim legal expert entitled to pronounce on religious matters

mugger an Indian crocodile

mugwump *N. Amer.* a person who is independent, neutral esp. in politics

Muhammad (*c.570-632*) Arab prophet and founder of Islam, born Mecca

mulatto somebody with one white and one black parent

Mulberry Harbour either of two prefabricated ports towed across the English channel to the Normandy coast to facilitate the supplying of the Allied armies in France consequent upon the D-Day landings

mulct 1) a fine 2) to fine somebody 3) to swindle (somebody); to swindle (something) from somebody

mule the offspring of a male donkey and a female horse

muliebrity womanhood, femininity; the condition of being a woman

mulierose fond of women

mulierosity fondness for women

mull a headland, a promontory

mullet a man's head of hair

mulligatawny spicy meat soup orig. from India

mulligrubs 1) state of depression, sulkiness 2) stomach-ache, colic

mullion an upright division between the panes of glass in a window

multifarious having many parts of great variety, many and varied; diverse

multiloquence much talking; verbosity

multipara woman who has given birth at least twice

multitudinous very many; vast (of a body of water)

mummery 1) pretentious, hypocritical, ridiculous or extravagant ceremonial procedures 2) a performance by actors in a traditional masque or mime i.e. by mummers

mumpsimus an error in which one persists after it has been exposed

Munchausen (a person who tells) an exaggerated story

Munchausen's syndrome a mental disorder in which a person feigns illness to obtain medical treatment

Munchausen's syndrome by proxy a psychiatric disorder in which the sufferer harms other people, usu. children, so that they require medical attention from which he apparently derives emotional satisfaction

mundane 1) everyday, ordinary, lacking interest 2) of this earthly world rather than a heavenly or spiritual one; secular

munificence generosity

munificent magnanimously generous in giving

munitions weapons, ammunition etc. used in war

murine to do with mice or rats

murrain a plague-like disease in cattle

muse a creative artist's (esp. a poet's) source of inspiration, usually an inspiring goddess or woman; to be absorbed in thought

Muses the nine patron sister goddesses in Greek and Roman mythology each of whom presided over a different art or science

muslin a delicate, lightweight, plain-woven, cotton cloth

mussitation muttering

Mussulman Muslim

mustang a small feral or semi-wild horse of Mexico and the south-western prairies of the U.S.

muster, pass muster to pass inspection as adequate; to 'get by'

must(h) sexual excitement in a male elephant or camel

mutable liable to change, fickle

mutant 1) something that has undergone mutation 2) a person who is deformed 3) *adj.* to do with change or mutation

mutation 1) a change 2) a genetic change which may affect subsequent generations

mutatis mutandis *Lat.* when the necessary changes have been made or taken into account

mutual experienced or expressed by each of two or more people about the other(s); reciprocal

mutt a mongrel dog

myalism a West Indian folk religion

mydriasis abnormal dilation of the pupil of the eye

mydriatic 1) a drug which cause such dilation 2) *adj.* to do with or causing mydriasis

myopia short-sightedness

myopic short-sighted; lacking foresight or planning

myosis = miosis

myriad 1) innumerable 2) a vast number

myrmidon a follower or henchman who carries out orders without question

myrmidons of the law policemen, bailiffs etc.

myrrh a fragrant gum resin obtained from certain trees and used, especially in the Near East, in perfumery, medicines, and incense

mythomania a pathological tendency (normal in children) to exaggerate or tell lies

mythopoeia the making of myths

N

nabob 1) a Muslim official or governor under the Mogul empire in India 2) a rich European who made his fortune in the East esp. in India 3) any person of great wealth

nacarat *n.* a bright, orange-red colour

nachträglichkeit (Freud) *Ger.* remembering events not as they were but in order to suit your present purposes

nacre mother-of-pearl

nacreous having a pearly lustre; iridescent

nadir the lowest point

naiad a nymph of the water

naïve innocent and gullible; simple and unsophisticated

Nama see **Hottentot**

nanism dwarfism

nano a thousand-millionth of...; a factor of 10^{-9} *Gk*.

nanos dwarf

nanosecond one thousand-millionth of a second

Nantes, Edict of 1598, granted some religious and civil liberties to French Protestants

napalm jellied petrol used in incendiary bombs and flame-throwers, etc.

napiform shaped like a turnip – large and round above and slender below

narcissism excessive love for oneself, one's physical appearance, etc.

Narcissus *Gk.myth* beautiful youth who fell in love with his own reflection in a pool

narcolepsy an illness characterized by uncontrollable attacks of sleepiness and drowsiness

narcotic (a drug) inducing drowsiness and relieving pain

nares the nostrils

narghile = hookah

narthex an antechamber or large porch in a church

nascent being born, beginning to exist, emerging

nasute having a long snout; having a keen sense of smell

natal to do with 1) birth 2) the nates or buttocks

nachträglichkeit
*(Freud) Ger. remembering events not as they were but
in order to suit your present purposes*

natant *adj.* 1) swimming 2) floating on the surface as if swimming

natation *n.* swimming

nates the buttocks

nautilus an active predatory marine mollusc

nave the main long central part of a church from the west door to the chancel, excluding the side aisles

Nazirite a Jew in biblical times who had taken certain vows of abstinence (also **Nazarite**)

neb a nose, snout or beak

nebbish (a) submissive, timid (person); (an) ineffectual, inadequate (man); a born loser

nebulous vague, hazy, wishy-washy

necessitarianism the doctrine that events are inevitably determined by preceding causes external to the will, aka **determinism**

necromancy 1) supposed communication with the dead to predict the future 2) black magic; sorcery; witchcraft

necrophilia sexual intercourse with corpses

necropolis a cemetery

necrosis the death of cells in tissue

nectar the drink of the gods

nefarious wicked

negate 1) to deny the existence of 2) to nullify; make ineffective

negatur it is denied (*Latin*)

negentropy negative entropy or a near synonym for information; reverse entropy or things becoming more in order

negritude conscious pride in the black African heritage

nekton the actively swimming aquatic animals in a sea or lake that move independently of water currents, including fish, turtles and whales

nem.con. with no one dissenting; unanimously (short for *Latin nemine contradicente*)

Nemesis Greek goddess of retribution or vengeance; the deification of retributive justice

nemesis 1) one's downfall 2) the inescapable agent that causes this; one's destroyer 3) an ever-present rival or enemy; a source of trouble

nemo dat quod non habet 'nobody can give what he does not own' a Latin tag from the law of sale of goods: you cannot transfer good title if you do not own the goods you are selling; there are some exceptions to the rule

nemoral to do with a wood or grove

nenuphar a water lily

neocracy government by upstarts

neogamist one who is newly married

neologism a newly-coined word or expression

neophobia a fear or dread of anything new

neophyte 1) a new convert to a religion 2) a newly-ordained priest 3) a novice in a religious order 4) any novice or beginner in a subject or activity

neoplasm a tumour

Neoplatonism a philosophical and religious system; combining the ideas of Plato with oriental mysticism, it began at Alexandria in the 3rd cent. and incorporated features from Pythagoras and Aristotle

neoprene a synthetic rubber-type polymer used in waterproof products

neoteny the retention of juvenile features in adulthood *adj.* neotenic, neotenous

neoteric modern, of recent origin

nepenthe, nepenthean 1) a tranquillizer; orig. a drug, possibly opium, mentioned in the *Odyssey* as a means of forgetting grief or trouble 2) anything that produces sleep, forgetfulness, or blissful dreaminess that induces oblivion of sorrow or eases pain

nephalism total abstinence from alcohol

nephalist a teetotaller

nephology the study of clouds

nephrology the branch of medicine concerned with the kidneys

nephrotomy surgical incision into a kidney

ne plus ultra *n.* the highest point; the most perfect state to which something can be taken

nepotism favouritism shown to relatives in appointing them to jobs

neritic to do with the shallow waters adjoining a coastline

nescient ignorant, without knowledge

nesh soft

Nestor the oldest and wisest man in a given situation

nether lower

Neue Sachlichkeit 'New Objectivity' 1920s and early 1930s German arts movement in reaction to Expressionism; reflecting the resignation and cynicism of the post-World War 1 period, the style was realistic using meticulous detail in smooth, cold, and static images

neural to do with a nerve or the nervous system

neuralgia severe pain along a nerve esp. in the head or face

neurasthenia nervous exhaustion and breakdown

neuritis inflammation of a nerve or nerves

neurology the study of the nervous system

neuron a specialized cell conducting nerve impulses

neurosis emotional maladjustment; a relatively mild mental disorder producing hysteria, anxiety, depression, or obsessive behaviour but not loss of touch with reality

neurotic afflicted by neurosis; tending to be emotionally unstable; excessively anxious or upset

neutral monism the view that both physical and mental phenomena can be explained or analyzed in terms of a single or common substance

neutron a neutral particle, i.e. with no electrical charge, about the same size as a proton and found in all atomic nuclei except those of ordinary hydrogen

newel 1) the central supporting pillar of a spiral or winding staircase 2) the stair-post, top or bottom, of a flight of stairs that supports the handrail, aka newel post

New World monkey an arboreal monkey of Central and South America having widely separated nostrils and a prehensile tail

Nibelung one of the Scandinavian race of dwarfs, and possessors of a hoard of gold and treasure wrested from them by Siegfried

nicety a fine detail or distinction

niche 1) a shallow recess in a wall 2) a suitable position in life or employment

nickelodeon a jukebox

niddering cowardly

nidificate, nidify to make a nest

niggard a miserly, mean or stingy person

niggardly frugal, tightfisted; stingy, miserly

nightjar = **whippoorwill** = **goatsucker** insect-eating bird with large eyes and greyish brown plumage; active at night, it has a characteristic discordant call

nihilism 1) the rejection of all principles, values and beliefs on the basis that they and life itself are all meaningless 2) the philosophical view that nothing has real existence

nihility nothingness

nihil obstat 'nothing hinders' official approval from the R.C. church that a book is not open to objection on doctrinal or moral grounds

Nike the Greek goddess of victory

nil desperandum do not despair

Nile at 4,187 miles is the longest river in the world

nimbus 1) a halo or luminous cloud of glory 2) a dark grey rain-cloud

nimiety the state of being too much; excess

nincompoop a stupid person

Nineveh important city of ancient Assyrian empire on the east bank of the Tigris opposite the present-day city of Mosul in northern Iraq; destroyed 612 b.c.

ninny a silly and weak person

Nippon Japan (in Japanese)

nirvana (*Buddhism*) blissful extinction; any ultimate state of satisfaction

nitid bright, glistening

nitre = saltpetre = potassium nitrate

nival permanently under snow

niveous snowy, snow-like

nobiliary particle a preposition such as *von* or *de* forming part of a title or surname and indicating noble rank

noble gas one which forms compounds only with difficulty or not at all

noble metal one which resists corrosion e.g gold or silver

noble rot a beneficent mould or fungus cultivated on certain white grapes to increase their sugar content and make possible the sweet wines of esp. Sauternes

noblesse oblige noble birth, privilege or rank obliges one to be high-minded, honourable, and generous

noctivagant wandering in the night

nocturnal concerning the night

nocturne a short, romantic, dreamy, musical composition intended to embody sentiments appropriate to the evening or night

nocuous noxious, harmful

noematic intellectual

noesis 1) the mental process by which knowledge is gained 2) the highest knowledge, as of universal forms

noetic to do with the intellect or mental activity

noisette 1) a small, round piece of meat 2) made or flavoured with hazelnuts

noisome offensive, disgusting, malodorous esp. foul-smelling

noli me tangere *Lat.* do not touch, no meddling

nom de guerre *Fr.* an assumed name

nom de plume *Fr.* pen name

nomenclature the terminology used in a particular discipline

nomic relating to the customary way of spelling

nominal in name only; token

nomothetic to do with general scientific laws

nonage the period of a person's immaturity or youth

nonce (**for the nonce**) for the time being, for the present

nonce-word a word coined for a particular occasion, e.g. Puseyite, gigmanity

nonchalant giving an impression of relaxed unconcern or indifference

non compus mentis *Lat.* not in one's right mind; insane

nondescript lacking distinctive characteristics; hard to classify; neither one thing nor another

none when it stands for not one, takes a singular verb: none of the partners is in the office today. Sometimes it = no one, no person, nobody, which also takes a singular verb: none of the bystanders was prepared to get involved. When it means no persons or not any the verb is plural: 1) none in the crowd were willing to take part 2) none of the delegates in the hall were listening to the speech

nonentity insignificant person or thing

nonpareil 1) unequalled, unique 2) an unrivalled person or thing

nonplussed surprised and confused; flummoxed

nosocomical starting in a hospital (of a disease)

nosography the description of diseases

nosology the classification of diseases

nosophobia fear of disease

nostalgia sentimental yearning for the past

nostalgic homesick

nostology gerontology

Nostradamus (*1503-1566*) French astrologer and physician; his two collections of predictions (*1555:1558*) remain the subject of controversy

nostradamus any quack doctor or charlatan

nostratic 1) to do with a hypothetical family of languages: Indo-European, Afro-Asiatic, Dravidian, Altaic, and Semitic, and other languages 2) the postulated ancestral language of this family

nostrum 1) a quack medicine 2) a pet remedy for social or political reform

notional imaginary or theoretical rather than actual

nott-headed, nott-pated having the hair cut bare

noumenal world in the philosophy of Kant, (*1724-1804*) the world as it actually is: cf. the **phenomenal world** which is the world as it appears to our senses

nous common sense

nouveau riche a person of recently acquired wealth esp. one perceived as lacking good taste

novantique new-old

novercal to do with a stepmother

noviciate 1) a novice in a religious order 2) the state or period of being such

noxious harmful, doing harm

noyade execution by drowning

nuance a subtle degree or shade of difference or variation perceived by the senses or the intellect e.g. in meaning, colour, or tone, feeling or expression etc.

nubile (of a woman) sexually attractive

nuciferous nut-bearing

nuciform nut-shaped

nucleus 1) the positively charged centre of an atom 2) the central and most important part of something

nugatory 1) trifling, worthless 2) not valid, inoperative, of no effect

nugget a (small) lump of gold or other precious metal in its natural state

nullifidian (a person) having no faith

nullipara (*adj*. **nulliparous**) a woman who has never given birth

number the number of ... takes a singular verb, a number / any number of ... takes a plural verb

numen a divine force guarding a place, inhabiting a natural object or guiding a person

numinous having a strongly religious or spiritual quality

numismatics the study or collecting of coins, banknotes or medals

nuncupative (of a will) declared orally by a testator, often somebody who is dying – a mortally wounded soldier or sailor or some other fatally injured person

Nuremberg city in Bavaria, venue for the Nazi Party congresses and rallies in the 1930s and the trials of former Nazi leaders after the Second World War

nurture training, upbringing; environment as distinct from heredity

nutant nodding

nymph a mythological spirit of nature imagined as a beautiful young woman

nympholepsy frenzy caused by the desire for the unattainable

nymphomania excessive sexual desire in a woman

nystagmus rapid involuntary movements of the eyeballs

O

oast a kiln/oven for drying hops

Oates, Titus (*1649-1705*) English fabricator of the **Popish Plot**

obbligato a musical accompaniment or instrumental part integral to a composition and not to be omitted in performance

obdurate 1) obstinate, stubborn 2) hardhearted

obeah sorcery from the Caribbean

obeisance 1) deferential respect 2) a bow or curtsy

obese fat, overweight

obfuscate 1) to make obscure or difficult 2) to confuse or bewilder

obi a sash worn with a Japanese kimono

obiter dictum, obiter dicta observations made in the course of a judgment which are not absolutely central to the decision the judge has to make and are not, therefore, legally binding as a precedent

objective *adj.* not influenced by personal feelings or opinions

objure to swear

objurgate to chide

oblate 1) (of a spheroid) flattened at the poles 2) a person living a religious life in a monastery, but not under its vows

oblanceolate (of leaves) shaped like the head of a lance reversed – having a broad rounded apex and a tapering base

oblation an offering to a god – the bread and wine in the Eucharist

oblique 1) slanting 2) not explicit or direct 3) indirect or evasive

obliquity the state or condition of being oblique

oblivious unaware of

obloquy 1) reproachful, censorious language 2) disgrace brought about by this

obmutescence persistent silence, dumbness, loss of speech

obnoxious extremely unpleasant

obnubilate to make dark or obscure

obscurantism opposition to enlightenment and the full facts of something becoming known

obscure dark, indistinct; remote from observation; not well-known; not easily understood

obsequies funeral rites, the burial ceremonies

obsequious displaying ingratiating servility; fawning; falsely humble

obsidian dark, glass-like volcanic rock formed from hardened lava

obsidional, obsidionary pertaining to a siege

obsignate to seal or confirm

obsolescent going out of use

obstetrics childbirth and midwifery

obstipation extreme costiveness

obstreperous boisterous; noisy and resisting restraint or control; aggressively and noisily defiant

obstriction obligation

obstruent (anything) causing obstruction

obtect, obtected (of a pupa) encased in a hardened secretion so that the wings, legs, etc. are held immovably to the body, as in butterfles

obtend to oppose; to allege

obtest 1) to supplicate, entreat 2) to call (a spirit or power) to witness 3) to object or protest

obtrude to impose or force (something) on someone

obtund to dull or blunt, to deaden

obturate to close, to stop up

occupatio
*a rhetorical device whereby one draws attention to
something by claiming an intention not to refer to it;
much used by politicians*

obtuse 1) irritatingly slow to respond, mentally or emotionally 2) not sharp; blunt 3) (of an angle) between 90 and 180 degrees

obverse 1) (of a coin, banknote or medal) the front with the head or principal design on it 2) the opposite or counterpart of a fact or truth

obvert to deduce the obverse of (a proposition)

obviate to do away with; to remove; to make unnecessary

Occident the West

occiput the back of the head

occlude to close up, to block, to stop up

occult *adj. & n.* (involving) the supernatural

occupatio a rhetorical device whereby one draws attention to something by claiming an intention not to refer to it; much used by politicians

ocelot a medium-sized wild cat of Central and South America; valued for its striped and spotted fur

oche the line behind which players must stand when throwing darts

ochlocracy mob rule

ochre 1) an earthy, pale yellow/brown/red clay pigment 2) a pale brownish-yellow colour

Ockham's razor the simpler answer: 'Entities are not to be multiplied unnecessarily' the principle enunciated by the English philosopher, William of

Ockham (*c.1285-1349*), that explanations should be kept as simple as possible and all extraneous matters excluded

O'Connor, Feargus (*1794-1855*) presented the Chartist petition in 1848; charismatic leader or Irish demagogue?

octad a group or set of eight

ocular to do with the eye(s)

oculist an eye doctor, **an opthalmologist**

odalisque a female slave or concubine in a harem

odeum, odeon a music-hall in ancient Greece

Odin *Scand.myth* a one-eyed god

odious arousing hatred, hateful, repulsive

odium widespread hatred or disgust

odoriferous having or giving off a smell

odorous having a distinctive smell

odyssey a long and eventful journey

oedema an abnormal collection of fluid beneath the skin; dropsy

Oedipus complex (in the psychology of Freud) the unconscious sexual impulses of a boy towards his mother and corresponding jealousy of his father

oenologist a wine expert

oenophile a lover of wine

oesophagus gullet

oestrogen female sex hormone that controls the reproductive cycle and develops and maintains female characteristics of the body

oestrus the period of sexual receptivity and fertility in female mammals (not humans); heat

oeuvre the body of work of an artist, composer, or author

offal the entrails and internal parts, (heart, liver, kidneys, tongue etc.) of an animal used as food; garbage, decaying or waste matter

Offa's Dyke frontier entrenchment marking boundary between England and Wales built by Offa, king of Mercia, in second half of 8th century

officinal available without prescription; over-the-counter

officious interfering, meddling; excessively forward in offering one's services or advice to others; intrusive; domineering

offing 1) the part of the sea that is distant yet visible from the shore 2) a position at a distance from the shore **in the offing** in the near immediate future

ogdoad a group or set of 8

ogee gentle curves in the form of a slightly bending elongated S shape

ogle to stare at lustfully, lecherously

-oid suffix indicating likeness, resemblance or similarity – anthropoid, humanoid

okapi a type of giraffe but with a shorter neck; lives in the forests of the Congo

Old World monkey includes macaques, baboons and mandrills; they have nostrils that are close together and nonprehensile tails; more closely related to anthropoid apes than are **New World monkeys**

oleaginous 1) oily 2) smarmy 3) slimily ingratiating

olent *adj.* smelling

olfactory pertaining to smelling, the sense of smell

olid foul-smelling

oligarchy government by a small group of people

oligophrenia feeblemindedness

oligopoly an industry in which the goods and services are provided by very few suppliers

oliguria the excretion of an abnormally small volume of urine

olio 1) a dish of many different ingredients 2) a miscellany

oliphant an ancient, ivory hunting-horn

olitory to do with kitchen-vegetables

olivine a usu. olive-green silicate mineral occurring in basalt and other igneous rocks

olla podrida 1) a stew from Spain, Portugal or Latin America 2) a miscellany

Ollendorff, Ollendorffian an artificial, unnatural, stilted expression of the kind that used to appear in 19th- century, foreign-language phrase books 'Unhand me, sir. I must ask you to desist; my husband is without'.

Olympus mountain in N.E. Greece, home of the gods of ancient Greece where Zeus held court

omertà *It.* a conspiracy of silence esp. within the Mafia

ominous indicating that something bad is going to happen; menacing, threatening

omnipotent all-powerful

omniscient all-knowing

omnium gatherum a miscellany; an assortment

omnivorous 1) feeding on a variety of foods of both plant and animal origin 2) devouring or able to consume or take in everything

omophagia *n.* eating raw flesh

omphalos the centre, the navel

omphalosceptic meditating while staring at your navel

onager 1) A small Asian wild ass 2) a catapult-like machine for hurling rocks in ancient and medieval warfare

onanism 1) coitus interruptus 2) masturbation

oncology the study and treatment of tumours

oneiric to do with dreams

oneiromancy the interpretation of dreams in fortune-telling

onerous burdensome, laborious

onkus 1) unpleasant 2) disorganised

onology foolish talk

onomancy, onomantic divination by names

onomastics the study of proper names esp. personal proper names

onomatopoeia 1) the formation of words which sound like the noise they describe 2) the use of such words – 'swish,' 'pop,' etc.

ontogeny the development of an individual organism

ontology the branch of metaphysics dealing with the nature of being

onus a burden or responsibility

onyx a semi-precious variety of agate with layers of different colours, used as a gemstone

oof money

oofy rich, wealthy

oogamy reproduction by the union of mobile male and immobile female cells *adj.* oogamous

oology the study, collecting of birds' eggs

opacity opaqueness; the condition of not being transparent

opal milky or bluish-white, semi-precious stone with iridescent reflections; reputed to bring bad luck

opalescent showing many small points of shifting colour against a pale or dark ground

opaque cannot be seen through, not transparent or translucent; difficult to understand

operose 1) laborious; tedious 2) industrious, busy

ophidian a snake

ophthalmologist an eye doctor, an **oculist**

opiate 1) involving opium 2) an opium-based drug

opine to hold and state as one's opinion

opossum American possum classified as a marsupial even though it may not have a pouch or merely one that is rudimentary

oppidan *n.& adj.* a town-dweller; to do with a town, urban

oppilation a stoppage, a blockage

opportune favourable, well-timed, convenient

opportunist a person who grasps opportunities, often unfairly

opprobrium 1) public disgrace, ignominy, infamy 2) shameful behaviour that causes this 3) shocked and disgusted condemnation

oppugn to question, to dispute

oppugnant combative, antagonistic or contrary

opsimath a late learner

optative expressing a wish e.g. the **optative subjunctive** Long Live the Queen!

optic relating to the eye or vision

optician a person qualified to prescribe and dispense glasses and contact lenses

optimum, optimal mean most favourable, most advantageous, but tend to be used as synonyms of 'best'

option 1) freedom to choose 2) thing that is or may be chosen 3) right to buy or sell a thing within a set time

optometry examining the eye for defects and prescribing correctional lenses or exercises but not drugs or surgery

opulent ostentatiously rich and luxurious; wealthy; abundant

opus a work; a numbered musical composition

opuscule a minor work

oracular prophetic; involving an oracle, obscure

oracy fluency in speech and the ability to understand it, *adj.* orate

oragious stormy

oral 1) spoken not written 2) to do with the mouth

orarian to do with the coast or shore

oratory the art of public speaking; eloquent speech

orb a sphere, a globe

orbicular, orbiculate, orbiculated circular, spherical

orbilius a flogging schoolmaster – from the name of the Latin grammarian who taught Horace in Rome in the 1st century b.c.; criticized by his former pupil, his name has become synonymous with a strict disciplinarian teacher

Orcadian 1) an inhabitant or native of the Orkney Islands 2) to do with the Orkney Islands

orchestrate 1) to bring different elements into an efficient relationship 2) to organize so as to achieve a desired overall effect

orchidectomy the surgical removal of one or both testicles

ordain 1) to order officially, to decree (that) 2) to confer holy orders on

ordinal number a number e.g. 8th indicating position in a series

ordinance an official order or rule; *N. Amer.* a municipal by-law; a city regulation

ordnance 1) heavy artillery; cannon 2) military supplies 3) the part of government that deals with military supplies

ordonnance the systematic arrangement of a literary or artistic composition or architectural plan

ordure excrement, dung

orectic relating to desires, appetites

oregano a Mediterranean aromatic herb

orgulous haughty, proud

oriel a large upper storey bay with a window – an oriel window – supported by brackets or cords

orient the special lustre of a pearl of the finest quality

Orient the East

orientate 1) to place or decide the position of 2) to familiarise, adapt, adjust to new circumstances

orifice mouth or other opening in the body

origami the Japanese art of ornamental paper-folding

orismology the science of defining technical terms

orison a prayer

ormolu gold-coloured alloy of copper, tin, and zinc, used to decorate furniture, clocks, mouldings, and other articles

ornate elaborately decorated

ornithology the study of birds

orogeny the origin and formation of mountains from the folding of the earth's crust

orography the branch of physical geography that deals with mountains

orotund 1) full, round, imposing, booming (voice) 2) pompous, bombastic, pretentious (writing, style)

orphic mystical or occult

orrery a clockwork model of the solar system

orthodontia, orthodontics dental treatment involving the straightening of crooked teeth and correcting bad 'bites' (malocclusions)

orthoepy the customary, correct pronunciation of words

orthognathous straight-jawed

orthography correct/conventional spelling

orthology the correct use of language

orthometry the correct writing of verse

orthopaedics medical treatment of the skeletal system, esp. the spine, bones, and joints

ortive rising; eastern

ortolan a European bunting, considered a great table delicacy

orvietan *n.* a supposed antidote or counter-poison

Orvieto a white wine from this region in central Italy

oryctérope Fr. an aardvark

oryctics the study of fossils

oryx large long-horned antelope of the dry regions of Africa and Arabia

oscheal to do with the scrotum

oscillate to move back and forth between two points

oscitancy, oscitance, oscitation 1) yawning 2) drowsiness, inattention

osculation = tacnode

osculatory *adj.* kissing

osier willow

osmatic, osmic concerning the sense of smell

osmidrosis = bromidrosis

osmosis absorption, mixing

osprey a large fish-eating bird of prey

ossify *v.tr.& intr.* 1) to turn into bone 2) to make or become inflexible

ossuary a container or room for the bones of the dead

osteal to do with bone

ostensible apparent or seeming

ostensive descriptive of non-verbal definitions or explanations e.g. by directly showing or pointing at something to indicate what is meant

ostentatious characterized by pretentious, showy, or vulgar display; designed to impress

osteomyelitis inflammation of the bone or bone marrow

osteopathy the treatment of medical disorders based on the manipulation of bones or muscle

ostinato a musical phrase or rhythm continuously repeated

ostler a stableman at an inn

ostracize to refuse to have anything to do with, to banish, exclude, expel from a community

otalgia earache

otic to do with the ear

otiose redundant, serving no practical purpose, superfluous

otology the study of the ear and its diseases

oubliette a dungeon with a trap door at the top through which a victim was dispatched

ouistiti a wistit or marmoset

oundy wavy

outlandish bizarre, strikingly unusual, conspicuously unconventional

outré *Fr.* beyond what is usual or proper, over-the-top

outside of although fairly common is considered to be incorrect or non-standard

ovate oval; egg-shaped

overbearing domineering

overt done or shown openly

overweening 1) opinionated, arrogant, conceited 2) immoderate or exaggerated

overwrought in a state of nervous excitement or anxiety; extremely agitated

ovine to do with or resembling (a) sheep

oviparous laying eggs which are then hatched outside the body

ovoid 1) egg-shaped 2) oval

ovoviviparous producing eggs that develop and hatch within the mother's body

ovum the female reproductive egg cell

Oxford comma (aka the serial comma) the optional comma in lists or enumerations before the final *and*; it tends to be included in American but omitted in British usage although it may be necessary to avoid ambiguity: he wrote to the Bishops of Manchester, Birmingham, and Bath and Wells

Oxford movement (*1833-1845*) aka Tractarianism or Puseyism, an attempt by Pusey and others to restore traditional Catholic doctrine in the Church of England; its practices and teaching are upheld in the High-Church wing of the Anglican Communion

oxymel a mixture of vinegar and honey

oxymoron a figure of speech combining two apparently contradictory terms – enjoys bad health; friendly fire

oxytocic accelerating childbirth by stimulating uterine contractions

oysterwench a low woman

ozone pure, fresh air

ozostomia foul breath

Ozymandias 'the king of kings' in Shelley's sonnet (*1817*) of the same name whose statue ends as a broken wreck in the desert sands

P

pabulum 1) food, fodder 2) vapid intellectual fare/entertainment

pacable that can be calmed or quietened; prepared to forgive

pace Lat. with due respect to (a person), despite the opinion of (a person)

pachyderm a very large, thick-skinned, mammal – elephant, rhinoceros, hippopotamus

pacific peaceful

paddemelon, paddymelon a small Australian wallaby

paean a hymn or song of joy and praise

paediatrician a doctor specialising in the treatment of children

paeon a metrical foot of one long syllable and three short in any order

pagoda multi-storeyed Buddhist temple or sacred tower in the Far East, usually pyramidal, with each storey having an upward-curving projecting roof

painterly characteristic of a painter; artistic

paladin 1) one of the legendary twelve peers of Charlemagne's court 2) a chivalrous knight, a knight errant 3) *fig.* a defender

palaeo- old, ancient, prehistoric

palaeography the study of ancient writing systems and manuscripts

palaeontology the study of fossils

palatable acceptable to one's taste or ideas

palatine concerning a palace

paletot a loose three-quarter length overcoat

palfrey a saddle-horse esp. for women

palimpsest 1) something which has been written upon more than once, the previous writing having been rubbed off to make room for the next 2) *fig.* rewriting a (hi)story; reinvention; an object or place that reflects layers of its history

palinal moving backward

palindrome a word or words that reads the same backwards or forwards – *madam*

palinode 1) a poem or song retracting something said in an earlier work 2) a recantation

palisade a fence

palisades *N. Amer.* a line of high cliffs

pall 1) a cloth draped over a coffin 2) a dark covering; a dark cloud 3) to become boring, less appealing or interesting through familiarity

Palladian the style of architecture introduced by the Italian architect Andrea Palladio (*1508-1580*); in London the Banqueting Hall and Lincoln's Inn Chapel are examples

palladium 1) a rare silvery-white metallic chemical element resembling platinum 2) a safeguard, a protection

palliasse a straw mattress

palliate to alleviate or relieve without curing; to make more bearable

palliative (something) relieving or alleviating a problem without dealing with the cause

pallid 1) pale 2) feeble, insipid

palmate shaped like an open hand

palmer a pilgrim

palmiped, palmipede *adj.* web-footed *n.* a web-footed bird

palpable 1) that can be felt or touched, tangible 2) very real, very obvious

palpabrel concerning eyelids

palsy paralysis with involuntary tremors

palter to act or talk insincerely; to equivocate

paludal living or occurring in a swampy, marshy habitat

palynology the study of pollen grains and plant spores – living and fossil

pan- all

panacea a cure-all, a catholicon

panache 1) dashing style 2) a plume of feathers

panaché 1) mixed 2) a shandy

pandect 1) a complete body of laws; a legal code 2) a treatise dealing with all aspects of a subject

pandemic (a disease) occurring over a very wide area

pandemonium wild confusion; uproar

Pandora's box a source of many unforeseen difficulties

panegyric speech or writing of praise; eulogy; encomium

paneulogism indiscriminating eulogy

pang pain

Pangaea the single supercontinent into which all the world's landmass is thought to have been grouped before it began breaking up about 200 million years ago

pangamic of indiscriminate mating

pangenesis a former theory of heredity, that each body cell produces hereditary particles that circulate in the blood before collecting in the reproductive cells

Pangloss, Dr. the eternal optimist philosopher in Voltaire's *Candide* (1759)

panjandrum a pompous, self-important official; one who has, or claims to have, considerable influence or authority

panoply 1) a full suit of armour 2) a striking, impressive display; a splendid array

panoptic taking in everything in a single view

pantechnicon a furniture van

pantheism 1) the belief that God is all things 2) a readiness to worship or tolerate all gods

Pantheon a circular temple in Rome dedicated to all the gods

pantheon 1) a temple for all the gods 2) a group of people – all the 'gods' figuratively and collectively in a certain field or era

panther the black leopard

pantoffle a slipper

pantology universal knowledge

panurgic able to do all kinds of work

panzers heavily armed German troops in the Second World War

papuliferous pimply

parabola a symmetrical curve formed when a cone is intersected by a plane parallel to its side

parabolic to do with a parable or a parabola

Paraclete the Holy Spirit

paradigm 1) an example, a model 2) a set of the inflections of a noun, verb, etc.; a declension, a conjugation

paradox an apparent absurdity or self-contradiction; a combination of contradictory features or qualities

paragoge, paragogue the addition of a sound or syllable to the end of a word – among(st)

paragon a model of perfection

paragram a pun

paralipomena things omitted from a text and added as a supplement

paralipsis a rhetorical device by which one fixes attention on a topic by pretending to ignore it: 'There are many drawbacks to your plan, not to mention the cost'

paralogism reasoning which appears logical but which is, in fact, unintentionally false – compare **sophism**

parameter variable quantity or quality that restricts what it characterizes

paramount chief in importance

paramour lover

paranoia 1) delusions of grandeur or persecution; unwarranted jealousy 2) excessive, unjustified suspicion and mistrust of others

paranormal beyond normal scientific explanation

paranormal, the the supernatural

paraphrase to summarise

parapsychology the study of interactions between minds, and between minds and the physical world; it involves investigation into mental phenomena such as telepathy, hypnosis and life after death; it also extends to extra-sensory perception and its kinetic counterpart, psychokinesis, which may be responsible for poltergeist disturbances and Uri Geller-type movements of and in objects without any apparent physical force

parasuicide attempted suicide not meant to succeed

parataxis, paratactic the placing, side by side of words, phrases, clauses, sentences etc. without explanatory or connecting words; the result is an abrupt, jerky style; the opposite of **hypotaxis, hypotactic**

paravane a device towed behind a minesweeper to cut the cables holding mines in place in the water

parboil to boil until partially cooked

parbuckle 1) a rope arranged like a sling for hoisting or lowering casks, tree trunks or other heavy, cylindrical objects 2) to raise or lower in this way

paregoric a medicine formerly used to relieve pain, diarrhoea and coughing

parembole an inserted phrase modifying or explaining the thought of the sentence – closer to the context than a parenthesis

parenesis persuasion

parenetic, parenetical hortatory

parergon supplementary or subsidiary work

paresis partial paralysis

paresthesia a burning or prickling sensation of the skin in the hands, arms, legs, or feet; temporary paresthesia is widely recognised as 'pins and needles'

pariah an outcast

Parian concerning fine white marble or porcelain

parietal to do with 1) the wall of the body or a body cavity 2) residence in a college and esp. visits from members of the opposite sex 3) prehistoric art on rock walls

pari-mutuel the name first given to the totalitizator form of betting in which those who have bet on the winners of a race share in the total amount wagered after the costs of management, taxes etc. have been deducted

pari passu Lat. 'with equal step', side by side; equally or equivalently; with equal pace, speed, or progress

parish-pump *adj.* parochial, provincial, of local interest only

parity equality

parka a warm, weatherproof, three-quarter length coat with a hood worn by, inter alios, Eskimos and mountaineers

parlance a manner of speaking; speaking in a particular way – *in legal parlance*

parlous perilous, precarious; dangerous

Parnassians a group of French poets of the second half of the nineteenth century (esp. Leconte de Lisle and Gautier) whose emphasis was on traditional verse-forms, impersonal lyricism, restricted emotion and the theory of 'art for art's sake'.

Parnassus a mountain in central Greece associated with Apollo and the Muses; regarded as the seat of poetry

paroccipital near the occiput

parochial 1) relating to a church parish 2) narrow in outlook

parody 1) a mocking imitation of the style of a work ridiculing the habits of the author, composer, etc. 2) something so badly done as to seem an intentional mockery; a travesty

paroemiographer a writer or collector of proverbs

paronomasia a pun; a play on similar-sounding words or phrases which are different in meaning and set in opposition to each other for effect – see e.g. **bells and smells**

paronym a word related to or connected with another word; a cognate

parousia the supposed second coming of Christ

paroxysm a fit

parrhesia boldness of speech

parricide the killing of a parent

parry to deflect

parse to analyze a sentence by breaking it down into its component parts; to deconstruct it

Parsee a Zoroastrian descended from the refugees who settled in Bombay

parsimonious unwilling to spend money; stingy

parteitag party conference (German)

parterre 1) an ornamental garden with paths between the beds 2) *N. Amer.* a theatre pit

parthenogenesis reproduction from an ovum without fertilization; virgin birth

Parthian shot a parting shot, a telling or hostile remark or gesture reserved for the moment of departure

parti pris n. a preconceived opinion; a prejudice; a bias *adj.* prejudiced, biased

partisan loyal to a particular cause, biased

part-song a usu. unaccompanied song with voices singing in harmony, rather than contrapuntally

parturition the act of giving birth; childbirth

parvenu *Fr.* an upstart

paschal relating to 1) the Jewish Passover 2) Easter

pasha, pacha a title (placed after the name) formerly used in Turkey and N. Africa for military leaders and provincial governors

pasquinade a lampoon or satire

passage of arms a fight; a quarrel

passé *Fr.* out of fashion; outdated

passe-partout *Fr.* 1) a master key 2) a simple picture frame

passerine *adj.* perching *n.* a perching bird

passible capable of suffering, feeling

passim *Lat.* here and there, scattered everywhere throughout the text

passle, passel a sizeable number, quite a few

passus a section of a longer medieval poem or story e.g. *Piers Plowman* is divided into several passus of unequal length

pasticcio *It.* musical work compiled from borrowings from elsewhere; a pastiche

pastiche a work that 1) mixes styles or 2) copies the style of another composer, writer, artist, or period

pastoral to do with 1) shepherds 2) (idealized) rural life 3) looking after one's flock (literal or metaphorical)

pastorate 1) an area or office presided over by a clergyman or pastor 2) a body of pastors

patagium wing-like membrane between the fore and hind limb of a bat

Patagonia a vast dry plateau region of southernmost South America, in Argentina (mainly) and Chile, extending from the Andes to the Atlantic; sparsely populated, it is used primarily for sheep and cattle grazing; larger than Texas, it is more than three times the size of the United Kingdom

Patavinity the style of Livy (*59 b.c.-a.d.17*) Roman historian, native of Patavium (Padua), hence provincialism

pate the head esp. the crown of the head

patella the kneecap

paterfamilias the (male) head of a family or household

paternalism an attitude towards somebody in one's charge of a father-type figure, benevolent but authoritarian ensuring their welfare whilst restricting individual freedom and responsibility.

paternity fatherhood

pathetic fallacy (John Ruskin in *Modern Painters* 1856) the attributing of human feelings and emotions to inanimate nature e.g. *the cruel sea*

pathogen any agent – bacterium, virus, or other micro-organism that can cause disease

pathological to do with disease

pathology the study of diseases

pathos evokes sorrow, pity, sadness, compassionate sympathy, concern, tenderness

patina 1) a green or brown film formed on copper and bronze 2) a similar film on other surfaces

patois a regional dialect

patrician a nobleman, an aristocrat; aristocratic; a well-bred person of cultivated tastes

patricide killing of one's father

patrimony property inherited from one's father or ancestor; property or estate which has descended in the same family

patristic concerning the early Christian writers or their work

patristics the part of Christian theology dealing with early Christian writings

patrology 1) patristics 2) a collection of the writings of the early Christian theologians

patronize 1) to treat condescendingly; to adopt a superior manner towards; to talk down to 2) to be a regular customer of 3) to encourage; to act as an active supporter of (a person, organization etc.)

patronymic *n. & adj.* (of) a name derived from the name of a father or ancestor

paucity smallness of number or quantity; scarcity; dearth

pavane, pavan a slow, stately dance

pavid timid, fearful

pavonine to do with a peacock or its tail; peacock-like

pawky drily humorous, sardonic

pawn an unimportant person whose actions are controlled by others

pax *Lat.* peace

payload the part of the load of a vehicle from which revenue is derived; passengers and cargo

payne to exert oneself, to take pains

pecan the nut from the species of hickory tree of the same name

peccable subject to sin; likely to sin

peccadillo a trivial sin or fault

peccant 1) sinning or guilty 2) causing disease

peccavi I have sinned – exclamation of one's guilt

pecking order a hierarchy of status among members of a group

Pecksniff a hypocrite, from the character of the same name in Dickens's *Martin Chuzzlewit* (1843 – 44)

pectoral relating to the chest or breast

peculation embezzlement

pedagogue a teacher esp. a pedantic one; a pedant

pedagogy teaching

pedant one who makes an unnecessary show of learning and attaches exaggerated importance to details of esp. scholarship

peddle to sell (goods) from place to place

pederasty, paederasty anal intercourse between a man and a boy

pedestrian dull, boring, uninspired

pedicular relating to or caused by lice

pedigree lineage

pedology the study of soils

peduncle a stalk

peer group a group of people of approximately the same age, status, and interests

peevish irritable

Pegasus *Gk. myth* the winged horse which arose from the blood of Medusa when Perseus cut off her head

pejorative disparaging, belittling, depreciatory

pelagic 1) to do with the open sea 2) (of fish, marine life) living in the upper waters of the open sea 3) (of birds) inhabiting the open sea, returning to land only to breed 4) (of geological formations) derived from material that has fallen to the bottom from the upper waters of the sea

pelf money acquired dishonestly

pellucid 1) transparent, translucent 2) extremely clear, limpid

Peloponnese southern peninsula of Greece, mountainous, joined to the rest of the mainland by the Isthmus of Corinth

pelt the skin of an animal with the hair, wool, or fur still on it

pen a female swan

penance an act showing sorrow or repentance for sin

penchant a liking, an inclination, a proclivity

pendentive the triangular portion of a dome cut off between two supporting arches at right angles to each other

pendragon a title conferred on an ancient British or Welsh war chief

pendulous hanging down so as to swing from side to side

penguins black and white flightless seabirds of the southern hemisphere – wings used as flippers

penitent feeling or showing regret that one has done wrong

penseroso, penserosa *It. adj.* melancholy; thoughtful

pensile pendulous; hanging down

pentadactyl, pentadactylous having five toes or fingers

pentagon a plane figure with five straight sides and five angles

pentagram a five-pointed star which has associations with magic and mysticism; the conventional representation of a starfish is in the form of a pentagram

Pentecost 1) the Jewish festival of Shavuoth 2) the Christian festival of Whitsuntide

pentecostal 1) relating to Pentecost 2) (in Christian use) emphasizing baptism in the Holy Spirit, evidenced by 'speaking in tongues', prophecy, healing, and exorcism

penultimate next to the last

penumbra 1) partial shadow 2) a fringe area of uncertainty

penurious 1) poor, hard up 2) unwilling to spend money; mean

penury poverty

peon a peasant, a Spanish-American unskilled worker

peotomy the amputation of the penis

pepita a nugget of gold

perambulate to walk about (a place); to stroll

perceive 1) to become aware or conscious of through the senses 2) to regard as

perceptible visible, observable

perception 1) the ability to become aware through the senses 2) the state of being or process of becoming aware in that way 3) the way a person regards something or someone – his or her 'take' on it or them

perceptive observant; having acute insight

percipient sensing, discerning sharply, keenly; perceptive

percolate to filter through

per contra on the other hand, on the contrary

percussion the striking of one body against another; *in mus.* descriptive of instruments (drums, cymbals, etc.) that are played by being struck

percutaneous through the skin

perdition eternal damnation; total ruin

peregrinate to travel or wander about from place to place

peregrination wandering

peregrine a falcon

peremptory 1) urgent or commanding 2) expecting immediate compliance without discussion 3) precluding discussion or debate; decisive; dictational

Pericles
(c.495-429b.c.) Athenian statesman, champion of democracy; promoted the culture of Athens in the golden age of art and letters

perennial lasting an indefinitely long time; appearing again and again, year after year

perestroika *Russ.* restructuring

perfervid particularly fervid; impassioned

perfidy treachery

perforant perforating

performative descriptive of a statement in which the speaker or writer performs an act – 'I resign'

perfunctory merely going through the motions, superficial, routine, mechanical

pergola an arched framework for climbing or trailing plants

peri a fairy

periapt a charm, an amulet

Pericles (*c.495-429b.c.*) Athenian statesman, champion of democracy; promoted the culture of Athens in the golden age of art and letters

periclinal dome-shaped

pericline a dome

perigee the point nearest to the earth in the orbit of the moon or a satellite

perigon an angle of 360 degrees

perihelion the point in its orbit when a planet or comet is nearest the sun

perilune the point at which a spacecraft in lunar orbit is closest to the moon

perinatal just before or after birth

per incuriam inadvertently, carelessly

perineum the area between the anus and the scrotum or vulva

peripatetic travelling around from place to place

peripeteia, peripety a sudden change in a person's fortunes – for the worse in a tragedy, for the better in a comedy

periphery the fringe or edge of something

periphrasis a roundabout way of saying something; a circumlocution

perissodactyla hoofed mammals with one or an odd number of toes on each foot – horses, rhinos, tapirs

perissological having too many words

perissology verbiage

peristalsis the worm-like movement by which the stomach, intestine, and bowels propel their contents

peristaltic to do with peristalsis

peristeronic pertaining to pigeons

peristeropod pigeon-toed

peristyle a row of columns surrounding a space within a building such as a court or internal garden or edging a veranda or porch

perjury lying on oath

perlocution speaking or writing which has an action as its aim but which in itself does not constitute the action, e.g. persuading

perlustrate to survey carefully

permeate to pass or spread through into every part of; to penetrate

permute to change the arrangement, order or sequence of

pernicious extremely harmful, destructive, ruinous, deadly

peroration the concluding part of a speech or written argument summing up what has been said; has overtones of pomposity

perpendicular vertical

perquisite a fringe benefit, a perk

perry an alcoholic drink made from fermented pear juice

perscrutation a thorough searching through

perse dark greyish-blue

per se as such, by or in itself

Persephone *Gk.myth* was abducted by Hades and made queen of the underworld but allowed to leave it for part of each year

perseveration inability to change behaviour; unadaptability

persiflage light, flippant, frivolous talk or writing; banter; raillery

persona non grata Lat. a person who is unacceptable or unwelcome

perspicacious shrewd, astute, discerning, having good judgment, insightful

perspicacity mental keenness

perspicuous easily understood, expressed clearly, lucid

pert 1) saucy, cheeky 2) jaunty

pertain to be relevant; to belong as a part

pertinacious extremely tenacious, stubbornly persistent, often to the point of obstinacy

pertinent relevant

perturb to disturb

perturbation a disturbance, disruption

perturbed made anxious or unsettled

peruke a wig

pervade to spread through, permeate

perverse wrong-headed; irrational; contrary (*kontrairee*); nonsensical; obstinately refusing, opposing or differing from what is reasonable or required

pervert *n.* a person whose sexual instincts deviate from what is considered to be the norm

perverted deviating from correct behaviour or beliefs esp. sexually deviant

pervious permeable; allowing passage through

pesky annoying

pestilence a fatal epidemic disease esp. bubonic plague

pestilent deadly

pestle a club-shaped implement for pounding substances in a mortar

petard a small bomb formerly used to blast into a fortification through a wall, doors, etc. **hoist with one's own petard** – your own scheme backfires on you

Peter principle people are promoted until they reach a level beyond their capabilities

petrel a seabird that flies far from land

Petri dish a shallow, circular, transparent dish with a loose cover, used for growing micro-organisms

petrified paralyzed with fear

petrify to make or become hard like stone; to paralyze with fear

petroglyph a rock carving

petrology the study of rocks

pettifogger 1) a lawyer who handles petty cases and indulges in sharp practice 2) a nit-picker on petty points

pettifogging quibbling about petty points, nit-picking

petto the breast

petulant peevish, irritable, childish

phage = bacteriophage

phalanger arboreal (tree-dwelling) Australian marsupial

Phalangist a member of a Lebanese Christian paramilitary organisation

phalanx a body of troops or police in close formation

phallic relating to or resembling an erect penis

phallocentric focused on the phallus as a symbol of male dominance

phallus an erect penis

phantasm an illusion, an apparition

phantasmagoria 1) a shifting sequence of real or imaginary images as seen in a dream 2) an optical effect which rapidly varies the size of images on a screen

Pharisaic, Pharisaical 1) concerning the Pharisees 2) self-righteous; hypocritical

Pharisee 1) a member of an ancient Jewish sect teaching strict observance of Jewish law and traditions 2) a person concerned more with the outward forms than the spirit of religion; a self-righteous person, a hypocrite

pharmacology the study of drugs

pharmacopoeia 1) a book-list of medicinal drugs 2) a stock of medicinal drugs

pharos a lighthouse

pharynx the throat

phatic *adj.* (in relation to speech) in the nature of general, social, chit-chat intended to 'break the ice' rather than convey any specific information – 'Good morning, how are you?'

phenetic classification the grouping of species according to their similarity of appearance cf. **cladism**

phenocryst a large or conspicuous crystal in a porphyritic rock

phenomenal world see **noumenal world**

phenomenology 1) the study of consciousness and the objects of direct experience (Husserl) 2) the study of phenomena as opposed to the nature of being

phenomenon 1) an occurrence, a fact, a situation 2) any remarkable person or thing

pheromone a chemical scent secreted by an animal, esp. an insect, affecting the behaviour or physiology of others of the same species

phial a small bottle for liquid medicine, a vial

Phi Beta Kappa the oldest fraternity in the United States of university students and graduates chosen on the basis of high academic standing

philander to make love triflingly

philanderer a womanizer, a male flirt

philanthropy the donating of money to good causes

philately stamp collecting

-phile a fondness or liking for

philippic a fierce verbal attack or denunciation; a tirade

philistine an uncultured person

phillumenist a collector of matchbox labels

philo- love of

philogynist one who is fond of or admires women

philology the study of language from a comparative or historical viewpoint

philomath a lover of learning

philomel, philomela a nightingale

philoprogenitive 1) having many offspring 2) loving one's offspring

philosopher's stone the mythical substance sought by alchemists – it was supposed to be able to change any metal into gold

philtre a drink supposed to arouse sexual desire; a love potion

phimosis abnormal narrowing of the opening of the foreskin, which prevents it being drawn back over the tip of the penis

phlegmatic placid, impassive, undemonstrative, emotionally calm

phlogiston a hypothetical substance once thought to be present in all combustible materials and to be released during burning

phocine relating to a seal or porpoise

Phoenicia an ancient country on the shores of the eastern Mediterranean, corresponding to modern Lebanon and the coastal plains of Syria

phoenix legendary Arabian bird, lives for 500 years, burns itself on its own funeral pyre, is then born again and rises from the ashes to live through another cycle – hence the emblem of resurrection and immortality

phoneme a basic and distinct unit of sound in a language that distinguishes one word from another (e.g. in *can, pan, bar, bad,* the *c*, the *p*, the *r*, and the *d*)

phonetic concerning speech sounds

phosphorescent luminous

photic to do with light

photosynthesis process by which green plants use sunlight to convert carbon dioxide and water into complex substances including the food required by animals

phototropism (in plants) orientation or growing towards the light

phratry a clan, a group of clans

phren the thinking principle, the mind

phrenology the now discredited study of the shape and size of the cranium as a supposed indicator of mental faculties and character

phronesis practical wisdom

phrontistery a thinking place

phthisis a wasting disease esp. pulmonary tuberculosis

phylloxera an insect that destroys vines – it wiped out Europe's vines in the 19th century

phylogeny the evolutionary development of a species, genus, or race

phylum a group or category of related things

physiognomy (judging character from) facial features

physiology the study of the normal functioning of living organisms and their parts

phytology botany

piazza large public square in an Italian town

pibroch music for the bagpipes

pica a craving for unnatural food in hysteria or during pregnancy

picador horseman in a bullfight who lances the bull in the neck

picaresque to do with rogues

picaroon a rogue, an adventurer

picayune 1) a small U.S. coin of little value 2) a person or thing of no consequence

pictograph, pictogram a pictorial symbol for a word or group of words as in cuneiform, hieroglyphics, written Chinese, and road signs

piebald spotted or patchy in black and white esp. in relation to a horse

pied-à-terre *Fr.* small flat or room kept for occasional use

pied-noir a French colonial born in Algeria

piety religious devotion

pilfer to steal

pilgarlic(k) 'peeled garlic' 1) a bald head; a man with a bald head 2) a pathetic person

pillage plunder

Pillars of Hercules the opposite rocks at the eastern end of the Strait of Gibraltar: the Rock of Gibraltar and the Jebel Musa in Morocco

pillory *n.* wooden frame on an upright post with holes for the head and hands of an offender holding him for exposure to public ridicule *v.* to expose to public ridicule

pimento 1) allspice 2) pimiento

pimiento a red sweet pepper

pince-nez glasses without sidepieces that are held in place by means of a clip over the bridge of the nose

pincer claw of a lobster or crab

pincer movement attacking an enemy on two flanks

pinchbeck *n.& adj.* imitation gold; cheap, tawdry

pinguid fatty, oily, greasy

pinion 1) the outer part of a bird's wing including the flight feathers 2) to cut off the pinion of (a bird) to prevent flight 3) to immobilize or restrain (someone) by holding or tying their arms or legs

pinking shears scissors with a serrated blade, used to cut a zigzag edge in fabric to prevent fraying

pinna the external ear, the auricle

pinnacle the highest point; a mountain peak

Pinyin transliterating Chinese characters into the Roman alphabet

pipe dream a fanciful or impossible plan or hope

piquant 1) having a pleasantly sharp, spicy or savoury taste 2) mentally stimulating

pique wounded pride, irritation, indignation or resentment from hurt pride or a slight *v.* 1) to excite or arouse (curiosity or interest) 2) to cause to feel resentment or irritation 3) to pride or congratulate (oneself), esp. in respect of a particular accomplishment

Pirandello Luigi (*1867-1936*) Italian dramatist, novelist and short-story writer; recurrent themes in his work are the relativity of truth and the changing personality of the individual; he was awarded the Nobel Prize for literature in 1934

pis aller Fr. a makeshift, a last resort, a stopgap

piscatorial concerning fishing or fishermen

piscine to do with fish; fish-like

pisiform pea-shaped

pismire an ant

pistole an obsolete, esp. a Spanish gold coin

pithy (of language) brief and forceful

pittance a tiny amount

pixilated, pixillated 1) behaving as if led by pixies; bemused; confused; bewildered; whimsical; eccentric; 2) drunk

pizazz, pizzazz an attractive combination of energy, vitality, and style

pizzicato played by plucking (e.g. the strings of a violin)

pizzle the penis of a bull; a whip made from a bull's pizzle

placate to calm, appease, pacify; to change hostility to friendliness

placebo an inactive substance that has no therapeutic properties given to a patient 1) to compare its effects with those of a real drug, or 2) for the psychological benefit to the patient who thinks he/she is receiving treatment

plagiarism passing off as one's own the work or idea of another

plagio- slanting, inclining, at an angle

plagiotropism a plant's growth at an angle to the vertical in response to a stimulus

plaid tartan

plainchant = **plainsong**

plain sailing arguably this might be written in the original nautical way as **plane sailing** on the basis that for short distances navigation could be by a plane chart as if the earth was a flat plane rather than a sphere

plainsong unaccompanied medieval church music

plaintive sounding sad

planchet a plain metal disc from which a coin is made

Planck, Max (*1858-1947*) German physicist who formulated the quantum theory; won Nobel Prize for physics (*1918*)

plangent (of a sound) loud and reverberating with a mournful tone; loud and sad

plankton minute drifting plants, protists and animals on the surface layer of a sea or lake

plantain a type of banana from the tropics

platitude an obvious, unoriginal, trite, banal remark

platonic not involving sex

platyrrhine New World or American monkeys with flattened noses, widely-spaced nostrils and prehensile tails cf. **catarrhine**

plaudits praise

plausible apparently reasonable, believable

plaza a large public square in a Spanish-speaking town

pleasance a secluded part of a garden of a large house

pleasantry a mild joke

pleasantries small talk

plebeian 1) of the lower social classes 2) unrefined 3) one of the common people; a coarse, unrefined person

Pleistocene of the epoch from about 1.6 million to 10,000 years ago

plenary 1) full or complete 2) (of a gathering) attended by all participants

plenitude abundance; fullness

plenipotentiary (a diplomat) with full powers of independent action, binding on his government

pleochroic (of some crystals) showing different colours when viewed from different angles

pleonasm redundancy; using more words than are necessary – *at this moment in time –the surrounding circumstances*

pleroma fullness, abundance; totality

plerophory, plerophoria full conviction

plethora an excess, orig. of blood in the body

plexus a network

pliant pliable, easily bent, flexible, not rigid

plight difficult situation

plosion the sudden, audible release of breath that occurs in the pronunciation of a stop consonant such as *b,d* or *p*

ploy trick or tactic

plumage a bird's feathers collectively

plumb to fathom

plumbism lead poisoning

plumiform feather-shaped

plunder to forcibly steal goods from esp. in time of war or civil disorder; to loot *n.* the action of plundering; property acquired in this way

plutocracy government by the wealthy

plutocrat a person whose power derives from his wealth

pluvial to do with rain

pneuma soul, spirit

pnyx (in ancient Athens) the public meeting place for discussing political matters; the assembly

poco *mus.* a little; rather

poco a poco little by little, gradually

pococurante a careless person; one who is indifferent

pococurantism carelessness; indifference

podagra gout affecting the foot

podiatry chiropody

podium a dais, a small raised platform for a speaker or conductor

Podsnap a pompous, self-satisfied, and self-important man, from the character of that name in Dickens's *Our Mutual Friend* (1864-5)

Podunk a typical, small, one-horse American town – from a place of that name in Hartford, Connecticut

poetaster an inferior, second-rate poet, a writer of poor verse

po-faced having a disapproving, humourless, solemn expression

pogoniate bearded

pogrom an organised extermination of an ethnic group (orig. of Jews in Russia)

poignant arousing sympathy, moving; keenly felt, touching

Pointillism painting with dots developed by the French painter Seurat (*1859-1891*); aka **divisionism**

Polaris 1) a star in the constellation Ursa Minor aka the Pole Star, the North Star 2) a U.S. ballistic missile fired from a submerged submarine

polarize to set at opposite extremes of opinion

polemic 1) a fierce verbal (oral or written) attack on, or defence of, a particular position 2) an argument or controversy *adj.* (also **polemical**) involving dispute, controversy

polemics the practice of disputation

polestar a guiding principle, a standard

policaster a poor, petty politician

poliosis premature greying of the hair

pollard to cut off the top and branches of a tree to promote new growth at the top

pollex the thumb

Pollyanna a cheerful optimist

polony = bologna

poltergeist 'a noisy ghost' who mischievously causes things to go bump in the night and throws objects about

poltroon a spiritless, lazy, good-for-nothing coward

polyandry polygamy in which a woman has more than one husband

polygamy *n.* having more than one wife or husband at the same time

polygeny, polygenism the theory that man evolved more than once, in several places across the earth, from several independent stocks

polyglossia the co-existence of several different national languages within a single culture

polyglot 1) (one who is) able to speak, write in a number of languages 2) (a book) written in several languages

polygraph an instrument that records variations in a person's pulse rate, blood pressure, and breathing rate, used as a lie detector

polygyny the state or practice of being married to more than one wife at the same time

polymath a person of considerable and wide-ranging knowledge or learning

polynomial having two or more names or terms

polyp 1) a sea anemone, a coral 2) a small growth from a mucous membrane as in the nose, usually benign and with a stalk or rounded base

polysemy (polysemic, polysemous) the existence of several possible meanings for a word or phrase

polysyndeton a rhetorical term for the repeated use of conjunctions

polysynthetic descriptive of languages (e.g. Eskimo) in which a single word, by means of affixes, can convey the meaning of phrases or clauses

pomade perfumed dressing for the hair

pome 1) an apple or similar fruit e.g. pear, quince 2) a small silver globe, filled with hot water, on which a priest, at mass, can warm his hands

pommel 1) a knob at the end of a sword-handle 2) the raised front part of a saddle

pomp a magnificent, ceremonial, or dignified display

poncho a cloak, similar to a blanket, with a hole in the middle for the head

ponderous heavy, unwieldy; laborious, dull, leaden

ponerology the doctrine of wickedness

poniard a small dagger with a slender blade

pons asinorum *Lat.* bridge of asses, the angles opposite the two equal sides of an isosceles triangle are equal

pontiff a pope

pontificate to speak in an over-authoritative manner; to adopt a preachy tone

pontine relating to bridges

Ponzi scheme a fraudulent investment scheme in which the payments of quick returns to the first investors are made from money invested by later investors

poop 1) the back, rear part or stern of a ship 2) a raised deck at the back of a sailing ship aka the **poop deck**

Pooterish self-important, bourgeois, narrow-minded and genteel – in the manner of Charles Pooter in *Diary of a Nobody (1892)* by G.& W. Grossmith

popinjay 1) a parrot 2) a fop; a coxcomb; a conceited person

Popish Plot a non-existent plot to murder Charles II of England and replace him with his Catholic brother James; it was a fabrication in 1678 of Titus Oates and others

porangi crazy; mad

porcine pig-like; to do with a pig or pigs

pornocracy the influence of courtesans esp. over the Papal court in the first half of the 10th century; government by whores

porphyry rock containing mineral crystals

portend to give warning that something untoward is likely to happen

portentous 1) warning that something momentous or calamitous is likely to happen 2) pompously solemn

portico a porch or covered walkway with columns supporting the roof; a colonnade

portiere *Fr.* a curtain over a door or doorway

portly plump

portmanteau a suitcase with two compartments

portmanteau word one word that is a blend of two other words – brunch (breakfast and lunch), smog (smoke and fog)

portoise, portlast the gunwale of a boat

portolan a book of sailing directions with charts, descriptions of ports, harbours, and coasts etc.

Portuguese man-of-war a type of jellyfish

poseur one who puts on airs and graces, who behaves affectedly

posey, posy pretentious

posit to put fotward as fact or as a basis for discussion, to postulate opp. to **sublate**

possum 1) an opossum 2) an Australian, New Zealand phalanger or other tree-dwelling marsupial **play possum** to pretend to be asleep, unconscious, or dead

post hoc, ergo propter hoc (*Lat.*) after this, therefore because of this (fallacious reasoning) – one thing follows another but that doesn't mean the second was caused by the first

posthumous occurring, appearing or awarded after a person's death

postiche inappropriately added after the work is finished; (anything) that is artificial, false; sham or pretence; a hairpiece; a false beard or moustache; a section of extra hair attached to a woman's real hair to give it greater bulk or length

postillion (in relation to a team or pair of horses drawing a coach or carriage without a coachman) the rider of the leading nearside horse

postliminy *international law* the right of restoration to their former status of persons and things taken in war

postmodernism a wide-ranging term that has been stretched so extensively across the arts, humanities and adjoining areas that it almost defies description, let alone definition; it is probably best thought of as encompassing anything avant-garde that has occurred since about 1960

postmodernity the way of life in Western society in the early part of the 21st century, reflecting in particular, the changes that have taken place in the workplace and esp. the advances in communication technology – the Internet, videos, Email and mobile phones etc.

postpositive (of an adjective, etc.) placed after the word modified

postulate *v.+ n.* to assume; an assumption

potable drinkable in the sense of non-poisonous; fit to be drunk

potage thick soup

potamic concerning a river or stream

potamology the study of rivers

potassium a soft, silver-white reactive metallic chemical element of the alkali / metal group

potassium nitrate a chemical compound used in gunpowders, fireworks, fertilizers and as a preservative for foods, esp. meats

potation 1) the act of drinking alcohol 2) an alcoholic drink

poteen whiskey distilled illegally in Ireland

Potemkin a sham; from the Potemkin villages named after the Russian army officer who erected them to impress Catherine the Great on her tour of the Crimea in 1787; it was claimed that they were mere facades

potent very powerful

potentate a monarch or ruler

pot-pourri 1) a mixture of dried, sweet-smelling, flower petals and herbs preserved in a vase to perfume a room 2) a mixture, a miscellany, a medley

potsherd a piece of broken pottery esp. one found on an archaeological site

pourriture noble Fr. noble rot

pox 1) a viral disease 2) syphilis

praepostor, prepostor a prefect or monitor at some British public schools

pragmatic practical as distinct from theoretical

pragmatics a field in linguistics involving the study of language from the viewpoint of the users

prandial to do with a meal

prank a practical joke; a mischievous trick

prankster one who plays pranks

prate to talk inconsequentially and at length

prater one who prates

prattle to chatter meaninglessly esp. in a foolish or childish way

pravity wickedness

praxis 1) practice as distinct from theory 2) usual practice or custom

praying mantis a grasshopper-like insect with a triangular head that waits motionless for prey with its forelegs folded like hands in prayer

precarious risky; insecure; perilous

precedence priority in order of rank

precedent an earlier case serving as an example or guide to be followed

precept a command, an order, a rule of conduct

précieuse the French equivalent of **bluestocking**

preciosity *n.* affectation, over-refinement esp. in language or manner *adj.* **precious**

precious stones pieces of mineral of great value esp. when used in jewellery; the four minerals traditionally regarded as precious stones are the ruby, the emerald, the diamond, and the sapphire, usefully collated under the acronym 'reds'

precipitant rushing abruptly

precipitate 1) *v.* to cause to happen prematurely 2) *adj.* hasty, rash, temerarious

precipitous like a precipice – very steep *(used only to describe physical conditions)*

précis a summary

precocial (esp. in relation to birds) having young that can feed themselves within a few days of hatching

precocious having developed or matured early or too soon

precular a beadsman

precurrent running forward; antrorse

predatory preying upon others

predicate 1) to base, to establish, to found 2) to assert (something) about the subject of a sentence or a proposition

predicative (of an adjective or other modifier) after the noun, in the predicate

predilection a preference, a partiality (for)

preemptive, preemptory doing something which makes action by an opponent pointless or impossible

prefigure to be an early indication or version of

prehensile (of an animal's tail or limb) capable of curling round objects and grasping them

prelapsarian *adj.* before the fall of humankind; innocent and unspoilt

prelate a high-ranking church dignitary – a cardinal, bishop, (all cardinals are now bishops), abbot or prior

premise, premiss a proposition on which an argument is based or from which a conclusion can be drawn

premonition (premonitory) (having) a strong feeling that something (unpleasant) is about to happen; presentimental

preoccupied engrossed in thought and inattentive to other matters

preponderance superiority in number, weight, or power

prepossessing attractive, pleasing

preposterous utterly absurd or ridiculous

prepuce 1) the foreskin of the penis 2) the fold of skin surrounding the clitoris

Pre-Raphaelite 1) a member of the school of painting founded in 1848 by D.G. Rossetti and others; they objected to the slick, sentimental, dark and murky style of Victorian art and wanted a return to the simple naturalism of the Italian painters who lived before Raphael (*1483-1520*) 2) (of women) having long auburn hair and pale skin

prerequisite a precondition

prerogative a right or privilege

presage *n.* a portent; an omen; a presentiment *v.* to be a sign or warning of something imminent

presbyter a church elder esp. of the Presbyterian Church

Presbyterian (in relation to a church) governed by elders, all of equal rank, e.g. the Church of Scotland

prescient having prior knowledge, knowing beforehand

prescribe to lay down as a rule or guide

prescription 1) a note from a doctor to a chemist verifying the medicine to be issued to a patient 2) basing a legal claim on long usage or custom

prescriptive 1) to do with the imposing of a rule for correct usage 2) legally established by long usage or the passage of time

presentiment a premonition (of misfortune), a foreboding

presentment the act of presenting; a presentation

prestidigitation conjuring, sleight of hand

prestigious highly regarded; the earlier sense of 'involving illusion, magic, or trickery' is now considered archaic

presumptuous taking liberties; overfamiliar; overconfident

pretension the asserting of an unsupported claim

pretentious claiming or demanding distinction or merit etc. to a greater extent than is warranted

preterition *n.* passing over, omitting

preternatural beyond what is natural – supernatural, unnatural

prevail to predominate; to hold sway

prevalent current, widespread in a particular area at a particular time

prevalid excessively strong

prevaricate to be evasive, to equivocate, to temporize

prevenancy complaisance; willingness to please others or accept their behaviour

prevenient preceding, coming before

previse to predict, to foresee, to forecast

priapic 1) phallic 2) having a persistently erect penis

priapism persistent erection of the penis

prig a smug, self-righteously, correct person who affects superior culture, morality, etc.

prima donna a leading female opera singer

prima facie *Lat.* at first sight; at first blush

primate 1) a bishop, archbishop 2) a lemur, bushbaby, tarsier, marmoset, monkey, ape, human

prime number a number divisible only by itself or 1, such as 2,3,5,7 and 11

primeval, primaeval belonging to the first age or ages of history

primigravida a girl or woman who is pregnant for the first time

primogeniture the state of being the first-born, and the corresponding right to inherit a deceased parent's entire estate

primordial existing at or from the beginning

primus inter pares Lat. first among equals

prince of the blood a son or grandson of a British monarch

pristine in its original condition

privatdocent (formerly in German-speaking countries) a lecturer paid by the students rather than the university or college

privateer 1) a privately-owned, armed ship, commissioned by a government to seize and plunder an enemy's ships 2) the commander of such a ship 3) one of its crew

privation the loss or lack of the necessities of life

privy to, to be to share in the knowledge of (information not generally available)

probate the official proving of a will

probity honesty, integrity, decency

proboscis long, flexible trunk or snout, as of e.g. an elephant, tapir

procephalic to do with the front of the head

proclivity a tendency, an inclination

procrastinate to put off doing something, to delay

procreation the reproducing of the species

Procrustean ruthlessly enforcing uniformity

Procrustes' bed victims of Procrustes (in Greek legend) were put on an iron bed; if longer than the bed, he trimmed off the overhanging bits; if shorter, he stretched them until they fitted it; hence, 'to place on Procrustes' bed', is to attempt to impose uniformity on people or things

proctology medical treatment of the anus or rectum

proctor 1) a university official with disciplinary functions 2) an invigilator at an exam in North America 3) generally, one who manages the affairs of another

procumbent lying face down; prone; prostrate

prodigal 1) wastefully extravagant; a squanderer 2) lavish; abundant

prodigious remarkably or impressively large

prodigy a usu. young person with exceptional abilities

proem a preface or preamble to a book or speech

profane contemptuous of anything sacred or holy *v.* to treat something sacred with irreverence

profanity swearing

profectitious from an ancestor

profess to claim one has (a quality or feeling)

profit à prendre
a right to take away something capable of ownership
from the land of another person; grass and herbage
(pasture); fish (piscary); wood (estovers)

proficiency competence, skill in using or doing something

profit à prendre a right to take away something capable of ownership from the land of another person; grass and herbage (pasture); fish (piscary); wood (estovers)

profligate 1) wasteful, extravagant, spendthrift 2) given over to loose living; dissolute

progenitive having reproductive power

progenitor 1) direct ancestor 2) originator, founder of a political, intellectual, or artistic movement

prognathous, prognathic having a projecting lower jaw or chin

prognosis a forecast or prediction

prognosticate to foretell, to prophesy

projective test any psychological test in which the respondent is asked to respond to vague material which projects unconscious ideas; the replies, when interpreted, are thought to reveal hidden aspects of the subject's personality

prolate (of a spheroid) having a polar diameter longer than the equatorial one cf. **oblate**

prolegomenon a critical or discursive introduction to a book

prolepsis 1) 'a flashforward' in storytelling 2) describing a future event as if it had already happened – *he was ensnared as soon as he stepped on the* *trapdoor* 3) anticipating and answering objections before they have been made *adj.* **proleptic**

proletarian (a member) of the working class

proletariat the working class

proliferate to reproduce rapidly; to increase rapidly in number

prolific highly productive; plentiful

prolix long-winded, wordy

prolusion a prelude

Prometheus *Gk.myth* stole fire from heaven; as a punishment Zeus had him chained to a rock where an eagle fed each day on his liver which, because he was immortal, grew again each night; freed by Hercules

promiscuous having many casual, sexual relationships

promontory a point of high land jutting out into the sea; a headland; a cape

promulgate to proclaim; to publish; to promote publicly

pronate to turn the palm downwards

prone 1) lying on the stomach with the face down 2) having a tendency towards something

propaedeutic introductory

propagate to breed or reproduce from parent stock

propensity an inclination or tendency

prophecy is the noun – a prediction

prophesy is the verb – to foretell, to predict

prophylactic 1) (a medicine) intended to prevent or protect against disease 2) *N. Amer.* a condom

propinquity nearness; proximity

propitiate to make (someone) well disposed; to win or regain the goodwill or favour of (somebody); to appease them

propitious favourable; boding well; auspicious

proponent a person who puts forward a theory, proposal, or project

propound to put forward (an idea, theory etc.) for consideration

propriety appropriateness, correctness esp. concerning standards of behaviour or morals

pro rata in proportion, proportionately

prorogue to discontinue the proceedings of a legislative body without dissolving it

prosaic dull

proscenium the very front part of a stage between the curtain and the auditorium

proscribe to prohibit, to outlaw

proselytize to convert, or attempt to convert (somebody) from one faith to another

Prosit! Good Health! Cheers!

prosody study of poetry

prosthesis an artificial body part

prostrate lying facedown

protagonist 1) the leading character in a literary work esp. a drama 2) the prime mover in some cause; purists claim there can be only one protagonist in relation to any one matter

Protagoras 5th-century b.c.. Greek sophist thinker who is remembered for his proposition 'Man is the measure of all things'; sharply criticized by Plato

protanopia colour blindness from insensitivity to red light

protasis (in a conditional sentence) the clause containing the condition

protean able to change shape or form; variable, versatile, adaptable, having the qualities of *Proteus* the Greek sea god who was able to change shape at will

proto- the first, the original

protocol 1) the codes of expected behaviour in any given situation i.e. the rules of conduct, the etiquette, and the formalities observed on official occasions or in relation to any procedure or group 2) the original draft of a diplomatic document esp. a treaty

proton a particle charged with positive electricity found in the nucleus of an atom

protrude to stick out

protuberant swelling out from the surrounding surface; bulging

proud projecting slightly from a surrounding surface

Proudhon P.J. (*1809-65*) Fr. socialist philosopher and writer, remembered for his famous assertion 'la propriété, c'est le vol' q.v.

provection the transfer of the final consonant from a word to the beginning of the next

provenance source, origin

provender dry food for horses; animal fodder

provincial to do with a province; unsophisticated; narrow-minded

provocateur a troublemaker

prow the front of a ship; the bow

proxemics the study of the amount of space people and animals set between themselves and others

proximity nearness, closeness

prunier a plum tree

prurient having an obsessive interest in sexual matters; sexually longing

psalter book of Psalms

psephology the study of elections, voting patterns, etc.

pseudonym a pen name; a fictitious name esp. one adopted by an author

psi the 23rd letter of the Greek alphabet, a composite consonant transliterated as ps

psittacine to do with parrots; parrot-like

psoriasis a skin disease which causes red, scaly patches

psychedelic 1) relating to drugs esp. LSD that cause hallucinations and apparent expansion of consciousness 2) having vivid colours and complex patterns similar to those experienced during hallucinations

psyche the soul; the spirit; the mind

psychosis severe mental derangement resulting in delusions and loss of contact with external reality

psychotherapy the treatment of mental disorders

ptarmigan a type of grouse

pterodactyl an extinct flying reptile

ptisan barley water

ptochocracy rule by paupers or beggars

ptochogony the production of beggars – wholesale pauperisation

Ptolemy ancient Egyptian dynasty

Ptolemy 2nd- century Greek astronomer who asserted the (spurious) geocentric view of the cosmos, which was adopted as Christian doctrine but superseded by the sun-centred works of Copernicus

ptosis the drooping of the upper eyelid

pubescence the start of puberty

pubescent having reached puberty, the period during which adolescents attain sexual maturity and become capable of reproduction

puce deep red to brownish-purple

puckish playfully mischievous, impish

pudency modesty

pudendum usu. in *pl.* **pudenda** the external female genitals

puerile childish, juvenile

puerperal to do with childbirth

pugilist a boxer

pugilistic to do with fist fighting

pugnacious eager to fight, argue or quarrel; combative by nature

puissant powerful

pulchritude beauty

pullulating 1) budding, sprouting 2) breeding rapidly or abundantly 3) teeming, swarming

pulmonary to do with the lungs

pulses (the edible seeds of) vegetable-type plants such as peas, beans, lentils – pulses are produced in pods

puma a large American wild cat, aka *panther*, *cougar*, *mountain lion*

pumice a light porous stone used mainly for removing hard skin

Punchinello Punch of the Punch and Judy show

punctilious precise, meticulous, painstaking in attention to detail

punctuated equilibrium the notion that evolution proceeds mainly in fits and starts rather than gradually at a constant rate

pundit a learned Hindu scholar; a person with an authoritative political view

pungent 1) having a sharp, strong taste or smell 2) (of remarks or humour) biting, caustic

pupa a chrysalis – the stage of a butterfly or moth between larva (caterpillar) and imago (adult)

purblind partly blind

purchase firm contact or grip

purdah the screening of muslim or hindu women by curtain or by clothing that conceals them completely

purgatory 1) *R. Catholic doctrine* place or state of spiritual cleansing of those who have to expiate venial sins before going to heaven 2) place or state of intense but temporary suffering 3) *fig.* agony, hell

purge to purify or cleanse (used in a variety of contexts)

purlieu a neighbouring area; outskirts; environs

purloin to steal

pursuivant 1) a follower or attendant 2) the lowest grade of officer of the College of Arms, ranked below a herald

purulent relating to or containing pus

purview scope, range, extent

Puseyite a follower of Pusey, one of the leaders of the Oxford Movement

pusillanimous lacking courage; faint-hearted; cowardly; timid

pustulant (an agent) causing the formation of pustules

pustule a small blister or pimple containing pus

pustulous producing pus, containing pus

putative supposed, assumed, generally considered or reputed to be

putrescent rotting

putsch an attempt by a political group or faction to overthrow a government

Pygmalion king of Cyprus, made a statue of a beautiful woman and fell in love with it; Aphrodite gave it life and the woman bore the king a daughter, Paphos

Pyramus Babylonian youth, lover of Thisbe; their tragic story is found in Ovid and *A Midsummer Night's Dream*

pyretic to do with fever

pyrexia fever

pyrite a type of iron ore resembling gold aka 'fools gold'

pyrosis heartburn

pyrotechnics 1) fireworks 2) a firework display 3) a brilliant or spectacular display

pyrrhic 1) (in relation to a victory) hollow, pointless, meaningless because the losses of the winner are too great to make victory worthwhile 2) a metrical foot of two short or unaccented syllables

pyx a box at the Royal Mint in which specimen gold and silver coins are deposited to be inspected annually

Q

qua as; in the capacity of; by virtue of being

quadrille 1) a square dance 2) a card game

quadriplegia paralysis from the neck down

quaff to drink with gusto, heartily

quagmire 1) a soft, swampy area of land that gives way underfoot; a bog 2) a complex or difficult predicament

Quai d'Orsai a street on the left bank of the Seine in Paris in which the office of the French Foreign Minister is located

quail a type of partridge but smaller

quaking 1) (esp. of the earth) shaking or trembling 2) shuddering with fear

qualm misgiving, doubt, hesitation due to conscience

quantify to express or measure the size of

quantum leap, quantum jump a sudden large increase or advance

quantum meruit *Lat.* as much as he has earned, the price to be paid for services when no amount was agreed

quantum valebant *Lat.* as much as they were worth, the price to be paid for goods supplied where no price was agreed

quaquaversal pointing out in all directions from a common centre

quarantine isolation of people or animals from abroad to prevent the spread of disease

quark a former hypothetical subatomic particle now known to exist

quarl a jelly-fish, a medusa

quarrel a square-headed arrow or bolt for a crossbow or arbalest

quarrender a kind of apple

quarter mercy shown to an enemy

quarter day(s) one of the four days in the year on which annual rent is to be paid and on which some tenancies begin and end

quarterings the coats of arms on a shield divided by horizontal and perpendicular lines, denoting the alliances of the family

quartz a hard, glossy, colourless mineral also used as a gemstone

quasar a star-like celestial object that is the source of intense electromagnetic radiation

quasi- seemingly; being partly or almost

quatrain (in poetry) a four-lined stanza or verse

Queen's evidence evidence for the prosecution given by a participant in the crime being tried

quenelle a small, seasoned ball or roll of pounded fish or white meat mixed with egg and sometimes breadcrumbs

querulous complaining

queue 1) a pigtail 2) *N. Amer.* a line

quicksilver 1) liquid mercury 2) moving or changing rapidly and unpredictably; mercurial

quiddity the essential nature of a person or thing

quidnunc a gossip, a busybody

quid pro quo something given or received in exchange for something else; in law consideration, – the essential element of a contract that is not by deed or under seal

quiescent in a state or period of inactivity

quietus death considered as a discharge or release from life

quincunx five objects arranged with one at each corner of a rectangle or square and the fifth in the middle

quintessence 1) the most perfect representation of a quality or state 2) an extract of a substance containing its central nature in its most concentrated form

quip a witty remark made on the spur of the moment

quire 25 sheets of paper; one twentieth of a ream

Quirinal one of the seven hills on which ancient Rome was built

quirk an oddity; a peculiar behavioural habit

quisling a traitor who collaborates with an occupying enemy; a fifth-columnist

qui vive, on the qui vive on the alert, on the lookout

quixotic like Don Quixote, absurdly chivalrous, impractically idealistic

Qumran the Dead Sea Scrolls were found in caves in 1947 at this site on the northwest shore of the Dead Sea

quodlibet 1) a theological or philosophical question for scholastic debate 2) a medley of popular tunes

quoin an external corner of a wall or building

quondam former

Quorn a vegetable protein – a substitute for meat

quorum the minimum number of people attending a meeting, needed to allow business to proceed

quotidian daily; everyday; ordinary; commonplace

R

Rabelaisian characteristic of the works of the French humorist and satirist, Rabelais *(c.1494-1553)* witty, eloquent, and colourful but often coarse

rabid 1) fanatical 2) to do with or having rabies

rabies a fatal, infectious, viral disease transmitted mainly by dogs; it results in the common name for the disease, hydrophobia (fear of water) as well as excessive salivation, convulsions, and paralysis

rack rent a market rent at the going rate, a full but not an extortionate or exorbitant rent

raconteur a storyteller

racy 1) slightly shocking 2) spirited and lively

raddle 1) red ochre (for marking sheep) 2) to colour with this or with rouge

raddled run-down, haggard, unkempt in appearance

radicate deeply rooted

radix root

raffish unconventional, slightly suspect, disreputable in an attractive manner

ragout a stew

raillery good-natured teasing, banter

raiment garments, attire, clothing

raison d'être the reason, justification or purpose for someone or something's existence

rake 1) a dissolute man in society; a roué 2) a slope, an angle 3) to direct (gunfire) along the length of a line of (a target)

rakish dashing, jaunty, somewhat dissolute, raffish

rallentando *mus.* gradually slowing down

ramate having branches

rambunctious rumbustious; boisterous

ramifications consequences

ramify to form branches, to branch out

rampant 1) unrestrained 2) unchecked 3) *her.* after the noun (an animal) standing on its left hind foot with its forepaws in the air and head in profile *(lion rampant)*

rampart a defensive embankment or wall around a fort, castle or city, with a broad top usu. surmounted by a walkway and parapet

rana the genus of the frogs

ranarium a place where frogs are reared

rancid (of decomposing food), foul-smelling, foul-tasting

rancour bitterness, hate, resentment

rank *adj.* 1) complete, utter, total, absolute 2) having a foul smell 3) growing too thickly

rankle to cause annoyance, to annoy

rant 1) to speak, shout, or write at length in a wild, impassioned way 2) a spell or piece of ranting

ranunculus a type of plant that includes buttercups, and crowfoots

rapacious extraordinarily greedy, greedily taking by force

rapport a close and harmonious relationship

rapprochement *Fr.* the return to a harmonious relationship

rapscallion a rascal, rogue

rara avis *Lat.* 'rare bird', someone or something uncommon, unusual or exceptional

rarefied 1) (of air) of lower pressure than usual; thin 2) very esoteric or refined

rascasse, la *Fr.* scorpion fish

ratel honey-badger

ratify to give formal consent to; to make officially valid

ratiocination reasoning esp. the oversubtle variety; the process of thinking logically

rationale the reasons or logical basis for a course of action or belief

rationalise to find reasons to justify or explain one's actions or attitudes

ratissage, le Fr. raking

ratite a bird unable to fly – emu, kiwi, ostrich

ratline a step on the rigging of a ship like a rung on a ladder – one of the small ropes fastened horizontally across the shrouds

raucous (of sound) loud and harsh; rough and boisterous

ravage to cause extensive damage to; to devastate

ravages damage, the destructive effects of something

ravenous extremely hungry

raze, rase to demolish, to flatten, to level

razzia a raid

reach an uninterrupted stretch of water on a river

reactionary opposing radical, political, or social change

reader a university lecturer immediately below a professor

ream 500 sheets of paper

reason is because... and **reason why** are tautologies; the notion of explanation is already implicit in 'reason'. In 'The Charge of the Light Brigade' ' their's not to reason why' is an instance of reason being used as a verb. The unexceptionable construction is 'The reason... is that'

rebarbative repellent, ugly

rebuff to snub; a snub

rebuke to criticize or reprove; a reproof

rebullition a renewed effervessence

rebus the representation of words by pictures or by combinations of pictures and letters

rebut to deny and give evidence or argument in support cf. **refute**

recalcitrant stubbornly disobedient, uncooperative

recant to renounce, to repudiate (publicly) a former opinion, belief or statement

recapitulate to summarise and state again the main points of; to repeat in concise form

recede to go or shrink back; to become more distant; to slope backwards

received pronunciation standard British English pronunciation of educated people in southeastern England

recension a revision of a text

rechabite teetotaller

recherché known only to connoisseurs; rare; rarefied or elegant; refined; much sought after

rechignement Fr. crabbedness

recidivist a habitual criminal, a repeat offender

reciprocal both given and received

reciprocity exchanging things with others for mutual benefit

recluse a person who lives alone and avoids people; a hermit

recognizance pledge made to a law court or magistrate; surety for this

recondite abstruse; little known; obscure

reconnaissance preliminary survey, exploration of an area for military purposes

reconnoitre to make a reconnaissance

recoup to regain (something lost or spent)

recreant 1) cowardly 2) a coward 3) an apostate

recrement refuse; waste matter; dross

recrimination an accusation in response to one from somebody else

recrudesce to break out again after a dormant period; to recur – the sense should be restricted to undesirable or unpleasant events

rectilinear, rectilineal in a straight line, relating to straight lines

rectitude morally correct behaviour

recurrent occurring repeatedly

recursant *(her.)* turned backwards, (of an animal) with its back toward the viewer

recusant a refuser, a rebel, formerly a Roman Catholic who refused to attend the services of the Church of England

recuse to challenge (a judge or juror), to reject; to refuse *adj.* **recusative**

recuse oneself to excuse oneself from judging a case because of a possible lack of impartiality

recussion the act of beating back, striking back

redact to prepare (something) esp. to edit, revise for publication

redeem 1) to make up for 2) to reinstate (oneself) in someone's good opinion 3) to free (humanity) from sin by the death of Christ on the Cross 4) to buy back 5) to pay off (a loan or debt) 6) to convert (bonds or shares) into cash 7) to exchange (coupons) for goods 8) to fulfill a promise

redemption 1) the act of redeeming 2) the state of being redeemed 3) deliverance from sin through the incarnation and death of Christ 4) recovery of something that has been pawned or mortgaged

redivivus brought back to life; reborn; returned to life

redolent 1) reminiscent, evocative, suggestive (of) 2) smelling (of) 3) fragrant, aromatic

redoubt a military defensive structure

redoubtable formidable; to be feared and respected

redound 1) to contribute (to) 2) to rebound (on or upon)

redress to remedy or set right

reductio ad absurdum *Lat.* proving the falsity of a proposition by showing its logical consequence is absurd or contradictory

reductive 1) making lower in status or rank 2) (in the arts) ignoring the possible complexities, significance, and meaning of a work by interpreting it narrowly and simplistically; presenting something in a simplified form

redundancy (in the literary context) using more words than necessary: it includes both tautology and pleonasm although some say all three mean the same *adj.* **redundant** no longer needed or useful; superfluous esp. as regards employment because of lack of available work

reedy like a reed, weak, thin, slender; (of a tone or voice) shrill; thin and high-pitched

refectory dining-room in a college or monastery

refectory table a long narrow dining table

reflective thoughtful

refocillate to revive

Reformation, the 16th-century movement for the reform of abuses in the Roman Church resulting in the establishment of the Reformed and Protestant Churches

refraction the bending of light waves, radio waves

refractory 1) stubborn, unmanageable 2) *med.* not responding to treatment (of a condition) 3) hard to work, resistant to heat (of a substance); hard to melt or fuse

refragable resistible; refutable

refulgent radiant, shining very brightly

refute to deny and prove (a statement) to be wrong cf. **to rebut**

regale to entertain lavishly or with stories and conversation

regenerate *adj.* reborn, renewed spiritually or morally

regicide the killing of a king

rehash to reuse (old ideas or material) in a slightly different form but without significant change or improvement

Reichstag the German parliament building in Berlin

reification the fallacy of regarding an abstraction as a material thing

reify to treat an abstract concept as if it was something concrete or permanent

reimburse to repay, to refund

reincarnation the coming back to life of a soul in another body

reins the kidneys

reiterate to repeat

rejoinder an answer, a reply, a retort

relegate to put in a less important position

relent to become less severe or more lenient

relevé *Fr.* next course after the soup at dinner

relief standing out from the surface, to a greater **(high relief)** or lesser **(low relief)** extent

reliquary a receptacle, repository or shrine for holy relics

remeant coming back

remiss negligent

remit *n.* a task or area of activity

remonstrate to protest or object forcefully

remove *n.* 1) a notional degree of remoteness or separation 2) (at a formal dinner) a dish to be changed while the rest of the course remains on the table

remplissage Fr. padding

Renaissance, the revival or 'rebirth' of art and letters in Europe during 14th / 16th centuries; began in Florence

renal to do with the reins or kidneys

rendition a rendering or performance of a dramatic, musical, or artistic work

renegade a deserter, a rebel or outlaw, one who has changed allegiance, a turncoat

renege to fail to keep a promise or agreement

reniform kidney-shaped

renitence, renitent resistance to pressure; disinclination

renounce (*formal*) to give up

rentier a person whose income comes from property and investments

rep fabric with a corded surface used for curtains and upholstery

repartee 1) a quick, clever, witty reply or retort in conversation 2) the ability to make such retort 3) conversation characterized by such retorts

repast a meal

repeal to revoke or annul (a law)

repeater a watch or clock that strikes again the previous hour or quarter-hour at the touch of a spring

repêchage a contest in which the runners-up in the eliminating heats compete for a place in the final

repercussions results, effects

repertoire the body of pieces known or performed by an artiste or company

repertory the performance by a company of the plays, operas, and ballets in its repertoire

repine to be discontented; to fret

replicate to reproduce; to duplicate; to make an exact copy of

repoussoir *Fr.* a strong piece of foreground (which gives depth to a picture)

reprieve 1) to cancel or postpone the punishment of 2) to abandon or postpone plans to close (something)

reprise 1) a repeated passage in music 2) a repeated performance of something 3) *v.* to repeat (a piece of music or a performance)

reprobate an unprincipled person; a rogue

repugnant 1) extremely distasteful; unacceptable 2) incompatible; inconsistent

repulsive disgusting

reredos a screen or wall decoration behind an altar

residuum a chemical residue

resigned accepting what seems inevitable

resilient readily recovering from difficulty

resolute bold and determined, constant in pursuing a fixed purpose

resonance a sounding back, an echoing; **resonate** to evoke a recognized feeling, to strike a chord, to ring a bell

resonant 1) sounding again 2) (of sound) deep, clear, and continuing to sound or ring 3) evoking or suggesting enduring images, memories, or emotions

respite a short period of rest or relief

resplendent dazzling, brilliant with colour or decorations

restaurateur a restaurant proprietor, restaurateur does not have an 'n' – not even in French

restive restless; resistant to control or discipline; refusing to keep still or silent

Restoration, the the re-establishment of the monarchy in England in 1660 on the accession of Charles II as king

resumé 1) a summary 2) *N. Amer.* a curriculum vitae

retard to delay; to make something late, delayed; to hold back the development or progress of

retch to make as if to vomit; to heave

retching ineffectual vomiting

retex to annul

reticle a network of fine threads or lines in the focal plane of an optical instrument to help accurate observation

reticulate *v.* to divide or be divided into a network or small squares *adj.* **reticulated**

reticule 1) a woman's network bag with a drawstring 2) a reticle

retiform net-like

retorsion retaliation

retort a sharp, angry, or witty reply

retract to withdraw; to draw back

retribution revenge

retroussé Fr. turned up at the end (a nose)

revanchism foreign policy based on revenge or the regaining of territory

revehent carrying forth; taking away

reveille a military wake up call usu. on a bugle

revel in to gain great pleasure from; to enjoy or relish

revelry noisy, unrestrained merrymaking

revenant one who returns esp. from the dead; a ghost

revendicate, (revindicate) to reclaim, to demand the restoration of

reverberate 1) (of a loud noise) to be repeated as an echo 2) (of a place) to appear to vibrate because of a loud noise 3) to have continuing serious effects

revere to have great respect for; to worship

reverie daydream(ing)

revetment a retaining wall

revile to criticise abusively

revindicate to revenge; to avenge

revirescence a return to a youthful or flourishing, vigorous state; renewal of youth or vigour

Reynard a literary name for a fox

rhabdomancy divining by the use of a rod esp. for underground water or minerals

Rhadamanthine *adj*. stern and incorruptible in judgment in the manner of Rhadamanthus, a judge in the underworld in Greek myth.

rhea large flightless S. American bird similar to, but smaller than, an ostrich

rheic relating to rhubarb

Rhemish from or to do with Rheims

Rhenish concerning the river Rhine

rhesus a monkey

rhetoric impressive and persuasive language, often oratory, to create an effect; now frequently used pejoratively to imply insincerity

rhetorical question a question to which no answer is expected but is used to make a statement for dramatic effect

rheum a watery discharge from the eyes or nose

rhinal concerning the nose

rhinestone an imitation diamond

rhinoceros large, heavily-built mammal with very thick skin, a massive body, three digits on each foot and either one or two horns on the nose

rhinology the branch of medicine concerned with the nose

rhinoplasm plastic surgery of the nose

rhizome a horizontal underground stem or root

rhopalic verse verse in which each succeeding word contains more syllables than the preceding word or each line is a foot longer than the previous one

rhumb line an imaginary line which cuts all the meridians at the same angle

rhyparographer a painter of genre or still-life pictures, esp. of low subjects

rialto a market or exchange (after the Rialto, the business centre of medieval Venice)

riant laughing, smiling

ribald humorous in a coarse, obscene way

rictus a fixed, unnatural gaping grin or grimace

rident laughing, grinning

rife widespread

rigescent growing stiff

rigmarole a lengthy and complicated procedure; a long, rambling story

rill a brook, a small stream

rime frost

ringer someone or something that looks very like another

riparian to do with the banks of a river

ripon, rippon a spur

riposte 1) a retort, a quick, clever reply 2) a quick return thrust in fencing

risible laughable; prone to laughter

risotto an Italian dish of rice, cheese, vegetables, meat, or seafood

risqué slightly indecent, indelicate, coming as a bit of a shock

rissole a compressed mixture of minced cooked meat and spices coated in egg and breadcrumbs and fried

rites of passage rituals or events marking an important stage of an individual's advance through life, e.g. marriage

riven split

rivet a short metal pin or bolt

Roanoke Island off the coast of North Carolina, is the site of the first attempted English settlement in America in 1585

roborant 1) tending to fortify, strengthening 2) a fortifying medicine; a tonic

rocaille decoration involving elaborate ornamentation with pebbles and shells

rocking-stone = logan, logan stone

rococo a term in the arts descriptive of the style which followed, and is similar to, baroque but which is lighter, more delicate, less ponderous, not as grand

and more detailed; often used negatively to signify something tasteless or pretentious, it has no specific significance in literature; in *mus.*

rode an anchor rope or chain

rodeo an exhibition or contest of cowboy skills

rodomontade boastful, bragging words or behaviour

rogue *adj.* 1) viscious and solitary – a rogue elephant 2) showing an undesirable variation from a standard esp. a cultivated plant 3) taking a rebellious stance; maverick *a rogue trade union*

roil 1) (of a liquid) to move in a turbulent manner; to make (a liquid) turbid by disturbing the sediment 2) *N. Amer.* to anger, annoy or irritate

roistering *adj.+ n.* merrymaking noisily

rollicking 1) *adj.* romping and frolicking, revelling 2) *n.* a reprimand, a bollocking

rollmop a rolled uncooked pickled herring fillet

roman-à-clef Fr. a novel in which real persons or events are depicted with invented names

Romanesque of or in the style of western European architecture from the 9th to the 12th century, i.e. rounded arches and massive walls

roman-fleuve a novel or sequence of novels dealing with the fortunes of a family over a prolonged period

Roman holiday entertainment or enjoyment at the expense of the suffering of others, orig. a holiday given for a gladiatorial combat

Roman nose a nose with a high bridge

Romanov the dynasty that ruled in Russia from 1613 until 1917

Romany 1) a Gypsy 2) the language of the Gypsies

rook 1) a type of crow 2) a cheat 3) to cheat

rookie an inexperienced newcomer

Rorschach test a personality test requiring the interpretation of a number of unstructured ink blots

rorty rowdy, roistering

roscid dewy

roscoe a revolver, a pistol, a handgun

Rosicrucians a secret occult society dating from the 17th century

rosin resin used esp. for rubbing on the bow of a violin or other stringed instrument

Rosinante a thin, worn-out old horse belonging originally to Don Quixote

rossignol nightingale

roster a list showing turns of duty or leave for individuals in an organisation

rostrum 1) the snout of an animal; the beak of a bird; the beak or curved prow of a ship 2) a platform

rota a list of duties to be done or people to do them in rotation

rote learning by heart, by memory without thought of the meaning

rotund (of a person) round or plump

rotunda a round building or room esp. one with a dome

roué a debauched man usu. an elderly one

roundelay a short simple song with a refrain

round robin 1) a tournament in which each competitor plays in turn against every other 2) a petition esp. one with signatures written in a circle to conceal the order of writing

rout an overwhelming defeat

roux a mixture of fat (esp. butter) and flour used in making sauces

royalty 1) money paid for the use of a patent or to an author or composer for each copy of a book sold or for each public performance of a work; a payment made by a producer of minerals, oil, or natural gas to the owner of the land 2) people of royal blood or status

rube *N. Amer.* a country bumpkin

rubella German measles

Rubenesque (of a woman) plump and attractive – like the women portrayed by Rubens *(1577-1640)* the Flemish painter

rubescent turning red, blushing

Rubicon, to cross the to take a step from which there is no going back

rubicund having a ruddy complexion

rubiginous rusty, rust-coloured

rubric (written in red) a direction with regard to a set procedure; a heading on a document

ructation *n.* belching; eructation

ruction a rumpus; a disturbance; a loud fight

rudaceous (of rock) made up of fairly large fragments

ruddock the robin redbreast

rudimentary 1) basic 2) immature, undeveloped

rue to regret

rueful feeling regret or sorrow

rufescent reddish

ruff a projecting starched collar or frill worn round the neck in the 16th and 17th centuries

rumbustious boisterous, unruly

ruminant an even-toed hoofed mammal of a type that chews the cud – cattle, sheep, antelopes, deer, giraffes

ruminate 1) to think deeply about, to ponder 2) (of a ruminant) to chew the cud

rummage to search through

rumpus an uproar, an angry dispute

rune 1) any of the letters of the earliest Teutonic alphabet; each letter was believed to have a magical significance 2) an obscure piece of writing using mysterious symbols *adj.* **runic**

rupture a break, breaking, or breach

Ruritania imaginary kingdom in south east Europe, the setting for the romantic adventure novels of the English writer Anthony Hope

ruse a trick, a stratagem

russet reddish-brown

rustic relating to the countryside

rut a recurrent period of sexual excitement and activity in certain male ruminants such as deer, goats, sheep, etc.; it corresponds to the period of oestrus in females

S

sabbatical paid leave orig. granted to university lecturers

sable 1) type of weasel with valuable dark brown fur 2) black

sabot a clog

sabotage wilful damage to machinery or materials, or disruption of work

sabre a cavalry sword

sabre rattling the display or threat of military force

Sabrina Roman name for the river Severn; also its poetic name – see Milton *Comus* (1637)

sabulous sand-like in texture; gritty

saccade 1) a small, rapid, jerky movement of the eye as it jumps from one point of fixation to another e.g. in reading or looking through the window of a moving train 2) a sudden jerk given to a horse on the reins

saccharine sugary, excessively sweet; over-polite or sentimental

sacerdotal to do with priests, priestly

sack to plunder and partially destroy (a place)

sacral to do with 1) sacred rites 2) the sacrum – the triangular bone at the bottom of the spine between the two hip-bones of the pelvis; aka the holy bone because it was used in sacrifices and it was thought the soul resided there

sacred cow something considered to be above criticism – a reference to the cow being held sacred by Hindus

sacrilegious disrespectful towards something considered sacred

sacristan the person in charge of a sacristy

sacristy a room in a church where the sacred objects, vestments, etc. are kept and where the clergy can get changed and prepare for the service

sacrosanct sacred, very holy and not to be harmed

sadist one who derives peasure from inflicting pain on others

sagacious showing great wisdom, very wise

sage 1) an aromatic plant with grey/green leaves used as a culinary herb 2) a wise man

salacious unduly interested in sexual matters; lewd, erotic; lustful

salad days one's raw youth

salamander an amphibian resembling a lizard or newt; once thought able to withstand fire

salchow (in figure-skating) a jump of one or more full turns in the air – named after the Swedish skater Ulrich Salchow *(1877-1949)*

salebrous rough, rugged

Salesian to do with the Roman Catholic educational religious order named after St. Francis of Sales

salicylism poisoning caused by an overdose of aspirin or other drug containing salicylic acid

salient standing out conspicuously, prominent

salientian a frog, a toad, an anuran

salivate to produce saliva

sallow (of a person's face or complexion) sickly yellow

salmagundi 1) a mixed dish of chopped meats, anchovies, eggs, and onions 2) a mixture, a miscellany

salmis *Fr.* a stew of roasted game

salmonella (a bacterium that causes) food poisoning

salon piece chamber music, light music for the drawing-room

salsify a European plant with a long, tapering, edible root used as a vegetable

saltant *adj.* leaping, dancing

saltation *n.* 1) leaping, jumping 2) a sudden transition 3) an abrupt evolutionary change

saltationists those who believe that evolutionary changes happen suddenly not gradually

saltatorial, saltatory *adj.* 1) leaping, dancing 2) relating to saltation

saltire a diagonal cross in heraldry

saltpetre potassium nitrate used for preserving foods and as a constituent of gunpowder and fertilizers

salubrious 1) healthy; health-giving 2) (of a place) pleasant; not run-down

salutary having a beneficial, albeit unpleasant, effect

salutation a greeting

salutatory to do with a greeting or salutation

salvage 1) to rescue (a ship or its cargo) from loss at sea 2) to save from loss or destruction

salve 1) a soothing ointment 2) something that soothes 3) to soothe

salver a tray

salvo 1) simultaneous firing of guns a) in battle b) as a salute or c) on a ceremonial occasion 2) sudden outburst of e.g. applause, criticism

sal volatile smelling-salts

samizdat Russian (formerly) clandestine publishing of banned writings in the former Soviet Union and the communist countries of eastern Europe

samovar a Russian tea urn

sampler a piece of needlework with different stitches to demonstrate the skill of the embroiderer

samsara Sanskrit the endless cycle of birth, death, and rebirth

samurai a member of a powerful military order in feudal Japan

sanctimonious affecting to be morally superior, holier-than-thou

sanction 1) to authorise, approve 2) a penalty imposed on a country

sanctity sacredness, holiness

sanctum sacred place esp. a shrine in a temple or church; a person's private room

sang-froid *Fr*. coolness; composure; calmness esp. under strain

sanguinary involving much bloodshed

sanguine confident, cheerful, optimistic

Sanskrit the ancient, classical, literary language of India

sap a trench

sapere aude *Lat*. dare to be wise

Sapir-Whorf hypothesis
the theory that the language we speak determines
what we can think and how we see the social and
material world; the conditioning effect of the mother
tongue is summed up in the title of a book by
Frederic Jameson 'The prison-house of language';
aka **linguistic relativism**

sapid savoury, tasty

sapient wise

Sapir-Whorf hypothesis the theory that the language we speak determines what we can think and how we see the social and material world; the conditioning effect of the mother tongue is summed up in the title of a book by Frederic Jameson 'The prison-house of language'; aka **linguistic relativism**

saponaceous to do with soap, soapy; unctuous, smarmy

sapor taste, flavour

saporous giving a taste or flavour

sapper 1) one who digs saps; a military engineer who lays or detects and disarms mines 2) (in the British army) a soldier in the Royal Engineers

Sapphic 1) relating to Sappho 2) lesbian

sapphire 1) bright blue 2) a transparent precious stone typically of that colour

Sappho Greek lesbian poetess of the early 7th century b.c. from Lesbos

saprostomous having foul breath

saprotroph fungus or bacterium that lives and feeds on dead organic matter

saraband a slow, stately old Spanish court dance

Saracens Arab Muslims esp. those who opposed the eight Crusades in the 11th – 13th centuries

sarcophagus a stone coffin which was thought to eat the flesh of corpses

sardonic bitterly, cynically humorous; mocking

Sargasso Sea a large area of the North Atlantic between latitude 20 degrees and 35 degrees N. and longitudes 30 degrees and 70 degrees W.. Ocean currents sweep clockwise round it, leaving its centre relatively still

sartorial relating to men's clothing, tailoring

Sassanian relating to or a member of the last native Persian dynasty that ruled from the early 3rd century a.d. until driven out by the Arabs in the late 7th century

Sassenach a Scottish word for an English person

sat, sitting 'I was sat there' is non-standard usage for 'I was sitting there'

sate to satisfy fully

satiate to provide with more than enough

satrapy (in ancient Persia) a province ruled over by a provincial governor – a satrap

saturnalia wild revelry

saturnine gloomy; (in appearance) dark and brooding

satyagraha passive resistance orig. in India by Gandhi against British rule

satyr a sylvan deity, part man, part beast (goat or horse) and very lustful

satyriasis an insatiable appetite for sex in men, corresponding to nymphomania in women

sauerkraut a German dish of chopped, pickled cabbage

saugrenu Fr. absurd, preposterous, ridiculous

saurian to do with lizards, lizard-like

sauté fried quickly in a little hot fat

sauve qui peut Fr. a stampede, a panic lit. save (himself) who can

savannah grassy plain of drier tropical and subtropical regions, with few trees

savant, savante a person of great learning, a sage

savate French foot boxing

savoir faire *Fr.* the ability to know what to say or do in any situation

savour (regarding good food or drink) to appreciate and enjoy to the full; to taste or smell with enthusiasm or relish

savoury *n.* a piquant or salty flavour esp. as an appetizer e. g. olives *adj.* 1) salty, spicy, sapid 2) wholesome, respectable

savvy shrewdness

saw a saying, maxim or proverb

sawbones a surgeon or doctor

scabbard a sheath for the blade of a sword or dagger; a sheath for a gun, other weapon or tool

scabrous 1) rough, (as if) covered with scabs 2) salacious, indecent, indelicate 3) scandalous, squalid and nasty

scallion a shallot or spring onion

scalloped in the form of a ribbed fan-shaped shell

scamp to skimp, to do something without thoroughness

scan 1) to look at quickly for relevant features or information 2) to analyse (verse) by examining the rhythmic structure 3) to examine closely 4) to traverse with a detector or an electromagnetic beam to obtain an image

scant barely sufficient

scapegrace a rascal, a scoundrel

scapula shoulder blade

Scaramouch a boastful coward – a stock character in Italian comedy

scarlet pimpernel a small annual plant with scarlet flowers closing in rainy or cloudy weather

Scarlet Pimpernel the assumed name of the hero of a series of novels (first published in 1905) by Baroness Orczy; a dashing, elusive English nobleman, he led a band of young Englishmen pledged to rescue the innocent victims of the French Revolution

scathing (of criticism) very severe

scatology 1) the scientific study of excrement, fossilized dung 2) a preoccupation with excrement, obscene literature, etc.

scatophagous feeding on dung

scaturient gushing like water from a fountain

scavenge 1) to search for anything usable among discarded material 2) to feed on decaying or discarded matter

scelerate, scelerous wicked, villainous

scend the upward movement of a vessel caused by a wave

sceptical unwilling to believe, doubting, questioning

scesis onomaton 1) a sentence constructed only of nouns and adjectives (usually in a regular pattern) 2) a series of emphatic, synonymous, repetitive, expressions

schadenfreude *Ger*. enjoyment of another's misfortune; gloating

scherzo a brisk, lively or playful instrumental musical passage forming part of a longer composition or movement e.g. a symphony or sonata

schilderwald *Ger*. a forest of signs

schism a split

schist slate; rock that can be split into thin layers

schizocephaly the practice of Maoris and others of preserving the heads of warriors

schizoid a socially inept, inadequate personality type with a mild form of schizophrenia

schlemiel an unlucky, bungling type who is easily victimised; a misfit

schlep 1) to drag 2) to do something when it's a drag 3) a drag

schlock shoddy, cheap, inferior goods

schmaltz exaggerated sentimentality

schmean to bribe, a bribe

schmuck a stupid, clumsy person

schnapps a strong alcoholic drink resembling gin

schnorrer a sponger, a beggar, a scrounger

scholium an explanatory note written in the margin of an ancient text by a scholiast (a commentator)

schooner 1) a sailing ship with two or more masts 2) a large glass for sherry 3) a tall beer glass

schtick, shtick an entertainer's esp. a comedian's act or routine

schtum, to keep to keep quiet, to say nothing

sciagram a picture or photograph made up of shadows or outlines

sciagraphy, skiagraphy the art of drawing shadows esp. the use of shading in technical or architectural drawing

sciamachy, skiamachy a fight with shadows or an imaginary enemy

sciatheric to do with a sundial

scienter *Lat.* knowingly, willfully

scilicet namely; that is to say

scimitar a curved sword that broadens towards the point, used originally in Eastern countries

scintilla a spark, hint, iota, trace, least amount

scintillate to sparkle

sciolism superficial knowledge, a smattering; holding forth on a subject about which one has only superficial knowledge

sciolist one who affects to be more knowledgeable than he actually is

sciomancy divination through consulting ghosts

scion 1) a young, usually male, member of a distinguished family 2) a shoot of a plant cut for planting or grafting on to another plant

sciophyte any plant that grows best in the shade

sciopticon a type of magic lantern

scissible, scissile that can be cut

scission a split, a division

sciurine to do with squirrels; squirrel-like

sclerosis hardening

sclerotic paralysed; rigid

scold a nagging, complaining, tiresome woman; a shrew

sconce 1) a bracket fixed to a wall for holding candles or lights 2) a small fortification or earthwork

scorbutic to do with scurvy

scoria 1) the frothy lava from a volcano 2) slag obtained from molten metal during smelting

scoriaceous pertaining to scoria

scorn contempt

scornful contemptuous

scortatory pertaining to lewdness

scotch to put an end to

scotoma a blind spot

scourge 1) a whip 2) a person or thing causing great trouble or suffering 3) to whip; to cause great suffering to

scree accumulated stones on the side of a mountain, on a hillside, or at the base of a cliff, aka **talus**

screed an overlong, monotonous speech or piece of writing

screw a propeller

scrim *N. Amer.* a transparent curtain that conceals or obscures

scrimshank to shirk, to skive

scrimshaw 1) to engrave designs on shells, whalebone, whales' teeth, ivory, etc. 2) anything engraved in this way

scrip paperwork indicating entitlement to stocks and shares

scrip issue a bonus issue of shares

scripopholy collecting share certificates and bonds as a hobby

scrivener a clerk, scribe, or notary

scrobe a groove in the rostrum of weevils or curculios

scrobiculate having grooves, furrows; pitted

scrofula a form of tuberculosis causing glandular swelling

scrotum the pouch of skin containing the testicles

scrumptious very appetizing or delicious

scrumpy rough, strong cider from the west country of England

scruples doubts about the morality or propriety of an action

scrupulous very conscientious or careful

scrutiny careful, minute examination

scry to foretell the future using a crystal ball

scuba an aqualung – from the acronym of **s**elf-**c**ontained, **u**nderwater, **b**reathing **a**pparatus

scud 1) to move swiftly in a straight line as driven by the wind 2) spray, rain, or clouds driven by the wind

scullion a menial who works in a kitchen, washes dishes etc.

scumble to soften the effect of a colour or line in a painting or drawing by applying a thin coat of opaque colouring

scuncheon the inner part of a door jamb or window frame

scurrilous (of language) vulgar, obscene, coarse, abusive

scut a short tail (of hare, rabbit, deer)

scutate shaped like a round shield; covered in scales

scutiform shaped like a shield

scuttle 1) to cause (a ship) to sink by making holes in the sides or bottom 2) to ruin (hopes or plans) 3) *N. Amer.* to abandon

scuzzy squalid; sordid; sleazy; disgusting

Scylla *Gk. myth* six-headed female monster who devoured sailors trying to navigate the narrow channel between her cave on the Italian side of the Strait of Messina and the whirlpool of Charybdis on the Sicilian side – two dangers such that to avoid one increases the risk from the other

séance *Fr.* a meeting of spiritualists at which attempts are made to make contact with the dead

sear 1) to scorch the surface of; to brand with a hot iron; to cauterize 2) to cause to wither or dry up

sebaceous fatty

sebaceous glands the minute glands in the skin which secrete oil to lubricate the skin and the hair

sebastomania religious insanity

sebum the oily secretion of the sebaceous glands

sec *Fr.* (of wine) dry

secability the capability of being divided

secco painting on dry plaster with pigments mixed in water

secede to withdraw formally from membership of

second-guess 1) to guess what is going to happen 2) to criticize or calculate with hindsight

secondment the temporary transfer (of a worker) to another position

second-order theorizing making theories about theories

secretaire an escritoire; a writing-desk

sectarian relating to a usu. religious group regarded as extreme in its beliefs or practices

secular 1) worldly; not religious, sacred or spiritual 2) occurring over a long period of time

securiform axe-shaped

sedate *v. & adj.* 1) to calm down or make sleepy 2) quiet, calm, and dignified; slow, unhurried

sedative *n.& adj.* (a drug) that has a soothing, calming, somnolent, or soporific effect

sedentary *adj.* sitting

sedition speech, writing or action encouraging rebellion against the government

sedulous steadily persevering, assiduous, diligent

sedulous ape, to play the to model one's own writing as closely as possible on the style of another writer

see the diocese of a bishop or the place within which his cathedral is situated

seemly *adj.* proper, fitting, suitable, appropriate

seethe to boil

segregate to separate

segue (in music and film) to move smoothly from one section or piece of music to another without pause or interruption

sehnsucht Ger. a yearning, a longing

seicento the style of Italian art and literature in the 17th century

seigniorage profit made by a government by issuing currency

seine a large net for catching fish

seismic to do with earthquakes

seismology the science of earthquakes

sejant sitting

selachian *n. & adj.* (relating to) sharks, rays, dogfish, skates

selatian *n. & adj.* a subclass of fish that includes sharks and dogfish

selcouth seldom known, rarely encountered

self-abnegation the denial of one's own interests in favour of others

self-aggrandizing the boosting of one's own ego and interests

self-deprecating tending to disparage oneself; modest

selva an equatorial rain forest in the Amazon basin

selvage, selvedge the nonfraying edge of a length of woven fabric

semantics the study of the meanings of words

semaphore a system of signalling by holding two flags in two different positions to represent letters of the alphabet

semblance the outward appearance of something

semester six months, a half-year course or term

seminal 1) to do with seed or semen 2) foundational 3) influential

seminary a college for the training of priests

semiology the general science of signs

semiotics the study of signs and symbols, their use or interpretation

semitic refers to the descendants of Shem, – Jews, Arabs, Aramaeans, Assyrians and others; today the term is used to describe the Jews

semoted separated; remote

sempiternal endless; everlasting

senesce to grow old

senescence old age

senescent growing old, elderly, aged

seneschal the steward or major-domo of the house of a medieval lord

senile old

senna 1) a Cassia tree, shrub or plant 2) a laxative made from its dried leaves and pods

sennight a week

senocular having six eyes

sensibility the ability to appreciate and respond to complex emotional or aesthetic issues; sensitivity

sensory to do with the 5 senses

sensual involving physical esp. sexual gratification

sensuous to do with the senses rather than the intellect; in practice the distinction between these last two entries is often ignored and they are used interchangeably

sententia Lat. an aphorism or maxim

sententious pompously moralizing esp. by the use of terse, pithy sayings, platitudes, or proverbs

sentient feeling, perceiving through the senses

sentinel a sentry

sepal one of the green leaf-like outer parts (the calyx) of a flower in bud

Sephardi a Jew of Spanish or Portuguese descent

sepia 1) the inky fluid secreted by the cuttlefish, or a brown pigment obtained from this 2) dark reddish-brown, similar to the colour of old photographs

sepsis putridity, rot; the presence of harmful bacteria

sept a clan

septicaemia blood poisoning

sepulchral 1) to do with a tomb or burial 2) gloomy; dismal

sequacious 1) disposed to follow others in a slavish, unquestioning way 2) following in logical sequence and regularity

sequelae symptoms or effects which are liable to follow certain diseases e.g. bronchitis after measles

sequester to seclude, set apart, isolate

sequestrate to seize, to confiscate

seraglio a harem

seraph (*pl.* **seraphim**) a member of the highest order of the nine orders of angels

serendipity the knack of making happy discoveries by chance

serial comma = Oxford comma

seriatim one after another

sericulture the breeding of silkworms

serif the short cross-line at the ends of printed letters – H compared with H

serigraph a printed design produced by means of a silk screen

sermonize to give a speech or write a piece that, like a sermon, assumes an air of moral superiority over the listener or reader

serpentine twisting and turning like a serpent or snake; tortuous; sly, treacherous

serranid, serranoid the family of heavy-bodied predatory fishes which includes the sea- basses

serration a series of teeth, points, or notches, as on a saw

serried arranged in a close series; standing close together

serum 1) the watery part of blood which separates out when clotting takes place 2) whey

servile 1) too eager to serve or please others 2) of or characteristic of a slave or slaves

sesquipedalian 1) (of words) long, having many syllables 2) given to using long words 3) a polysyllabic word 4) a user of such words

sessile 1) having no stalk or peduncle (of flowers or leaves) 2) fixed in one place; immobile (of an organism e.g. the barnacle)

seta a bristle

setaceous bristle-like; bristly

setiferous, setigerous having bristles

sett the burrow of a badger

Sèvres the fine porcelain made at this town near Paris

sextant 1) an optical instrument used in navigation and surveying for measuring angular distances and taking altitudes 2) the sixth part of a circle

sexton a person who looks after a church, its property and churchyard and who may also act as bell-ringer, gravedigger etc.

shade a ghost

shades the departed spirits, or their abode, Hades

shagreen 1) sharkskin used as an abrasive or as a decorative covering 2) untanned leather with a rough surface

shaman a priest-doctor of shamanisim, a tribal religion of various peoples of northern Asia and Native Indians of north-west America

shanghai to force to join a ship's crew

Shangri-La an imaginary paradise on earth

shanks's pony *n.* walking

shard a piece of broken pottery, glass etc.

shebang a thing, matter, or situation

shebeen an illegal drinking den

shechita the Jewish religious slaughter of animals

shelduck, sheldrake (the male) a large duck, usually brightly-coloured

shibboleth 1) a distinctive trait associated with a particular group which sets the group apart but which is now regarded as outmoded 2) orig. a test-word for detecting Ephraimites who could not pronounce "sh" (Judges xii. 4-6)

shicker drunk, a drunk

shiksa a non-Jewish girl or young woman

shillelagh an Irish cudgel of blackthorn or oak

Shintoism the ancient national religion of Japan

shivaree *N. Amer.* a noisy mock serenade to newly-weds

shoal 1) shallow water 2) a sandbank visible at low water

shogun the military ruler in feudal Japan (till 1867)

short shrift rapid and unsympathetic dismissal; curt treatment; little time between condemnation and execution or punishment

shrew a turbulent woman, a scold; a bad-tempered, nagging woman

shrine 1) a place of worship hallowed by association with a sacred person or object 2) the tomb of a saint or other holy person 3) a reliquary 4) an alcove containing a holy image 5) a place or site venerated and visited because of its history or association with a famous person or event

shrinkage the loss of merchandise in a retail store due to shoplifting

shrive 1) to hear a person's confession 2) to confess one's sins to a priest

shroff to separate out counterfeit currency from the genuine

shroud a sheet in which a corpse is wrapped for burial; something that envelops or obscures

shrouded enveloped in darkness

shtoom silent

sib 1) a sibling 2) a blood relation

sibilant hissing

sibling a brother or sister

sibyl prophetess

sic transit gloria mundi
so passes away the glory of the world;
a reference to the fleeting nature of human vanities

sibylline prophetic

siccative a substance used to accelerate the drying of certain liquids – paints, inks, etc.

sic 'thus' a word used after a quotation to show that, lest it be thought that the quotation has been misprinted, it is here printed exactly as in the original

sic transit gloria mundi *Lat.* so passes away the glory of the world; a reference to the fleeting nature of human vanities

sidereal to do with the stars

siderodromophobia the fear of trains

sidle to move sideways or edge along esp. stealthily or furtively

Siegfried or **Sigurd** a hero in Germanic and Norse mythology

Siegfried Line a line of defences built by the Germans along their western front opposite the Maginot Line, prior to and during the Second World War

sienna a yellowish-brown type of clay used as a pigment in painting

sierra a long jagged mountain range

sigmoid shaped like the letter S

signal striking, remarkable, outstanding

signet a person's seal used with or without a signature

silage any green crop compacted and stored in airtight conditions for use as food for livestock

silica a hard, glossy mineral which occurs naturally as quartz and is used in the manufacture of glass

silicon a brittle, non-metallic element used in transistors, solar cells and alloys

silicone a durable synthetic resin used in oils, water-repellents, adhesives, and prosthetic replacements for bodily parts etc.

silo 1) an airtight pit or tower used to store silage or grain 2) an underground chamber for housing a guided missile

Siluria the ancient name for the south-eastern part of South Wales

silvan = sylvan

silver bullet a simple solution to a complex problem

simian to do with or resembling monkeys or apes

simile a figure of speech in which one thing is likened to another thing of a different kind – *as tall as a tree*

simoniac one who practises simony

simon-pure real, authentic, genuine

simony dealing, trafficking in ecclesiastical privileges, e.g. advowsons, pardons, etc.

simpatico similar in attributes or interests; having like mind or temperament; likeable; compatible

simper to smile in a silly, self-conscious, affected manner

simplistic treating complex issues as simpler than they really are

simulacrum a likeness, a semblance, an image

simulate to imitate; to feign; to pretend

sinapi mustard of Egyptian origin

sinapism mustard plaster, a medical application containing mustard

sinecure employment with little or no work to do; a cushy job

sine die Lat. (of a court hearing etc.) adjourned indefinitely without a date being fixed

sine qua non 'without which not' *n.* a thing which is totally indispensable

sinew the strong fibrous tissue connecting muscle to bone; a tendon or ligament

single stick 1) a wooden stick used instead of a sword for fencing 2) fencing with such a stick

singularity (in astronomy) a point of infinite density at the centre of a black hole

singultus hiccup

sinister on the left-hand side; evil or dangerous

sinistral to do with the left side or the left hand; left-handed

sinology the study of all things Chinese

sinuous bending in and out, winding

siren a woman who is attractive to men but dangerous; a temptress

sirocco a hot wind from N. Africa blowing across the Mediterranean to southern Europe

Sisyphus *Gk. myth* was condemned in Hades to roll a large stone to the top of a hill from which it always rolled down again, hence eternal punishment; the sheer futility of it was taken by the French existentialist, Albert Camus, as a leitmotif for human existence itself

sitology the science, the study of diet

sitophobia 'fear of food,' an aversion to eating (usu.) a certain type of food

sitzfleisch Ger. staying power, persistence, endurance in the sense of being able to sit something out for a long time or sitting it out after you are no longer welcome

sizar a student at Cambridge or Trinity College, Dublin who receives financial help from the college, formerly an allowance of victuals from the college buttery

sjambok a whip of rhino hide from South Africa

skein 1) a loose coil of yarn, wool, or thread 2) a flock of wild geese or swans in flight, typically in a V-shaped formation

skelp to slap, to smack

skeuomorph an object made in a form which closely copies the form and function of another object but which is made in a substitute material

skewbald 1) marked with patches of white and another colour (not black) 2) a horse with this colouring

skewer a spit or pin pushed through meat for roasting or through smaller pieces of meat and vegetables for grilling

skid row a run-down part of a town for down-and-outs, vagrants, alcoholics etc.

skink a lizard *adj.* **scincoid**

skirl, skirling the sound of bagpipes

skirmish a minor fight or conflict

skirr a whirring or grating sound, as of the wings of birds in flight

skittish 1) lively and unpredictable, playful, frisky 2) (of a horse) excitable, nervous, easily frightened, highly strung, inclined to shy

skua a type of gull, brownish, about two feet long, predatory and rapacious, forces other birds to drop or disgorge the fish they have caught

skulduggery underhand, unscrupulous behaviour; trickery

skulk to sneak or slink away; to hide or move around secretly, in a sinister or suspicious manner

skunk to defeat resoundingly

slake to satisfy (a desire), to quench (one's thirst)

slather 1) a large quantity 2) to spread thickly 3) to squander **open slather** free rein; a free-for-all

slattern a sluttish, slovenly woman or girl

slaver 1) saliva running from the mouth 2) servile flattery; drivel, nonsense 3) to let saliva dribble from the mouth 4) to show excessive sentimentality over, or desire for; to drool over

sled a sleigh, sledge, toboggan

sleight of hand manual dexterity in performing conjuring tricks

slew 1) to turn or twist about; to slide, swing or skid sideways 2) a large number of, a large quantity of

slingshot a catapult

sloth 1) sluggishness, laziness, idleness 2) a sluggish, slow-moving, arboreal, edentate mammal of tropical America with long arms that hangs upside down from branches and feeds on vegetation

slough 1) an outer covering that is shed – e.g. the cast-off skin of a snake; dead tissue that drops off from a wound 2) a swamp, a bog, a marsh 3) despair, hopelessness *v.* to shed, discard

slovenly 1) sloppy, untidy and dirty 2) slipshod, carelees, casual

slubberdegullion a slob, a slovenly person

smarmy excessively flattering or ingratiating

smegma a sebaceous secretion under the foreskin

smelt is preferred to smelled; a small silvery fish that resembles a trout

smidgeon a small amount, a soupçon

smut 1) a small flake of dirt or soot 2) obscene or indecent language or images

snafu *n.* 1) a confused or chaotic state; a mess 2) *v.* to throw into chaos, acronym from: Situation Normal All Fucked Up

snarky *N. Amer.* sharply critical

sobersides a sedate and solemn person

sobriquet *Fr.* a nickname

Socinian an adherent of the Unitarians, Laelius and Faustus Socinus (uncle and nephew), Italian theologians of the 16th century who denied the doctrine of the Trinity and the divinity of Christ

sockdolager 1) a heavy decisive blow or remark 2) an outstanding person or thing

sodality a fellowship or fraternity

sodden soaked through

soi-disant self-styled

soigné, soignée *Fr.* well-groomed, fashionable, elegantly sophisticated

sojourn a stay, a temporary residence *v.* to stay temporarily

Sokal hoax two science academics, Alan Sokal and Jean Bricmont, alarmed at propositions from maths and physics being cited in support of esp. French literary theories, concocted a spoof article couched in the very language they considered to be so inappropriate and in 1996 an American learned magazine printed it without comment

sola topi a lightweight sun hat worn in the Tropics and made from the pithlike stem of the sola plant

solecism a grammatical mistake; a faux pas, a gaffe

solferino purplish red

solicitous caring; showing interest or concern

solidus a forward slash (/)

soliloquy the speaking of one's thoughts aloud when alone; a monologue

solipsism 1) the theory that only the self exists, can be known: self-existence is the only certainty 2) selfishness, self-centredness

solstice the point in the ecliptic at which the sun is farthest from the equator – the summer solstice (about 21 June in the northern hemisphere) when it touches the tropic of Cancer, is the longest day of the year; the winter solstice in the northern hemisphere when it touches the tropic of Capricorn is approximately 22 December, the shortest day

solvent financially sound

somatic to do with the body, as distinct from the mind

somatotonic extrovert, aggressive, assertive – supposedly characteristic of a typical **mesomorph**

sommelier a wine waiter

somnolent sleepy; sleep inducing

sonorous deep, rich, full (sound); pompous, imposing, grandiloquent (speech)

soothsayer a fortune teller; a prophet

sop a bribe; a 'sweetener'

sophism an apparently sound argument which is actually specious and intentionally so – compare **paralogism**

sophisticated 1) having or appealing to fashionable and refined tastes and habits 2) intelligent, knowledgable, or able to appreciate culture and the arts 3) (of machines or methods) complex and using advanced technology 4) (of a person) aware of and able to interpret complex issues

sophistry the use of sophisms

sophomore a second-year student

soporific somnolent

sorcerer, sorceress a wizard, magician or person claiming to have magic powers

sordid 1) (of motives etc.) not honourable, mercenary 2) dirty, squalid

sordine a damper or other device to deaden the sound of a stringed instrument

sordino, sourdine a mute for a bowed or wind instrument

soroptimist a member of an international club of the same name for professional and business women

sorority a club for female students; sisterhood

sorus a heap esp. a cluster of spore-cases on the underside of a fern frond

sotto voce *Lat.* in a quiet voice

soubrette the stock character of a saucy maid in a stage comedy

sough to make a sighing sound like the wind

souk a market-place in Muslim countries; an Arab bazaar

soupçon a small amount, a smidgeon

sourdine 1) a soft stop on an organ or harmonica 2) another word for **sordino**

sovereign supreme, excellent

sovereignty supreme power or authority of a state to govern itself

sow 1) to plant seed 2) the female pig

spadassin a swordsman, a bravo

spades – in spades in large amounts; in the extreme; to a high degree

spagyric relating to alchemy

spandrel an almost triangular shape or space formed by a 90 degree angle enclosing one of the outer curves of an arch

Spanish fly a beetle, the dried body of which is used as an aphrodisiac

spartan strict and simple with no luxuries; austere

spasm a sudden involuntary contraction or tightening of the muscles

spasmodic occurring in brief, intense, abrupt bursts at irregular intervals

spat a slight, small-scale quarrel

spatchcock a chicken or gamebird split open and grilled

spate a flood, a torrent, a deluge

spatula 'a little broad blade' used 1) by doctors for holding down the tongue 2) in cooking 3) for stirring, mixing paint and spreading plaster

spawn to lay eggs

spawning (of a fish, frog, etc.) laying eggs, oviparous

speciesism human disregard of the needs of other animals

specious seemingly sound, authentic but not really so; deceptive

spectre a ghost

speculum an instrument which widens the cavities, opens the passages of the human body and thereby aids medical examination

speech act theory is concerned with an utterance regarded as an action esp. as regards its intention, purpose or effect; this developing area of linguistic philosophy takes the analysis of language beyond the old dichotomy between statements that are true and those that are not.

spelean cave-dwelling; to do with caves

speleology 1) the study of caves 2) potholing, the exploring of caves

speleotherapy treatment for asthma in disused mines where the air is free of pollen, dust mites and other irritants that cause an allergic reaction

spelunker one who studies, explores caves

spencer 1) a type of jacket 2) a vest worn by women

sperm whale hunted for its spermaceti (from which cosmetics, candles and ointments are made); it is also the source of ambergris used in the manufacture of perfumes

sphaeristerium a tennis-court

sphenoid wedge-shaped; a bone at the base of the skull

spheroid a globe-like solid figure that is almost but not perfectly round

sphincter a ring of muscle round an orifice esp. the anus

sphinx 1) an ancient Egyptian stone figure 2) an enigmatic or inscrutable person

sphragistics the study of seals and signet rings

sphygmic to do with the pulse

sphygmomanometer an instrument for measuring blood pressure in the arteries

spiel salesman's patter

spigot 1) a stopper inserted into the vent-hole of a cask 2) a tap

spillikin a splinter of wood, bone or plastic

spillikins a game involving a heap of spillikins from which the players try to remove one spillikin at a time without disturbing the others

Spinoza 17th-century Dutch philosopher who rejected the dualism of Descartes; he held that reality is all one substance, including God and nature, and that everything that exists is a part of this one substance

spitchcock an eel split and grilled or fried

spitfire a person with a fierce temper

splenetic 1) to do with the spleen 2) spiteful, peevish, bad-tempered (a condition once thought to emanate from the spleen)

spoilage 1) something spoilt 2) the act of spoiling or the state of being spoilt; damage

sprachgefühl
a gift for learning and using language;
a feeling for language(s)

spoils valuables seized in war

spoliary the place in a Roman amphitheatre where the bodies of the dead gladiators were taken

spoliation *n.* plundering, pillaging

spondee a metrical foot of two long or two stressed syllables

spoondrift, spindrift; spray blown from the waves

spoonerism transposing the initial sounds of words: 'You hissed my mystery lecture', after the Rev. W.A. Spooner *(1844-1930)* Warden of New College, Oxford

spoor the track, trail, or scent of an animal

sporadic occurring irregularly or only in a few places

spore a reproductive cell of lower plants, algae, fungi, protozoans, bacteria, etc. capable of development into a new individual

sprachgefühl Ger. a gift for learning and using language; a feeling for language(s)

sprezzatura Ital. studied unconcern, insouciance esp. in art or literature; the difficult made to look easy; the effortless technique of a great artist

sprichwort Ger. a saying, a proverb, an adage

spry (of an old person) lively

spumescent producing or resembling foam or froth

spurious false, counterfeit

squalid 1) dirty, unpleasant, wretched 2) morally repulsive; sordid, disreputable

squamous sealy, flaky

squander to waste, to spend extravagantly

squib 1) a small firework that hisses before exploding 2) *N. Amer.* a short news item 3) a small or weak person 4) *N. Amer.* a short or weak kick or hit

squillion an extremely large but indefinite number

squinch a stone arch across an interior angle of a square tower to support a superstructure such as a dome

squinny to peer; to look with a furtive glance from the corner of the eye

squireen a small-scale squire

stabile a free-standing abstract structure in art – a static mobile

staccato with each note or sound sharply separated or detached from the others; with a jerky, abrupt delivery

staid respectable and unadventurous

staithe a wharf from which coals, in particular, may be loaded into vessels

Stakhanovite an extremely hard-working person – from the name of the exceptionally industrious Russian miner, A.G. Stakhanov

stalactite a tapering structure of lime deposit hanging from the roof of a cave

stalagmite a tapering column of calcium salts rising from the floor of a cave

stalemate 1) a draw in chess 2) a deadlock

stalking-horse 1) a horse or screen with a hunter hiding behind it as he stalks his prey 2) a pretext concealing a person's real intentions 3) (in politics) a weak candidate put up to trigger off an election so that a stronger candidate may emerge

stamina endurance, the strength to keep going

stammtisch Ger. a table reserved for regular customers

stanch, staunch to stop the flow of blood

stannary a tin-mining district in Cornwall

stannic relating to or containing tin

St. Anselm's ontological argument for the existence of God God must be the greatest being that ever existed. But existence in the mind is inferior to existence in reality. As God is the greatest conceivable being, He must also exist in reality as well as in the mind

stanza a verse or group of lines in a poem

staple main, important or principal *n.* 1) a main item of trade or production 2) a main or important element of something

starboard the right-hand side of a ship or aircraft when one is facing forward

Star Chamber an English court (abolished in 1641) sitting in closed session, it heard cases involving the security of the state; noted for the severity of its judgments

stasis the stopping of circulation of any of the body fluids – the blood in its circulation or the food down the intestinal canal

status quo *Lat.* the present position

status quo ante *Lat.* 'state in which before', the previous position

Statute of Limitations law laying down time limits for bringing legal proceedings

steatopygia excessive fat on the buttocks

steed a horse

steenbok a small African antelope

steganography secret, concealed, hidden writing; the precursor of cryptography

steinbock the Alpine goat

stellar 1) to do with a star 2) having the quality of a star performer

stelliform star-shaped

stenography shorthand writing

stenotopic able to tolerate only a narrow range of environmental changes

stentorian very loud-voiced, in a loud and powerful voice

steppe a large area of flat grassland without trees esp. in Siberia

stercoral, stercorary, stercoraceous to do with dung, excrement

stercorarian one who points out that the bread of the Holy Communion passes through the digestive system and is evacuated like any other food

stereo- three-dimensional

stereotype a standard, conventional, image or idea of a person or thing

stern the rear part of a boat or ship

sternutation sneezing

stertorous (of breathing) heavy and laboured, resembling snoring

stet 'let it stand', *Lat.* an instruction to disregard an alteration in a text

stethiaeum the front half of a bird

stevedore a docker

stickler one who insists on a certain quality or type of behaviour

stigma a mark of disgrace or shame

stilo novo *Lat.* new style according to the Gregorian calendar – introduced in 1582 and still used today

stilted stiff, self-conscious, unnatural, artificial

stint 1) to be miserly with (something) 2) a fixed amount of work or time

stipple to mark a drawing or painting with numerous short strokes, dots or specks

stipulate to lay down as a specific requirement

stochastic statistically random

stoic, stoical indifferent to pleasure or pain; showing great self-control; not showing one's feelings; impassive

Stoicism the school of philosophy founded by the Greek philosopher, Zeno, *(340-270 b.c.)* in a colonnade or porch (a stoa) in Athens; opposed to Epicureanism, it promoted the notion of indifference to pleasure or pain

stolid showing no emotion or interest; phlegmatic

stomatic to do with the mouth

stood, standing 'I was stood there' is non-standard usage for 'I was standing there'

stooge 1) an actor who feeds lines to a comedian or acts as the butt of his jokes 2) a subordinate who is taken advantage of by someone in a superior position

storiated, historiated, storied recorded in history or in a story; fabled

storm petrel a small dusky seabird that rarely lands except to lay its eggs aka Mother Carey's chicken

stormy petrel 1) a storm petrel 2) a troublemaker or one who portends trouble

stout quite fat, heavily built

strabismus a squint

Stradivarius highly valued violin or other stringed instrument made by A. Stradivari in Cremona, Italy in 17th or 18th century

straitened impoverished

stramineous light like straw, strawy, straw-like

strammel straw

strand a shore

strangury painful retention of or difficulty in discharging urine

strappado torture in which the victim was hoisted by a rope tied to his wrists and then suddenly allowed to drop to the ground or until his fall was checked by the rope

stratagem a game plan

streptomycin a bacterial antibiotic used to treat tuberculosis

stria *pl.* **striae** a scratch, stripe or streak; a linear mark, ridge, or groove

striation a stripe, a furrow, a ridge, a groove

stricture a sternly critical remark

strident 1) (of sound) loud, harsh and grating 2) putting forward a point of view in an excessively forceful way

stridulator one of the insects (cicada, grasshopper, locust, and cricket) that makes a shrill creaking sound by rubbing its legs or wings together

strigose (botany) having bristles or stiff hairs; (entomology) ridged, furrowed or grooved

stringent strict

stringer a local reporter who provides items of news to a national newspaper or news agency

stripling a young man

strobe = strobe lighting or stroboscope

strobe lighting a flashing beam of very bright light produced by a perforated disc rotating in front of a light source

stroboscope an instrument producing a very bright flashing light which makes moving people appear stationary

strumpet a whore

strut *n.* a structural part of a framework designed to support or strengthen it

struthious ostrich-like

Stubbs, George *(1724-1806)* 18th-century English painter of esp. horses

stucco plaster used for coating outside walls or moulding into architectural decorations

stud a stallion kept for breeding

stultify to impair, to make ineffective

stunt to hinder the growth of

Sturmabteilung *Ger*. Hitler's nazi terrorist militia, the Brownshirts

Sturm und Drang German literary movement of the latter half of the 18th century, characterised by high emotional unrest – the storm and stress of its title – it was often concerned with the individual's revolt against society

Stygian to do with the Styx, mythical river of the underworld; dark, gloomy, hellish

stylite an ascetic anchorite living on top of a pillar in Egypt, Mesopotamia, Syria, Turkey, and Greece in and after the 5th century; Simeon Stylites (c.390-459), thought to be the first person to have done this; lived in that way for 30 years

stymie to obstruct, to hinder

suave smooth-mannered

subcaudal beneath the tail

subcontiguous almost touching

subcontinuous nearly continuous but with slight gaps

subcordate heart-shaped

suberose corky

subfusc 1) dull, gloomy 2) formal clothing at some universities

sub judice *Lat.* under judicial consideration and consequently banned from public discussion elsewhere

subjugate 'to bring inder the yoke', to bring under one's power or control; to conquer

subjunctive together with indicative, imperative, and infinitive is one of the four moods of a verb; it arises where situations are conceived as possible or contingent, but not asserted as facts: *God save the Queen; If I were you; be that as it may; God forbid; far be it from me; so be it*

sublate to deny – opp. to **posit**; to remove; to assimilate (a smaller entity) into a larger one

sublimate to divert esp. a primitive sexual impulse into a higher cultural, or socially more acceptable activity

subliminal affecting someone's mind without their realising it

subliminal advertising employs subliminal images that influence the viewer unconsciously

sublittoral close to the seashore

sublunary 1) under the moon 2) belonging to the material, not spiritual world; earthly

suborn to bribe

subpoena a writ ordering somebody to attend court

subreption fraudulent concealment; misrepresentation

subrogation the putting of a surety (who has paid the debt) in the position of the creditor thus entitling the surety to payment from the original debtor i.e. from the person he guaranteed

sub rosa *Lat.* in secret; in strict confidence, private

subscribe to agree with, to give support or approval

subservient subordinate; servile

subside to sink to a lower or normal level

subsidiarity the principle that, as far as practicable, the function of government should be exercised at the local level

subsist to continue to exist

substantiate to support with evidence, to prove

substitute *v.& n.* (to put) a person or thing in the place of another; it does not mean 'replace' so the football commentator who says 'The striker has been *substituted*' is, technically, in error – he means replaced; the substitute is substituted

subsume to include (something) under a wider classification

subtend *v.* to extend between or under; to be opposite to

subterfuge a trick or deception used to achieve a goal

subtrahend the sum, quantity or number to be subtracted from another

subvention a subsidy

subvert to undermine, to overthrow, to overturn

subvirate a stunted, underdeveloped specimen of a man or manhood

succès de scandale Fr. a success due to notoriety or a thing's scandalous nature

succès d'estime Fr. success in terms of critical appreciation rather than public acclaim or commercial gain

succinct (of speaking or writing) concise

succour help, assistance, aid, relief, comfort and support in times of distress *v.* to give support or aid to

succubus a female demon who supposedly had sex with sleeping men

succulent 1) juicy, tasty 2) a plant, e.g. a cactus, that can exist in very dry conditions by using water stored in its fleshy tissues

sudatory, sudorific causing sweat

sudor sweat

suffragan an assistant (bishop)

suffuse to spread through or over (something)

suicism selfishness

sui generis unique

sui juris Lat. legally competent to manage one's own affairs, independent

suist *Lat.* a self-seeker

sulcate furrowed, grooved

sully to make dirty; to soil or stain; to damage the integrity of; to ruin someone's reputation

sulphur 1) an inflammable yellow, mineral substance, aka brimstone 2) the material of which hell-fire and lightning were thought to be made

sulphurous *fig.* hellish; passionate; fiery, hot-tempered

sultan a Muslim sovereign or ruler

sump 1) a receptacle in which excess liquid collects in engines, machines, mines, etc. 2) a cesspool

sumpsimus a correct expression displacing one that is incorrect but common

sumptuary descriptive of laws that control personal spending esp. on luxury items

sumptuous of a size or splendour suggesting lavish expense

sunder to separate, to split apart, to sever

supellectile pertaining to household furniture; ornamental

superannuated 1) retired with a pension 2) too old or outdated to be effective or useful

supercilious haughtily superior, contemptuously indifferent

superego the part of the mind that acts as a self-critical conscience cf. **ego** and **id**

supererogation the performance of more than is required

superfluous more than is sufficient or required

supernumerary *adj.* 1) present in excess of the customary or required number 2) not belonging to the permanent staff but engaged for additional work; (of an actor) appearing on stage but not speaking *n.* 1) a person or thing that exceeds the required number 2) a substitute or assistant 3) an actor who has no lines to say; an extra

superordinate 1) a higher category within a system of classification; a **hypernym** 2) (a person) of superior rank or status

supersede to take the place of; to take over from; to supplant

supinate to turn the palm of the hand upwards

supine 1) lying on the back with the face upwards 2) passive, inactive, lethargic from moral weakness or indolence

suppeditate to supply

supplant to supersede and replace

supplicate to ask in a humble manner, to make a humble request

suppositional supposed; based on or involving supposition

supposititous hypothetical

supposititious fraudulently substituted for the real thing, spurious; counterfeit, false, forged

suppository a solid medicine in the shape of a cone or cylinder which dissolves after being inserted into the rectum or vagina

suppurate to produce or discharge pus

supputation *n.* calculating, computing

surcease 1) to cease 2) a cessation

surety 1) a guarantor 2) a guarantee

surfeit an excessive amount esp. in relation to eating or drinking

surly bad-tempered, gruff, grumpy

surmise 1) to suppose on scanty evidence; to guess 2) a supposition, conjecture or guess

surmount to overcome; to get over

surpass to exceed

surreal transcending the accepted conventions of reality; emanating from the subconscious – dreamlike, hallucinatory, disorientating

surreptitious stealthy, sly, sneaky; covert, clandestine

surrogate a substitute, a deputy

surveillance close watch

susceptible 1) giving in easily to 2) vulnerable to 3) easily influenced or affected by

suss to figure out

susurration, susurrus a whispering, murmuring, rustling noise

susurrant whispering, murmuring, rustling

sutler a camp follower who sold provisions esp. liquor to the soldiers

suzerain an overlord

suzerainty dominion over a dependent state esp. with regard to controlling its foreign affairs

svelte attractively slender, graceful, elegant

Svengali someone who has a mesmerising, sinister influence over another

swab 1) a mop 2) a wad of absorbent material used in medicine and surgery

swain a young man from the country

swarthy of dark complexion

swasivious agreeably persuasive

swatch 1) a sample of cloth or fabric 2) a number of these bound together in book form

swathe, swath a broad strip esp. of grass or corn when mown or reaped

sweetbread the pancreas or thymus gland of an animal, esp. as food

sybarite one who is devoted to luxury

sychnocarpous bearing fruit many times

sycophant a flatterer; a toady: one who flatters persons of influence

syllogism deductive, but possibly invalid, reasoning; of the 256 possible syllogistic permutations, only 24 (some say only 19) are valid

sylvan to do with woods; wooded

symbiosis a living together for mutual benefit or because of mutual dependency

sympatric taking place or existing in the same or overlapping geographical areas

symplectic placed in or among, as if woven together

synaesthesia, synesthesia stimulation of one part of the body producing a sensation in a different part or parts; stimulation of one sense producing a subjective sensation or image of another sense or senses, e.g. an impression of colour evoked by a sound

synapse the minute gap between two nerve cells across which nerve impulses are transmitted

synchronic concerned with matters occurring at the same time without considering historical antecedents

synchronicity the apparently meaningful coincidence of events with no discernible causal connection

syncopation *mus.* the making of weak beats strong and vice versa

syncope 1) the omission of sounds or letters from within a word, e.g. *victuals* is pronounced *vittles* 2) fainting

syncretism the combining or reconciling of different religions, cultures or schools of thought

syncretize to attempt to amalgamate and harmonize differing schools of thought, religious beliefs, etc.

syndactyl 1) web-footed 2) having webbed fingers

syndrome a group of signs or symptoms occurring together and thereby indicating a disorder or disease to which a particular name is given

synecdoche a figure of speech in which 1) a part of something is used to describe the whole ('all hands on deck' for all sailors), or 2) vice versa ('Lancashire beat Yorkshire' referring to the two cricket teams)

synergy increased efficiency achieved by individuals or things working together rather than on their own

synonym a word or phrase having the same meaning as another word or phrase in the same language

synopsis a summary, an overview

synthesis the combining or combination of components into a whole

synthetic artificial, not genuine, insincere, unnatural

syphilis a sexually transmitted bacterial disease

systemic affecting the body or system as a whole and not just a particular part

syzygy 1) either a conjunction or opposition when three celestial bodies e.g. the sun, the earth, and a planet esp. the moon lie in a straight line 2) any pair, usu. of opposites or correlated or connected things

T

tabard a sleeveless jacket or jerkin consisting only of front and back pieces with a hole for the head

tabefaction a wasting away

tabescent wasting away

tableau a group of motionless figures representing a scene

tabula rasa *Lat.* a blank tablet, a clean slate – the human mind at birth with no preconceived ideas

tachism, tachisme abstract painting with blobs of paint on canvas, originated in the 1940s in France

tachycardia abnormally rapid heartbeat

tachyon a hypothetical particle that travels faster than light

taciturn untalkative; uncommunicative in speech; saying very little

tacnode a point at which two branches of a curve have a common tangent, each branch extending in both directions of the tangent

tad a touch, a small amount

Taffia (joc.) the Welsh mafia

tagmeme the smallest unit of grammar in tagmemics

tagmemics a type of grammatical analysis pioneered by the American linguist K.L. Pike in the early 1950s

talion the law of retaliation, *lex talionis*

talisman a stone, ring or other small object believed to act as a charm to protect the holder from evil and bring good luck; a good luck charm

talon a claw of a bird of prey

talus 1) the large bone in the ankle 2) scree 3) the sloping side of a wall

tamarin a small South American monkey, similar to a marmoset

tangential peripheral; having only a superficial connection or relevance, just touching

Tantalus a king in *Gk. myth* whose detention in Hades was exacerbated by his inability to reach fruit and drink tantalisingly close at hand – hence the derivation of the word **tantalise** to tease or torment by the sight or promise of what is unobtainable

tantamount to equivalent to; virtually the same as

tantony the smallest pig in the litter

tantras Hindu or Buddhist mystical or magical writings

Taoism a Chinese philosophy/religion which shows 'the right way' (tao) of life through virtue to prosperity, longevity and immortality

tapir pig-like mammal of tropical America and S.E. Asia with a short, flexible proboscis, three-toed hind legs and four-toed forelegs

tapster a barman

taradiddle, tarradiddle a lie, a fib

tarantella a Neapolitan dance

tarantula a large spider

tarn a small mountain lake

tarragon a plant with narrow aromatic leaves, used as a herb in cooking

tarsus the ankle

Tartar, Tatar 1) a member of the Tartars, the 13th-century marauding Asiatic tribes who overran much of Asia and Eastern Europe 2) **tartar** a savage, violent-tempered, fearsome person

Tartuffe a hypocrite, from the name of the central character of Molière's play of the same name (1664)

tatami a rush-covered straw mat – a traditional Japanese floor covering

tatterdemalion a scruff, a ragamuffin

tattoo 1) a signal by drum or bugle for soldiers to return to their quarters 2) a military display or pageant 3) any drumming or tapping 4) *v.&n.* (to make) an indelible design on the skin

taurine of or resembling a bull

tautology the repetition of an idea in different words: *pair off in twos; 7.30 p.m. in the evening; revert back; past history; free gift* 2) an empty statement composed of simpler statements in a way that makes the statement true whether the simpler statements are true or false: *either it will snow tomorrow or it will not snow tomorrow*

taw 1) a marble 2) a game of marbles

tawdry 1) tatty, tinselly, gaudy 2) sordid, sleazy

taxidermy preparing, stuffing, and mounting animal skins to give them a lifelike appearance

taxonomy classification

tchotchke 1) a decorative little object; an inexpensive, showy trinket 2) an adorable person esp. a small child 3) a pretty girl or woman

teal 1) a small freshwater duck 2) a dark greenish-blue colour

teamster a lorry driver

tectonic to do with 1) building or construction 2) the earth's crust and its distortion due to large-scale movements within it

teem (with) to be full of, swarming, abounding, or crawling with

teeming and lading stealing money by means of false book-keeping entries

teetotal never drinking alcohol

tegestology collecting beermats

tegular 1) to do with a tile or tiles; tile-like 2) overlapping like tiles

tegument an integument esp. of a flatworm

telaesthesia awareness of things remote in space or time by extra-sensory or psychic perception

telamon, telamones a column or pillar in the form of a male figure supporting an entablature, aka **atlas**

telegnosis knowledge of faraway happenings, not obtained through any of the normal senses

telegony the supposed influence of an earlier mating with a male on the offspring of subsequent matings of the same female with other males

teleology 1) the idea that there is evidence of purpose, order and design in the universe which points to the existence of a cosmic designer 2) the study of the purpose of things and the explanation (now largely discredited) of phenomena by reference to the purpose they serve

Tell it not in Gath Do not let your enemies hear it – Gath being the birthplace of Goliath

tellurian 1) to do with the earth 2) an inhabitant of the earth

telluric concerning 1) the earth or soil 2) the earth as a planet

telmatology the study of peat-bogs

telpher, telpherage an overhead transport system involving electrically-driven trucks or cars being suspended from and running along aerial cables or rails

temerarious rash; recklessly daring, precipitate

temerity rashness, boldness; foolish disregard for danger

tempera a method of painting using powdered pigments mixed with egg yolk and water

temperance abstinence from alcoholic drinks

temperate 1) self-restrained; moderate; without extremes of heat and cold 2) showing moderation or self-restraint

template 1) a shaped piece of rigid material used as a pattern or mould 2) a model or example

tempi *pl.* of tempo

temporize to act evasively, to equivocate; to stall in order to gain time; to play for time

tempus fugit Lat. time flies

temulent drunk, intoxicated

tenacious holding firmly; persistent or stubborn

tendentious promoting a particular point of view; biased

tendril a slender shoot by which a climbing plant attaches itself for support

tenebrosity darkness

tenebrous dark, gloomy

tenesmus a desire to empty the bowels and straining to do so but with little or no effect

tenet a principle or belief

tensile 1) to do with tension 2) capable of being stretched

tensile strength the greatest tension or stretching a substance or material can withstand without breaking

tentative uncertain, not fixed; provisional; hesitant

tenuity thinness

tenuous thin, weak, slender, flimsy

tenuto (of a note in music) to be held for or beyond its full time value

tepee a wigwam

tephra rock fragments and ashes from a volcano

tephromancy divination by inspecting the ashes of a sacrifice

tepid lukewarm

tercel a male hawk

tergiversator 1) a turncoat; an apostate 2) one who is ambiguous, evasive; an equivocator

termagant an aggressive, turbulent woman, a virago, a shrew

terminus ad quem *Lat.* an end or finishing point; an aim or goal

terminus a quo *Lat.* a starting point; the earliest possible date

termite a white ant that causes considerable damage to timber

tern a gull-like seabird with a forked tail

terpsichorean 1) to do with dancing 2) a dancer

terrapin a small freshwater turtle, aka **water tortoise**

terrene 1) to do with the earth 2) on dry land 3) worldly

terrestrial 1) concerning the earth, the ground or dry land 2) (to do with television), broadcasting other than by satellite

terrine 1) pâté 2) a pâté dish

terse (of speaking or writing) sparing with words, brief, abrupt, to the point

tessellated of mosaic pattern; chequered

testaceous reddish-brown like terra cotta

testimonial 1) a recommendation of the character or worth of a person or thing 2) a tribute given for services or achievements; a public tribute to someone esp. in sport, a game or event held in honour of a player who receives part of the monies raised

testudinal to do with or resembling a tortoise or turtle; tortoise-like

testudineous as slow as a tortoise

testudo an overhead protection for Roman soldiers – a mobile arched structure or overlapping shields

tetanic to do with tetanus

tetanus an acute infectious, bacterial disease causing rigidity and spasms of the muscles, aka **lockjaw**

tetralogy four related works of literature, drama, cinema or music

Teutonic German, Germanic

thalassic to do with or living in the sea

thalassocracy the government of a country which controls large expanses of the seas; supremacy on the seas

thalassotherapy the use of seawater in health treatment

thanatology the study of death

thanatopsis a meditation or reflection on death as in a poem

thaumaturge a miracle-worker

thaumaturgy miracle-working

theave a young ewe

thelytokous producing only female offspring

theocracy government by priests in the name of God or a god

theodicy the vindication of God and divine providence in spite of the existence of evil

Theophilanthropy a religion drawn up under the French Directory in 1796 to take the place of Christianity

theopneusty divine inspiration

therapeutic curative

therblig (in time and motion study) any task that can be analysed

therianthropy psychological or spiritual identification with a particular animal

Thermidor the eleventh month of the French revolutionary calendar from 19th July to 18th August; the 9th Thermidor of the Republican year 2 (27th July 1794) is the date of Robespierre's fall and the end of the Reign of Terror

Thersites an ugly, cowardly, evil-tongued Greek soldier at the time of the Trojan War who railed against his senior officers

thersitical loud and abusive; foul-mouthed

thespian an actor

theurgy divine, supernatural magic or miracles

thew muscle strength

thoral nuptial

thorax, thoracic the chest, to do with the chest

thrall slavery – **in thrall to** overawed by, spellbound by, in the power of

thrasonical boastful, bragging

threnody a lament

thresh to separate out by beating the grain from the husk or straw

throe a pang or pain

Thunderer, The nickname of The Times newspaper

thurible a censer, a container in which incense is burnt

tic a twitch or spasm

ticket-of-leave man (formerly) a British prisoner who, having served part of his sentence, was allowed out of prison on certain conditions i.e. present-day parole

tide time, season – Yuletide, Whitsuntide

tiffany thin silk-like gauze muslin

tigon the offspring of a male tiger and a lioness

tilde the diacritical sign ~ , a wavy line placed over certain letters and vowels in esp. Spanish and Portuguese

tilth 1) the tilling, cultivation of land; tillage 2) the condition of soil that has been tilled

timbre the distinctive character or quality of a voice or musical sound

timbrology the study of stamps; stamp-collecting

time-barred (in relation to legal claims) too late to be pursued by the issue of proceedings

time-server a person who changes his views to suit the prevailing circumstances or fashion

time warp 1) an imagined distortion of time (and space) whereby people, objects, events of one age can be moved to another 2) a state in which the features characteristic of an earlier period are crystallized i.e. time appears to stand still (living in a 1930s time warp)

timorous timid or nervous

timpani kettledrums

tincture 1) a medicine made by dissolving a drug in alcohol 2) a slight trace 3) *colloq.* an alcoholic drink

tinker a mender of brass or tin kettles, pans

tinnitus persistent ringing or buzzing in the ears

tintinnabulation the tinkling sound of bells

tirade a long speech of angry criticism, denunciation or accusation

Titan 1) *Gk.myth* one of the giant gods 2) a person of great strength, size, intellect or importance 3) a satellite of Saturn

titfer *Brit.slang* a hat

tithe (formerly) one-tenth (a tithe) of the annual produce of the land paid as a tax to the church

titillate to arouse, to excite pleasurably esp. in a sexual way

titivate to make smarter or neater

titubation tottering, staggering, stumbling, as if drunk, but usu. caused by injury to the cerebellum or spinal chord

titular 1) concerning a title 2) in name only – to do with a formal position or title not involving any real authority

tmesis (esp. in colloquial speech) the insertion into a compound word of an intervening word or words – *abso-blinking-lutely*

toady a flatterer; to act obsequiously

tocology, tokology childbirth; obstetrics; midwifery

tocsin an alarm bell or signal

toddy a drink of (usu.) whisky, hot water, sugar and lemon juice

tome a volume; a large scholarly book

tonal relating to tone

tonality 1) the presence of a key in a musical composition 2) the colour scheme in a painting

tong a Chinese secret society formerly reputed to be involved in organized crime

tonic a medicine which gives tone and vigour to the system

tonsorial to do with a barber or his trade

tonsure complete or partial shaving of the head of a monk or priest; the part of the head, usu. the top, that has been shaved

tontine a group scheme whereby annuities are paid to subscribers; as the members die the payments to the survivors or survivor increase

toothsome 1) (of food) temptingly tasty 2) (of a person) sexually attractive and alluring

topography the representation on a map of the surface features of a region; the surface features in question

topology the study of the geometrical properties of a figure unaffected by smooth changes in shape or size or distortion of the figure by elastic deformation, e.g. stretching, twisting, knotting, bending, or squeezing, but not breaking or tearing

toponym a place-name derived from the topography of the place – High Salvington on the Downs in Sussex is such a place

topos a theme that crops up from time to time in literature – *ubi sunt* and *carpe diem* are examples

toque a tall white hat worn by a chef

torch song a sad or sentimental song of unrequited love

toreador a bullfighter

torpescent becoming torpid

torpid sluggish, lethargic

torpor sluggishness, inertia (mental or physical), lethargy

torque 1) a necklace of twisted metal 2) force that causes rotation 3) the ability of a shaft to cause rotation

Torquemada Tomás **de** *(1420-1498)* Inquisitor-General at the time of the Spanish Inquisition; he took ruthless measures against heretics and was responsible for the expulsion of the Jews from Spain.

torrid extremely hot, burning

torschlusspanik Ger. 'door shut panic' – the frenzy as people fight to rush through a door before it is slammed in their face; mid-life crisis

torsion *n.* twisting

tort a civil wrong (negligence, defamation etc. but not breach of contract) for which the tortfeasor is legally liable

torticollis stiff neck, wry-neck

tortilla a pancake (Mexico); an omelette (Spain)

tortuous twisting or turning

torturous involving pain or suffering

torus shape of a ring doughnut or of a tyre

totalizator a machine for registering bets on a race and calculating how the stakes are to be divided among those backing the winner

totem 1) an emblem or symbol of a group; a natural object or animal symbolising a clan or family esp. among N. American Indians 2) a representation of such

totemic 1) to do with a totem 2) symbolic, emblematic

totty girls or young women collectively considered as sexually desirable

toucan a fruit-eating bird of tropical America; it has a large brightly coloured bill

tour de force Fr. an amazing feat

Tourette's syndrome brain disorder characterized by involuntary twitches and outbursts of obscenities

tournedos a small, round, thick cut from a fillet of beef

tout court Fr. simply, only, merely

toxicology the study of poisons

toxin a poison

toxophily archery

tracery ornamental pattern(s) formed by the tracing, or interweaving, of the mullions in the head of a Gothic window

tract 1) a large area of land 2) a system of organs or glands that has a particular function: the *urinary tract* 3) a religious pamphlet

tractable easily controlled; docile; easy to deal with; acquiescent

Tractarianism another name for the **Oxford Movement**

tractate a treatise

traction drawing, pulling

traduce to speak ill of; to misrepresent; to defame

tragalism lust, lechery

tralatitious relating to transference of words, metaphorical; handed down from generation to generation, traditional

trait a characteristic; a distinguishing feature or quality

trajectory the path of something moving through space

trammel 1) to constrain, hinder or impede 2) a triple-mesh fishing-net 3) an impediment, a hindrance, a restriction

tranche a portion, a slice

transcend 1) to be or go above or beyond; to be superior to 2) to surpass

transcendent pre-eminent, surpassing; above or beyond what is expected or normal in physical human experience; not part of the material universe

transcendental supernatural, superhuman, exalted, metaphysical, mystical; based on intuition or innate belief rather than experience

transcendental meditation a method of meditation and mental relaxation derived from Hinduism involving the silent repetition of a mantra

transcribe to put into written or printed form; to write or type out

transept (in a cross-shaped church) one of the two short wings or arms at right angles to the nave

transfigure to change in appearance

transfix 1) to impale; to pierce through with a pointed object 2) to cause somebody to be motionless, rooted to the spot

transient lasting or staying for a short time only

transition, transitional change

transitive (of a verb) that takes an object

transitory not permanent; short-lived

transliterate to write or spell (a word etc.) into the corresponding letters of another alphabet or language

translucent allowing light to pass through, but not transparent

transmigration (of the soul) the passing into a different body after death

transmogrify to transform something in an extraordinary way

transpose to cause to change places

transubstantiation a change from one substance into another, esp. the bread and wine of the Eucharist into the body and blood of Christ

transume to make an official copy of a legal document

Transylvania a large, wooded, and mountainous region of northwest and central Romania; as the setting of the novel *Dracula* (1897) by Bram Stoker it has certain inevitable, sinister associations

trappings the accompanying objects or visible signs

trauma injury, wound; emotional shock with lasting effect

travail toil

travertine a porous rock

travesty a mockery, a caricature, a parody

treatise a learned written work dealing with all aspects of a particular subject

trebuchet a large sling-like military machine used in medieval siege warfare for hurling rocks at castle walls, etc.

tree line (on a mountain) the altitude above which no trees will grow; (towards the poles) the line of the latitudes north or south of which no trees will grow

tref, trefa not kosher

tremulous physically trembling or shaking usu. with fear

trenchant cutting; sharp; incisive, vigorous

trepan a small cylindrical saw for perforating the skull

trephine an improved form of trepan with a guiding centre-pin

trepid fearful

triage (the process) to decide the order of treatment of patients or casualties

tribulation trouble, suffering, a hardship, an affliction

tribune 1) a platform, dais or rostrum 2) a champion of the people

trichechine like a walrus or manatee

trichology the study of the hair, the scalp, and baldness

trident a three-pronged spear

trigamy the state of having three wives or husbands at the same time

trigraph a group of three letters representing one sound e.g. *sch* in schedule

triphthong a combination of three vowels pronounced in one syllable; three written vowel characters representing the sound of a single vowel (as the 'eau' in tableau)

tripod a three-legged stand supporting a camera

tripos the final honours examination for a B.A. degree at Cambridge university

triptych three pictures or panels hinged together vertically

triskaidekaphobia abnormal, superstitious anxiety regarding the number 13

trisketion Celtic symbol consisting of three legs or lines radiating from a centre

tritanopia colour blindness from insensitivity to blue light

trite hackneyed, unoriginal, worn out by too much use, clichéd

triturate to grind to a fine powder

triumvirate a group of three powerful people or rulers

Trocadero, Battle of The French took the fort of Trocadero which controlled access to Cadiz on 31st August 1823. The battle gave its name to various buildings in Paris and elsewhere.

troglodyte 1) a person who lives in caves 2) one who lives a solitary and eccentric existence

troilism sexual activity involving three people

troll 1) to walk, stroll 2)(in folklore) a giant or dwarf living in a cave 3) to sing out loudly, happily 4) to fish by drawing the bait along in the water, often from a boat

trompe l'oeil *Fr.* painting or design giving the illusion of reality esp. by creating a three-dimensional effect

trope figurative or metaphorical use of a word or phrase – metaphor, metonymy, synecdoche, etc.

tropical to do with a trope; figurative

tropism the tendency of a plant to grow towards or away from an external stimulus

tropology the use of metaphors in writing or speaking

troubadour a French lyric poet composing and singing in Old Provençal in southern France in the late Middle Ages

trounce to defeat heavily in a contest

troupe a group of entertainers who go on tour to different venues

trouper 1) an entertainer with long experience 2) a reliable and uncomplaining person

trouvaille *Fr.* a lucky find; a godsend; a windfall

truchmanry the office of an interpreter

truckle to give in, to submit

truculent eager or quick to argue or fight; aggressively defiant

truffle an underground fungus regarded as a delicacy; strong-smelling and rich-flavoured, it resembles a mushroom or rough-skinned potato

truism a remark or statement that is obviously true and says nothing new or interesting

truncate to shorten

trutinate *v. tr.* to weigh

truttaceous to do with or like a trout

tryst a secret meeting of lovers

tsantsa the shrunken head of an enemy kept as a trophy by the Shuar group of the Jivaro people of Ecuador

tsar, tzar, czar 1) an emperor of Russia before 1917 2) a person with great power and authority in a particular field

tsunami a very large sea wave caused by an earthquake under the sea or some other disturbance

tubercle a small lump or swelling on a bone

tuberculosis a disease caused by the growth of tubercles in the lungs

tubicen a trumpeter

tubicinate to blow a trumpet

tucket a flourish on a trumpet

tuft-hunter one who tries to become acquainted with persons of rank or importance

tumbrel, tumbril a cart used to take condemned persons to the guillotine during the French Revolution

tumescent swelling, becoming swollen

tumid 1) swollen 2) pompous, bombastic

tumulus an ancient burial mound; a barrow

tundra vast, flat, treeless, cold Arctic region with permanently frozen subsoil – between the perpetual snow of the Arctic and the tree line

tungsten hard, steel-grey metallic chemical element

tunicate having concentric layers like an onion

turbary the legal right to cut turf or peat for fuel on common land or on another person's land

turbid 1) muddy, cloudy 2) thick, dense 3) muddled, in turmoil; unclear, confused

turbillion a whirl, a vortex

turbinaceous turfy, peaty

turbinate shaped like a spinning top or an inverted cone

turbine machine or motor driven by a wheel that is turned by a flow of water, steam, gas, air, or other fluid

turbulent 1) wild and unruly 2) involving sudden changes and conflicting elements 3) agitated, disturbed; restless, chaotic

turdine relating to thrushes

tureen a soup-dish

turf war a dispute between criminals or gangs over the right to operate within a particular area

turgescent becoming or seeming swollen

turgid 1) swollen 2) pompous, bombastic – turgid and tumid mean much the same

Turing test a test for intelligence in computers devised by the English mathematician, Alan Mathison Turing *(1912-1954)*

turnkey a jailer

turpitude depravity, wickedness

turret 1) a small tower on a building esp. a castle 2) an armoured revolving tower for a gun

turtle an aquatic or marine tortoise

tushery the use of affectedly archaic language

tussive to do with a cough

tussock a tuft or clump of grass

tutoyant intimate, affectionate

tutu a ballerina's costume of either a bodice and a very short skirt (classical) or a long and bell-shaped one (romantic)

tykhana in India a basement place to rest in during the hottest part of the day

tyrant a cruel and oppressive ruler

typhiology the science of blindness and the cure of the blind

Tyre the former major Phoenician commercial city and port on the Mediterranean coast; famous for its silks and purple dye, it is the site of present-day Sur in Lebanon

tyro, tiro a beginner, a novice

tzigane a Hungarian gypsy

U

über *Ger.* over, super

Übermensch *Ger.* superman

uberrima fides (contracts) of the utmost good faith esp. those involving a duty to disclose to a prospective insurer all relevant information before it decides whether to enter into the insurance contract

ubiety the state of being in a definite place

ubiquitous everywhere at once, omnipresent

ubi sunt 'where are they?', a recurring theme in literature and esp. lyric poetry in which the writer bemoans the passage of time and the disappearance of lovers, friends and aquaintances.

udal freehold land in Orkney and Shetland

Uffizi art gallery and museum in Florence – one of Europe's finest

uhuru freedom *(Swahili)*

Uitlanders Britons (and others) who went to live in Transvaal and Orange Free State after gold was discovered in 1886; foreigners

ukase an edict or decree in Russia

uliginose, uliginous growing in wet, swampy places

ullage the amount of liquid missing from a container which would need to be added to make it full; loss from evaporation or leakage

ulotrichous, ulotrichan having tightly curled, woolly hair

Ulster is not the same as Northern Ireland and to describe it thus is annoying to many Irish people; of its 9 counties, 3 – Cavan, Donegal, and Monaghan – are in the Republic

ultracrepidarian (someone) straying outside their field of competence

ultramarine brilliant deep blue

ultramontane believing in the supreme authority of the pope

ultra vires Lat. 'beyond the powers', unauthorized

ululate to howl

umami an exceptional delicious taste

umber a dark yellowish-brown pigment

umbrage offence

umbrageous 1) shady or forming a shade 2) inclined to take offence

umlaut a vowel change in Germanic languages indicated by a mark of two dots (e.g. ü) over a vowel

uberrima fides
(contracts) of the utmost good faith esp. those involving
a duty to disclose to a prospective insurer all relevant
information before it decides whether to enter into the
insurance contract

umrah the voluntary lesser pilgrimage to Mecca made at any time of the year

unabashed not abashed – not embarrassed, ashamed, or disconcerted

unadulterated pure with nothing added; not mixed with anything else, undiluted

unalloyed not mixed, pure

unambagious 1) direct; clear 2) definite

unambiguous having a totally clear meaning which is capable of only one interpretation

unassailable unable to be attacked, questioned, or defeated

unavailing achieving little or nothing

unbiddable disobedient, not docile

unbidden 1) uninvited 2) voluntary, spontaneous

unbridled unrestrained

uncertainty principle the position and velocity of a particle cannot both be measured exactly at the same time

uncharted not on any map

unchartered without a charter or written constitution

uncials the forerunners of present-day capital letters

unciform in the shape of a hook

uncinate hooked

unconscionable 1) unforgiveable, excessive, unreasonable 2) unprincipled, unscrupulous

uncouth rude, awkward, uncultivated in speech or behaviour; lacking in good manners or refinement

unction 1) anointing with oil 2) the oil itself 3) unctuousness

unctuous smarmy; oleaginous; insincerely earnest

undaunted not intimidated, discouraged or disheartened

undertaking 1) a promise, a guarantee 2) a project, an assignment, a task 3) a business, a commercial venture

undertow a current below the sea's surface moving in the opposite direction to the surface current

underwrite to guarantee, to undertake to finance

undulating wavy

unduly excessively

unequivocal definite; absolutely clear in meaning; leaving no doubt

unexceptionable not open to objection, beyond reproach or criticism

unexceptional ordinary, rather dull

unfathomable 1) incapable of being fully explored or understood 2) impossible to measure the depth or extent of

unfledged 1) not yet having developed the feathers necessary for flight 2) not fully developed; immature

unfrock to defrock; to deprive a priest of ecclesiastical status

unguent an ointment, a lubricant

ungulate a hoofed mammal – horse, pig, deer

unicameral having only one legislative chamber

unicorn mythical, horse-like creature with one straight horn on its forehead

unilateral involving only one side

unimpeachable completely honest and reliable; beyond reproach

uninterested indifferent, unconcerned, bored, cf. **disinterested**

uniparous giving birth to only one offspring at a time

unique the only one of its kind; it cannot be qualified so you cannot say 'rather' or 'fairly' unique.

unkempt untidy, scruffy

unlettered illiterate, uneducated

unmitigated absolute, total, out-and-out, downright

unpractical = impractical

unprecedented novel, unparalleled, never having happened before

unreconstructed die-hard, stubbornly holding to outdated political thinking or views

unregenerate unreformed, unrepentant, stubbornly persisting in old prejudices

unremitting not ceasing

unrequited not reciprocated

unscathed without suffering any injury

unseemly improper, inappropriate, unbecoming

unslakeable that cannot be slaked, quenched, or satisfied

unsolicited not requested

unstinting not holding back; given or giving without restraint

untempered not lessened, moderated, or mitigated

*Untermensch pl. **untermenschen*** a person regarded as racially or socially inferior – *Ger.* 'underperson'

untimely happening at an unsuitable time

untoward 1) out of the ordinary, unexpected, unusual 2) unseemly or improper 3) characterized by misfortune or annoyance

untrammelled able to act freely and without restrictions; not restricted or hampered

unwitting not aware of the full facts

unwonted not customary, not usual

upbraid to reproach, reprimand, reprove

upstage to divert attention from, to outshine

ur – primitive; original; earliest – **ur-text**

uraeum the back half of a bird

urban concerning a city

urbane (esp. of a man) suave, courteous, refined, sophisticated, elegant

urn 1) a vase for the ashes of a cremated person 2) a large container with a tap, for making and keeping tea or coffee hot

urology the branch of medicine dealing with the urinary system

ursine to do with a bear or bears; bear-like

ur-text an original or earliest version of a text

urticate to sting like a nettle

urtication stinging or prickling sensation like a burn

usitate *adj.* according to custom

usitative *adj.* expressing usual action

usquebaugh whisky

ustion the act of burning; cauterization by burning

ustorious *adj.* burning

ustulation *n.* burning

usucaption, usucapion *Roman law* the acquisition of a title or right to property by uninterrupted and undisputed possession for a prescribed period

utraquistic subterfuge
the practice, in relation to a word that has two meanings
which are close or overlap, of using the word in both
senses during the same discussion without pointing out
that the sense required the second time is different from
the sense already used, aka legerdemain

usufruct the right to enjoy the use of someone else's property without damaging it

usurp to seize by force and without authority; to supplant (someone in power)

usury lending money at exorbitant rates of interest

uterine concerning the womb or uterus

utilitarianism 1) an action is right if it is useful, if it brings about happiness, or is for the benefit of a majority 2) the ultimate good is the greatest happiness of the greatest number

utmost good faith = uberrima fides

Utopia an imaginary place where everything is perfect

utraquistic subterfuge the practice, in relation to a word that has two meanings which are close or overlap, of using the word in both senses during the same discussion without pointing out that the sense required the second time is different from the sense already used, aka legerdemain

Utraquists, aka **Calixtines** asserted the right to communion in both kinds – *sub utraque specie* – the wine from the cup (calix) as well as the bread

uxoricide the killing of one's wife

uxorious excessively submissive, doting on and devoted to one's wife

Uzi a sub-machine gun of Israeli design

V

vaccinate = inoculate

vachery a dairy

vacillate to waver mentally; to keep changing one's mind

vacuous (of the mind) lacking thought or intelligence, vacant, empty, without content or substance

vade mecum *Lat.* a handbook or guide kept constantly to hand

vagarious concerning vagaries; irregular or erratic

vagary a change that is neither expected nor explained; a whim; a caprice

vagitus the cry of a new-born child

vagrant (a person) wandering from place to place without a home or a job; (one who is) homeless, a tramp

vainglorious boastful

valediction the action of saying farewell; a farewell

valedictory *n.* + *adj.* farewell

valency the combining power of an element

valetudinarian a person who is chronically unwell or complaining about their health

valgus *Lat.* knock-kneed

Valhalla *Scand. myth* the hall in which the dead heroes in battle feast with Odin

Valkyrie any one of Odin's twelve maidens who scour the battlefields for dead heroes to take to Valhalla

vallation an earthwork wall providing military defence; a rampart; fortification

vancourier a precursor, a forerunner

Vandals Germanic marauders who overran parts of Europe in the 4th – 5th centuries before settling in N. Africa

Vandyke a small pointed beard; a goatee

vanguard the front

vapid insipid; spiritless; dull and uninteresting; boring

vaporous to do with moisture in the atmosphere; misty, hazy, steamy

vapours, the depression

vapulation a flogging

variegated having irregular patches of colours

varlet a rascal, a rogue

varus *Lat.* bow-legged

vascular concerning the system of vessels for carrying blood, sap, water, and nutrients

vasiform vase-shaped, duct-shaped

vasodilation the widening, enlarging of blood vessels which decreases blood pressure

vatic prophetic

vaticinate to prophesy; to foretell the future

vaunt to boast about or praise (something)

vaunt-courier a forerunner

vaurien, vaurienne Fr. a worthless person

vector a carrier

Veda ancient Hindu scriptures

Vedanta Hindu philosophy based on the Upanishads

vedette *Fr.* 1) a mounted sentry stationed beyond the outposts of an army to observe the enemy 2) a female media star

vegan a person who does not eat or use animal products

vegetate to live in a dull or boring way with no mental stimulation; to stagnate intellectually

vehemence intense, passionate emotion or conviction

vehement showing strong feeling; powerful, passionate, intense

velleity volition at its lowest level; a very slight inclination

vellum parchment from the skin of a calf

vellicate to twitch

velour, velours a velvet-like fabric

venal capable of being bribed, corruptible

venatic, venatical to do with hunting

vendanges, les Fr. the grape-picking; the grape harvest

veneer a thin covering

venefical poisonous

venenate to poison

venerable worthy of respect, reverence

venerate to revere

veneration great respect; reverence

venery 1) hunting 2) the pursuit of sexual gratification

venial (of sins in the R.C. church) minor, forgivable, excusable, pardonable

venom poison from the bite or sting of certain snakes, scorpions

ventouse a cup-shaped suction device which, applied to a baby's head, sucks it out of the uterus instead of it being drawn out by forceps

ventre à terre Fr. at full speed

ventricose, ventricous having a pot-belly

venue the site where an event takes place

verbal noun a gerund

verbatim in the exact words used; word for word

verbiage excessively lengthy speech or writing

verbosity the use of too many words

verboten Ger. forbidden

verdigris a green or bluish coating or patina on copper, brass, or bronze exposed to damp

veridical, veridicous truthful, accurate

verification *n.* the proof that something is true

verisimiltude the appearance of truth

verism naturalism in art or literature

verismo naturalism in Italian opera; its chief exponent was Puccini *(1858-1924)*

veritable genuine, actual

verity truth

verkrampte adj.+ n. S.Afr. Africaans ultra-conservative, reactionary

verligte *adj.+ n. S.Afr. Afrikaans* liberal, enlightened, progressive

vermeil gilded silver or bronze; vermilion

vermicular worm-like, wavy

vermiform resembling a worm

vermilion brilliant red

vernacular 1) to do with ordinary, not grand buildings 2) the language of the ordinary people

vernal of or occurring in Spring

vernier a supplement to a measuring instrument having smaller, finer subdivisions than the main scale to increase accuracy in measurement

vernissage a private viewing before the opening of a public exhibition

versal *is short for* universal

verso the left hand, even-numbered page of an open book; the reverse side of a piece of paper meant to be read aloud

vertebrate an animal with a backbone or spinal column

vertex the highest point

vertiginous causing dizziness

vertigo dizziness

vervain a herbaceous plant used in herbal medicine

verve vigour, spirit, and style; energy and enthusiasm

vesica the bladder

vespertine to do with the evening

vespiary a wasps' nest

vested interest a financial or other stake in something

vestige a very small remaining amount; a trace

vestigial remaining; forming a small remnant or trace of something

veteran car one made before 1905

vex to annoy

vexatious annoying, harassing

vexillogy the study of flags

vexillum a flag

via dolorosa *Lat.* 'the sad road' a long ordeal

viable capable of independent existence

vial = phial a small bottle for liquid medicine

vicarious experienced at second hand, not directly; occurring from a feeling of identification with another

vice-chancellor the official in charge of a British university

vicegerent a deputy

vicissitude a change of circumstances or fortune often for the worse; in plural ups and downs

victuals food

videlicet, viz namely

vie to compete

vigil staying awake at night to keep watch or pray

vigilant keeping careful watch

vigilante a member of a gang who avenges crimes as if he was a policeman

vignette a brief description or sketch

vilify to defame

vilipend to treat or regard with contempt

villein a serf, a peasant

vinaigrette 1) vinegar-oil salad dressing 2) a small decorative bottle or box used for holding an aromatic restorative such as smelling salts

vindemial concerning the vintage

vindicate 1) to clear of blame 2) to justify

vindictive revengeful, vengeful

viniculture, viticulture the cultivation of grapevines for wine making

vinous relating to wine

vintage the wine obtained from a particular harvest of grapes

vintage car one made between 1919 and 1930

vintner a wine merchant

viraginity the state or condition of being a masculine woman

virago a man-like woman, termagant, shrew

virement the transferring of items from one financial account to another

virgate like a wand or rod; slender, straight

viridity, viridness verdure, greenness, verdancy

virile manly

virilism the abnormal development of male characteristics in a woman

virtu 1) expertise in the fine arts 2) objets d'art collectively

virtuoso a brilliantly performing musician

virulent 1) full of poison 2) venomously hostile

vis-à-vis 1) in relation to 2) as compared with; as opposed to

visage face

viscera the intestines, entrails, guts

visceral 1) as a gut feeling 2) intuitive, instinctive

viscerotonia the personality type most closely associated with an endomorph body type; hedonism and conviviality are its principal characteristics cf. **cerebrotonia, somatotonia**

viscid sticky

viscosity stickiness

viscous sticky

Visigoths the Western Goths; having invaded the Roman Empire (between the 3rd and 5th centuries) and conquered much of southern France, they established a kingdom in Spain where they were finally defeated by the Moors in 711

visionary a person with 1) foresight 2) fanciful not practical ideas

vista an extensive view

visor, vizor 1) a transparent flap on a helmet that can be pulled down to protect the face 2) a small moveable screen attached above the windscreen in a motor vehicle and as protection against the glare of the sun 3) a stiff peak on a cap

vitellus egg-yolk

vitiate 1) to spoil or impair the quality or efficiency of 2) to destroy or impair the legal validity of

vitilitigation vexatious litigation

vitious flawed, imperfect, faulty

vitreous to do with glass, hyaline

vitrine a show-case made of glass for delicate objects, curios, etc.

vitriol sulphuric acid; bitterness, hatred, malice; caustic criticism

vitriolic (usu. of language) severely bitter, malicious or harsh

vituline resembling a calf or veal

vituperate to vilify, revile

vituperation bitter, abusive censure

vituperative bitterly abusive

vivace *mus.* in a lively fashion

vivandière Fr. a female satler

viviparous giving birth to live young creatures, not hatching them as eggs

vivisepulture burial alive

vizier a senior official in the former Ottoman empire

vocable a word considered with reference to its form rather than meaning *adj.* capable of being voiced or spoken

voire dire the preliminary examination on oath of a prospective witness, by the judge 'to speak the truth'

volar relating to the palm of the hand or the sole of the foot

volatile dangerously unstable; changing quickly in mood; explosive

volitant 1) flying 2) having the power of flight

volition the use of one's own will in e.g. making a decision

volte-face an about-turn, a complete about-face

voluble talking with facile fluency and at length

voluptuary one devoted to luxury and sensual pleasure; a sensualist

voluptuous sensual; curvy and sexually appealing

volute a spiral scroll being the top part of an Ionic column or pillar

voodoo a religious cult practised in and around the Caribbean esp. Haiti; originating in West Africa, it mixes superstition and witchcraft with some Roman Catholic ritual and is characterized by communication (by trance) with deities and ancestors, serpent worship, magic and the like

voracious ravenous, extremely hungry

vortex a whirl of air, water or flame: a whirlpool, cyclone, or whirlwind – it sucks in anything close

Vorticism in England, a short-lived *(1912-1915)* literary and artistic movement; allied to cubism and futurism, it attacked the sentimentality of 19th-century art and was characterized by a sharp, machine-oriented style

vorticose rotating quickly; whirling

votary, votarist a devotee, adherent, or follower

votive in fulfilment of a vow

vouchsafe to condescend or deign to give, grant, or disclose

voulu Fr. contrived, forced

vox angelica an organ-stop that produces a soft, wavy effect or tone

vox humana an organ-stop with a tone resembling the human voice

vox pop interviews with members of the public on radio or television

vox populi public opinion

voyeur a person who derives satisfaction from watching others when they are naked or engaged in sexual or other activity; a peeping Tom

vraisemblance French for verisimilitude, the semblance of truth or reality in literary works

vulcanize to harden (rubber) by treating it with sulphur at a high temperature

Vulgate the official, late 4th- century Latin version of the Bible as used by the Roman Catholic Church

vulgate 1) the accepted version of an author's text and the one most commonly used 2) everyday, colloquial speech

vulnerable at risk of being attacked or harmed

vulpine to do with a fox; foxy

vulva the external female genitals

W

wag a habitual joker; a humorous or witty person

wagon-lit a sleeping car in a European train

Wahabi, Wahhabi a member of a Sunni Muslim sect of Islam, dominant in Saudi Arabia

waif a stray, homeless person or animal esp. a forsaken child

wainscot a panelling usu. of wood applied to the walls of a room

wainwright a builder or repairer of wagons

waive to forgo

wake *n.* a watch beside a corpse before burial; attendant lamentations and (occasionally) merrymaking

wallaby a small Australasian kangaroo

Walloons the French-speaking people of southern and eastern Belgium

Walpurgis night the eve of May Day – the night of 30th April

Walter Mitty a daydreamer who fantasizes about a life much more exciting and glamorous than his own, from the fictional character of that name created by US humorist James Thurber (1894-1961)

wan very pale as a result of exhaustion, illness or unhappiness

wanderjahr Ger. a year spent travelling, off work, or wandering

wanderlust a very strong desire to travel

wane to grow smaller

wanton 1) without motive, provocation, or justification 2) maliciously and unnecessarily cruel

wapiti a large North American deer

warfarin an anti-coagulant used as a rat poison and to treat thrombosis

warlock a male witch, a man who practises black magic

warp, woof warp is the threads stretched out from top to bottom or lengthwise on a loom to be crossed by a woof or weft which is the threads woven into and crossing the warp

warping towing or hauling a ship

warthog a wild African pig with wart-like lumps on the face and large, curved tusks

wastrel a spendthrift

water-buck a large African antelope that lives in herds near water

water pipe = hookah an oriental tobacco pipe

watershed 1) the dividing line of high land that separates two adjacent waters that flow to different outlets 2) a dividing line or turning-point

water table the level below which the ground is saturated with water

water tortoise = terrapin

wattle 1) loose skin hanging from the throat of a turkey and certain other birds 2) rods or stakes interwoven with twigs or branches, used to make fences, walls etc. 3) an Australian acacia tree

wax 1) to grow larger, to increase in size 2) to become (wax lyrical)

waybill a list of passengers or goods being carried on a ship or vehicle

wayfarer a person who travels on foot

waylay to intercept in order to attack

wayzgoose a printers' annual outing or dinner

weal a red, raised mark on the skin from a blow

weald a formerly wooded district of southeast England

wean to accustom (an infant) to food other than its mother's milk

weanling a newly weaned child or animal

wean someone off to make (someone) give up a habit or addiction

weasand windpipe, trachea

weasel words words used to evade a direct statement or commitment – *we will do our best to…*; an equivocation

weazen thin, sharp

Weber, Max *(1864-1920)* German sociologist who attributed the rise of Western capitalism to the Protestant work ethic

webster a weaver

weeds = widows weeds

weevil a beetle with a long snout that feeds on plants

weir a dam built across a river

welkin the sky or heaven

welsh to fail to honour an obligation

weltanschauung Ger. 'world-view', a particular philosophy or view of the world and human life itself or a view which is typical of a period

weltgeist Ger. the world-spirit

weltschmerz Ger. 'world pain', sadness, melancholy caused by the depressing state of the world

wen a large overcrowded city **the great wen** London

wheedle (to try) to persuade someone to do something by coaxing or flattery

wheeze a trick, a deception, subterfuge

whet 1) to sharpen 2) to excite or stimulate

whey the watery part of milk

whey-faced pale (from fright)

Whigs the former name for the British Liberal Party

whilom former, formerly

whippoorwill = nightjar = goatsucker a nocturnal bird with a distinctive call; feeds on insects caught in the air

whit a bit

whited sepulchre a hypocrite, a wolf in sheep's clothing Matthew xxii:27

who or **whom**? **who** is nominative and the subject case: the man who came to dinner. **whom** is accusative, the object case and is also used after a preposition: Whom shall we support? To whom shall we give our support?

Whom is not to be used with the verb 'to be' except where that verb is in the infinitive: The man whom we understood to be a judge. The woman whom he knew to be Rachel, now opened the door. BUT The woman who he knew was Rachel now opened the door.

Who or whom is always decided by the role of the pronoun within the clause it introduces.

If it is not clear which is required, the advice is to re-jig the wording to convert it into a him/he construction. 'Who did you meet at the station? Paul Smith? I met him on the platform.' Technically, therefore, the question should have been 'whom did you meet?' But in conversation the strict rules of grammar are relaxed – whom is considered to sound too pedantic.

The him/he construction test does not work when the relative pronoun follows a preposition in a relative clause.

whorl a ring of leaves or flowers round the stem of a plant

widget any small device, mechanism or gadget, the name of which is forgotten or unknown

widow's mite a small monetary contribution, given by one who can barely afford it (Mark xii:42)

widow's weeds black clothes worn by a widow in mourning

wildebeest a gnu

wile trickery, a ploy; a devious or cunning stratagem

will-o'-the-wisp = ignis fatuus pale, flickering light seen over marshland at night

wimple a cloth head-dress, similar to a hood, formerly worn by women and still by some nuns

window strips of foil dropped from aircraft to counteract an enemy's radar system

window dressing 1) an arrangement of an attractive display in a shop window 2) a skilful but superficial or misleading presentation (in a selectively favourable way) of something that has significant drawbacks

winkle to pry open or out

winnow 1) to use wind or a current of air to separate grain from chaff 2) to sift; to separate out (an unwanted element)

winsome attractive, appealing, charming

wiseacre a wise guy, a clever dick, a know-all

wistful sadly pensive; wishful, yearning, longing for something

wistit = wistiti =ouistiti = marmoset a small tropical American monkey

wit 1) the ability to use words or ideas in a clever, amusing, and imaginative way 2) a person having that ability 3) practical intelligence

withering scornful

withers the highest part of a horse's back at the base of the neck above the shoulders

without prejudice a letter written with these words at the top cannot be read out in court; so anyone wanting to make an offer to settle a matter can use this rubric to prevent the letter from being construed as an admission of liability

wizened dried up, withered, wrinkled with age

Woden, Wodan, Wotan other names for Odin

wolverine, wolverene the largest of the weasels, hunted for its fur – aka glutton, Gulo gulo, carcajou, Gulo luscus

wombat an Australian marsupial which resembles a small bear

without prejudice
a letter written with these words at the top cannot be
read out in court; so anyone wanting to make an offer to
settle a matter can use this rubric to prevent the letter
from being construed as an admission of liability

wont habit, custom *adj.* accustomed, used

woo 1) to try to gain the love of a (woman) 2) to coax or urge

wooden spoon the prize for finishing last in a race or competition

wop (*offensive slang*) an Italian

worst to defeat, to get the better of

wrack seaweed

wraith a ghost

wreak to cause or bring about

wreathe 1) to form or shape into a ring or wreath 2) to encircle or surround with, or as if with, a ring or wreath

wrest to extract forcefully after grappling for

wrought (of metals) beaten out or shaped by hammering

wry 1) (of humour) drily mocking, sardonic, pawky 2) having twisted features (of a facial expression) denoting amusement or displeasure

wunderkind Ger. a child progidy, a whizzkid

wuss a weak, ineffectual person

wyvern, wivern a type of dragon with wings and a serpent's tail

X, Y, Z

Xanadu an imaginary idyllic place, from Coleridge's poem *'Kubla Khan'* (1816)

xanthocroid having a light complexion and light hair

xanthous 1) yellow 2) having light brown or yellowish skin

xantic yellow

Xanthippe the shrewish wife of Socrates; a shrew, a conjugal scold

xeric adapted to a dry environment

yang (in Chinese philosophy) the active male principle of the universe

yaw to veer

yean (of a sheep or goat) to give birth

yin (in Chinese philosophy) the passive female principle of the universe

ylem (in the big bang theory) the primordial matter of the universe from which the basic elements are said to have been formed

zaftig having a full, rounded figure; buxom; curvaceous

zander the European pike-perch fish

Zapotec a native of Oaxaca, a state of southern Mexico

zeal great enthusiasm or energy for a cause or objective

Zealand the largest and most populous island of Denmark; Copenhagen is its major city

zealot a fanatic; an extreme enthusiast; one who has extreme passion or devotion for a particular cause or idea

zeitgeist Ger. 'the spirit of the time' the way people think and feel in a particular period

zenith the highest point

zephyr a soft, gentle breeze esp. from the west

zeugma a rhetorical device that applies one word in two different senses – she closed the door and her heart to him

ziggurat (in ancient Mesopotamia) a platform temple tower in the shape of a stepped pyramid

zikr a dervishes' circular dance

Zinfandel a red wine from California

zingaro an Italian gypsy

zeitgeist
*Ger. 'the spirit of the time' the way people think
and feel in a particular period*

Zionism a movement to establish a Jewish nation in Palestine and, since 1948, for the development and protection of Israel

zircon a hard mineral used as a gemstone and in industry

zodiac (diamond-like) a band in the sky divided into twelve equal parts (signs of the zodiac) each named from a constellation formerly situated in it

zoëtic vital

zoiatria a veterinary surgery

zoic to do with animals

zoilism fierce criticism, characteristic of Zoilus 4th-century b.c. Greek commentator

zombie 1) a revived corpse 2) a lifeless, totally unresponsive person

zoosemiotics the study of animal communication

Zoroastrianism ancient dualistic Persian religion founded in 6th century b.c.; still has adherents in northeast India and Iran

zucchini courgette

zugunruhe Ger. the migratory restlessness of birds

zweite gesellschaft Ger. second-rate people

zygomatic bone the cheekbone

zygote a cell formed by the union of two gametes

zymurgy fermentation in brewing, distilling, wine-making, etc.